POLITICAL THOUGHT
in INDIC
CIVILIZATION

Thank you for choosing a SAGE product!
If you have any comment, observation or feedback,
I would like to personally hear from you.

Please write to me at **contactceo@sagepub.in**

Vivek Mehra, Managing Director and CEO, SAGE India.

Bulk Sales

SAGE India offers special discounts
for purchase of books in bulk.
We also make available special imprints
and excerpts from our books on demand.

For orders and enquiries, write to us at

Marketing Department
SAGE Publications India Pvt Ltd
B1/I-1, Mohan Cooperative Industrial Area
Mathura Road, Post Bag 7
New Delhi 110044, India

E-mail us at **marketing@sagepub.in**

Subscribe to our mailing list
Write to **marketing@sagepub.in**

This book is also available as an e-book.

POLITICAL THOUGHT in INDIC CIVILIZATION

Edited by
Himanshu Roy

Los Angeles | London | New Delhi
Singapore | Washington DC | Melbourne

First published in 2021 by

SAGE Publications India Pvt Ltd
B1/I-1 Mohan Cooperative Industrial Area
Mathura Road, New Delhi 110 044, India
www.sagepub.in

SAGE Publications Inc
2455 Teller Road
Thousand Oaks, California 91320, USA

SAGE Publications Ltd
1 Oliver's Yard, 55 City Road
London EC1Y 1SP, United Kingdom

SAGE Publications Asia-Pacific Pte Ltd
18 Cross Street #10-10/11/12
China Square Central
Singapore 048423

Published by Vivek Mehra for SAGE Publications India Pvt Ltd and typeset in 10.5/13 pt Sabon by AG Infographics, Delhi.

Library of Congress Control Number: 2021944402

ISBN: 978-93-5479-157-4 (HB)

SAGE Team: Rajesh Dey, Syed Husain Naqvi, Madhurima Thapa

Contents

Preface

Under the influence of colonial education and a Eurocentric focus on studies in the social sciences and literature in post-colonial India, Indic thought, part of Indic traditions, and its academic explanatory tools rooted in the history and social ethos of the 'Indons', as termed by Herodotus, the Greek historian, for the residents across the river Sindhu, has been on the margins in mainstream academia. Ideas, ideologies, frameworks, reference points and many other significant tools of scholarly discussions and writings are so much under the influence of Western thought that they not only fail to appreciate Indian realities in their historical contexts and contextualized present but also produce strange results that may at times be contrary to the realities, which lead us to tempered conclusions and altered solutions unfit for our social requirements. The all-pervasive impact of the colonial mind and its lingering effects in post-colonial India continues to have a negative impact our curriculum and thought, affecting Indianness in academic discourse.

It will be apt here to demonstrate the colonial construction of the knowledge formation through the role of the Asiatic Society in colonial India. As it is well known, the Asiatic Society was formed in 1784 in Kolkata by 38 Europeans. There was no Indian member in it; neither was it open for them for the next 40 years. The objective of it was to investigate everything: from nature to geography to forms of governance, institutions, science, agriculture, language, etc., to understand the colony and the subjects. It was an institutionalized beginning to Orientalize knowledge, that is, to interpret India for the British from the colonial lens. The pandits and maulvis were engaged to interpret the text, but they were not part of the decision-making process; neither were they engaged in the final publication of the texts. Their names and contributions were never recognized. Sanskrit alphabets were translated into Roman alphabets with diacritical marks. This transliteration was then adopted by the European academia to learn Sanskrit. It impacted the understanding and interpretation of Sanskrit texts and the history of India.

Similarly, the Census Commission, the Archaeological Survey and such institutions created their interpretations of India. The reports of the Commission and of the gazettes of the military–civil–judicial officers were the other methods of knowledge formation. The academic discourse on the pre-colonial and colonial Indian history is still primarily guided by the colonial constructs which were deliberately distorted by the colonial state that had replaced the Mughal state. As its power consolidated, it began to develop its ideological apparatus to seek the legitimacy of the subjects to its rule. The missionaries, the Asiatic Society, the training manuals of the civil services, the printing press, the Census Commission, the Archaeological Survey and other such institutions and the social divisions of Indian society (caste, religion, gender and language) facilitated this process of the judicial procedure, educational policy and modern institutions and aided the operation of the ideological apparatus.

The contemporary discourse in the social sciences and humanities in Indian universities has consequently become fragmentary, Oriental and Westernized. The larger subterranean popular praxis of Indian citizens and their non-bookish discourse has, however, remained Indic and holistic, with their distinct diverse local ethos existing with pan-Indic commonalities. These praxis and ethos have also been changing to fit the changing structural, technological, topographical and political requirements of the multilingual localities. From the ideational bliss of Rigveda to the 'Total Revolution' of Jayaprakash Narayan, it has been a long civilizational history of ideas, open to new currents of change, but it has refused to be blown over of its Indian-ness. Strong research based on Indic terminologies and its frames of references shall not only give due justice to the historical past of the land but shall also impact the way contemporary events and processes are analysed. It is imperative that the discourse set around the

Indic thought is developed and deployed as an effective tool for comprehending and interpreting even contemporary social and political processes.

Indic traditions, of which thought is an integral part, underline that a process or phenomena can be understood in numerous ways. *Ekam Sat Vipra Bahudha Vadanti* is an often-repeated quote from Upanishad. It means that truth is one, but sages call it by different names. This indicates inherent acceptance of a culture of debate in our society. There is celebration of diversity, unlike the idea of tolerance, which is European and indicates intolerance. It is not to argue that these are the only sets of tools, but it is to emphasize that these tools are on the margins and rarely deployed. Although references to Indic texts is quite common in our daily lives or even deployed for explaining phenomena at a more general level, they do not find equal references in social science texts or higher academic books and research papers. However, a convincing answer would emerge if Indic thought, which is rooted more in the context in which the process emerged, is deployed effectively.

One illustration can be very relevant here, that is, the definition of dharma, which is more often translated as religion. A glance at the true meaning of dharma tells a different story. Dharma is defined as that which upholds, sustains and uplifts; it does not define the object that is being upheld, sustained or uplifted. It does not imply any specific object (living or inanimate) and thus applies to all possible objects. It represents a 'principle' or a 'quality of being' that can be widely used in a variety of contexts to mean a variety of different ideas. In the 'Karna Parva' of Mahabharata, Krishna explains dharma to Arjuna in the following words: *dharanat dharma mityahu dharmo dharayate prajaha Yat syad dharanasamyuktam sa dharma iti nischayaha*. Dharma sustains the society. Dharma maintains the social order. Dharma ensures well-being and progress of humanity. Dharma is surely that which fulfils these objectives. This was precisely the context and meaning in which Gandhi underlined that religion and politics are inseparable.

This narrative seeks to retrieve, resurrect and analyse this Indian-ness in its history. It also intends to posit this Indian-ness as the pivot of academic curriculum and public discourse. The objective is to engage the academics of different disciplines of social sciences on different themes derived primarily from Indic traditions. This book brings together interdisciplinary perspectives of history, sociology, literature and politics in interpreting different themes of Indic philosophy. It weaves the heuristic interpretations of different disciplines with their methodological insights into a holistic pedagogical volume. The arguments, facts, themes and interpretations presented there are usually not found in the mainstream academic narratives.

To arrive at the standard format of pedagogy, four workshops were held in the past four years at different academic centres of India: Developing Countries Research Centre (DCRC), University of Delhi, Department of Political Science, Goa University, Department of Political Science, DDU College, University of Delhi and Nehru Memorial Museum and Library, Teen Murti House, New Delhi. I thank Professor Sunil Choudhary, Director, DCRC, Professor Rahul Tripathi, Head, Department of Political Science, Goa University, Principal Hemchand Jain, DDU College, University of Delhi and Mr Shakti Sinha, then Director, NMML, for organizing the workshops. I also thank Abhijit Baroi, Commissioning Editor and Rajesh Dey, Managing Editor, SAGE, for their unstinted support, and Vikas Kumar, a research scholar in Political Science for his secretarial assistance. Finally, I thank my contributors for their brilliant works.

Introduction

Indic Society

Indic thought has been changing over the centuries, incorporating and internalizing diverse new ideas; it also continued with the old ideas, recycling and reinterpreting them in new forms. The changes have been adaptive and incremental both at the popular and elite levels. The social rupture at pan-Indic level has been rare; the rupture, if at all, has been more local and cultural.[1] The organizational structural changes evolved over the centuries were more due to internal economic reasons or were given a push by invaders. These changes were multidimensional and multi-layered. The memoirs of different foreign travellers to India or the treatises written by different Indians at different times in history reflect this.

Diversities have been an integral part of Indic social praxis and thought. Every Hindu family has a family deity (*kul* devi/devata). Every village has its deity (*gram* devi/devata). Every region, sub-region has its local deity. These diverse deities of families and villages are celebrated by each one of these units; and the festivals that take place on different occasions involve every person. In pre-modern India, these diversities were the usual part of the social life which were more pronounced in absence

[1] Yogendra Singh, *Modernization of Indian Tradition* (New Delhi: Thomson Press, 1973), 28.

of any episcopal order, particularly in Hinduism. The existence of mass number of free peasantries scattered over lakhs of villages with their small landholdings acted as bulwark against any episcopal order, theocracy, papacy and caliphate. The diffused landholdings among different castes and the insular village life gave birth to their large number of gods and sects that constituted a loosely federated kind of polymorphous religion of Hinduism which was in contradistinction to the Christ-sized gods owned by the churches and the landlords who thrust their gods upon the serfs and slaves. Slaves were owned by their masters; serfs were owned by their lords and churches had vast landholdings. More their properties, more were the numbers of serfs and slaves; and in the same proportion developed the pre-eminence of Christ, Mohammad, Christianity and the caliphate, which was contrary to Indic social life reflected in thought, praxis and polity.[2]

The expanding cultivable land in India and settlement of new villages ensured opportunity of livelihood for everyone despite inscriptive graded social structure and differential customary laws. The inscriptive caste structure provided labour for cultivation and professional services in the villages, which were always in short supply. Those who came to India from outside or were from indigenous tribes were merely placed within these folds of the castes, which were divisions of work or specialized services in the villages. It was also hereditary as it ensured a perpetual supply of labour and services in midst of shortages. But it did not foreclose the vertical and horizontal mobility of castes. Even the religions which came to India from outside or the religions which emerged in India were no exception to it. This opportunities to livelihood through expanding cultivable land provided freedom to individuals which was not existing to serfs and slaves who were dependent on their owners.

---

[2] Brajadulal Chattopadhyaya, *The Making of Early Medieval India*, 2nd ed. (New Delhi: Oxford, 2012), xxvii; and *The Concept of Bharatavarsha* (Ranikhet: Permanent Black, 2017), 21–25; Richard M. Eaton, *India in the Persianate Age* (New Delhi: Allen Lane, 2019), 10–11.

From Kabul–Kandahar to Dhaka and Kanyakumari to Himalaya and the Indian Ocean, there were hardly 15 crore Indians during the Aurangzeb's regime. Indian villages had always felt the shortage of labour, which also provided opportunities for mobility of labour as well as trade and commerce, as villages were not autarkic, self-sufficient or self-reliant, as it is commonly understood. While the villages provided culture diversities, the trade and commerce—local, regional and international—and similarities of caste structure across regions provided uniformity of culture, which was reflected in religion represented by universal Indic gods, mantras, epics, texts, marriage, worships, rituals, celebration style of festivals, designs of temples, etc. This had emerged over the centuries from the common idea of *Jambudvipa* and *Bharatavarsa*, which corresponded to the land between the ocean in the south and Himalayan in the north.[3] It reflected the subtle, subterranean feeling of oneness among the residents, bounded by cultural–religious unity transcending different political kingdoms that had emerged from time to time.

Polity

Premised on this geography, culture and livelihood, the polity that emerged over the continent until the arrival of political Islam reflected this base of oneness in great traditions while simultaneously being diverse in little traditions in its functioning and structure; and the idea behind this kind of polity had also emerged from the same premise of great and little traditions of livelihood, opportunities, expansion of cultivable land, ease of survival and prosperity due to international trade and the existence of individual freedom. In the formulation and application of laws, taxation, policing, governance, the consent, support and acceptance of the residents, subjects were sought in public sphere. The opulence of the rich was noticeable, as reported by foreign

---

[3] For details, see Himanshu Roy, *Secularism and Its Colonial Legacy* (New Delhi: Manak, 2009), xxi–xxii, 13–16.

travellers, and their gap with the subjects was wide, yet there was no theocratic state or episcopal order forcing the subjects to serfdom and slavery or forcing them to attend church. The relative absence of forced labour or heavy taxation despite the existence of imperial regimes reflects the acceptance of the polity as there was no radical rupture against the polity. The perpetual shortage of labour, the open acceptance of new migrants, their mobility and wide opportunities of livelihood forced monarchs to be conciliatory in their functioning, lest their subjects migrate to other kingdoms in search of better taxation and freedom. This situation had also forced the monarchs to abstain from being theocratic, or not to force their personal religions on their subjects. Rather, in public domain, they were forced to support all the sects. Temples, monasteries in public spaces were usually not destroyed by them in their territorial expansion and conflicts as these places, particularly pan-Indic, universal gods, represented similar faiths and culture of subjects. Local deities representing localities and sub-regions might have been occasionally displaced or carried away.[4] But the destruction of local deities or Indic gods that occurred after the arrival of political Islam in India was not occurring in pre-Islamic India.

The pre-Islamic India, or the society even during the political rule of Islam, has been well described by foreign travellers who visited India in its long history, or is available in inscriptions. For example, in the inscription of Raja Raj Chola II, a vivid description of village life, education, trade, taxation, etc., is recorded. The functioning of the village assembly was democratic; decisions taken were collective; there was popular participation; caste structure existed but inter-caste marriages were held. 'The violation of the law was firmly dealt with through punishment by the village assembly.' There were 260 students in school who were taught by 19 teachers.[5] They 'learnt Sanskrit, Vedic studies besides learning to recite Thiruvaimozhi, the Tamil hymns of

[4] For details, see Eaton, *India in the Persianate Age*, 23, 28.
[5] For details, see S. Jeyaseela Stephen, *Pondicherry under the French* (New Delhi: Primus, 2018), 21–23.

Nammalvar'. Al-Biruni also mentioned about inter-caste marriages, which were common among members of certain castes.[6] Similarly, on education, it will be apt to cite the British official's reports of the early years of the British East India Company's rule about the three presidencies, which mentioned that the school education was very advanced at that time.

Education

Before the Company sieged the power in Bengal in 1757, there were 80,000 schools in Bengal alone, with one school for every 400 students. Even in the 1830s, there were 100,000 schools in Bengal and Bihar. In Madras and Bombay presidencies, Munro and Prendergast, respectively, recorded that there existed at least one school in every village. This was in the 1820s. In the 1850s, Leitner mentioned about similar state of education in Punjab. More importantly, this education was inclusive. In the Madras presidency, in the Tamil- and Malayali-speaking territories, there were 70 per cent and 54 per cent Shudras students, respectively, reported by the British during 1822–1825, when Indic village education was on the decline due to colonial rule. Campbell, the district collector of Bellary in Karnataka accepts this decline in 1823. Equally inclusive was the composition of the teachers who were from different castes, including Shudras. Many of them taught students at their homes who also used to come from distant localities; and they were from all castes. The subjects were grammar, arithmetic, language and scripts. It was *gyan*, *bhasha gyan* and elementary mathematics. But there were few variations across different regions.

Beside schools, there were institutions of higher education; but they did not necessarily exist in every district, just as schools existed in every village. In Madras presidency, there were 1,094 *agraharams* with 5,439 students from different castes. Teachers and students from economically weaker sections were taken care of by

---

[6] Al-Biruni, *India* (New Delhi: National Book Trust, 1983), xv.

the society through charitable funding. The students were taught poetry, metaphysics, theology, Vedas, law, logic, astronomy, mathematics, ethics, medicine, etc. Then, there were Arabic and Persian institutions which also focused on Islamic theology, grammar, logic, astronomy, medicine, etc. The different tiers of institutions, *maktabs*, madrasas, libraries and *khanqahs* imparted different standards of education. *Maktab* was the school, madrasa was the college and *khanqahs* was the Sufi centre. Teachers were usually paid in cash and kind of which there exists a record in the Malabar region.

After the arrival of Islam, the universities such as Nalanda and Vikramshila were no longer existent. The destruction of Nalanda by Bakhtiyar Khalji was the last nail in this pre-Islamic Indic university, which had survived three major destructions. Even after Khalji's villainous act, Nalanda survived for another 200 years with much lesser number of students and teachers. It withered away by the 15th century.[7] Islam, to an extent, had impacted the education of Indic traditions by introducing Arabic script and Persian as the state language. Also, its sword forced Hindus to retreat with their knowledge from the regions where Islam had acquired power. Al-Biruni records that 'Hindu sciences have retired far away from those parts of the country conquered by us, and have fled to places which our hands cannot yet reach.'[8]

Culture and Economy

An interesting history of the pre-Islamic Indic civilization was that those who came to India settled down and became integral part of its social matrix. They rarely returned to their homelands; the returnees were few: most of them were travellers, traders, invaders and looters. The settlers did not carry forward their identities or tried to convert the locals to their identities; rather, they merged with the locals. But after the arrival of political

[7] For details, see Hartmut Scharfe, *Education in Ancient India* (Leiden, Boston, Koln: Brill, 2002), 150–151.
[8] Al-Biruni, *India*, 10.

Islam, Muslim rulers settled down in India but did not merge their identity with the locals as it had happened in the past; rather, they expanded their religious cultural identities through conversions, bringing in technology, food, clothes, architecture, gods, language, scripts, military warfare technology, taxation system and administrative structure from their homelands and made it an integral part of Indic civilizations over the centuries through administrative polices, political praxis and religious propagation. It was an organized, deliberate design under which they successfully converted a part of Indic population to Islam and its culture, which were Arabic, Persian and Central Asian. It may be clarified here that changes have been an integral part of Indic civilization. But this kind of religious conversion from Indic to Arabic or to Greco-Roman before the arrival of political Islam was not recorded.

Economically, India has been a powerhouse of wealth for centuries in the pre-colonial history. International trade through land and sea has been its forte, as recorded in different literature and inscriptions.[9] Across the coastal regions, merchant settlements, both Indian and foreign traders, have been existing. Similarly, Indian traders have been trading across different regions of the world, from Central Asia to Africa to Southeast Asia. Until the 1750s, approximately one quarter of the GDP of the world was generated by India. Bullion came from every trading country that traded with India. Except for horses and precious metals, India imported least; whereas, it exported spices and textiles to different regions of the world. The wealth was unevenly distributed, most of it was concentrated into business and ruling elites.[10] The land was known across the world for its wealth and opportunity; therefore, traders, looters, invaders and settlers came to India from across the world as it provided them opportunities of better life and safety. Those who settled down here became part of this cultural mosaic within a generation or two. Only

---

[9] Stephen, *Pondicherry under the French*, 2–3, 25–28.
[10] William Dalrymple, *The Anarchy* (London: Bloomsbury, 2019), 411.

the followers of Islam who came from outside maintained their distinct religious identities and turned to Arabia for their spiritual succour or for the continuation of their cultural traditions. Even local converts who converted from Hinduism, Buddhism and Sikhism unfortunately imitated them. Their names were changed from Indic to Arabic; their food, clothes, manners of worship, everything changed. They did not go back to Arabia; they created Arab culture in India. The conversion separated the families, uprooted converts from their culture as they imitated Arabs and created a new religious–cultural identity in society that generated social tension. Fortunately, for Indic civilization, the majority of Muslims remained fitted into their caste framework which kept them rooted in Indic culture despite their conversion and imitation of Arabs. From time to time, there were movements within Islam in India to make these converts more Arabic in their culture. Those who had come from the Arab world were co-opted as upper caste among the Muslims. This whole development led to the formation of three broad caste blocks among them: Ashraf, Ajlaf and Arzal; the last two were equivalent to Other Backward Castes and Scheduled Castes, respectively.[11] As the turmoil in the Arabic world worsened, more numbers of Muslims migrated to India in search of their safety and livelihood. During the rule of Muslim rulers, these migrants were large in number who settled down in different regions of India,[12] but the bulk remained in North India, from Baluchistan, Sindh to Punjab, Delhi and Uttar Pradesh.

In this social backdrop, Indic thought was reflected in its philosophy, dance, music, temples, Vedas, epics, puranas and smritis, which were diverse but still represented the unity of the civilizational culture across political kingdoms, best reflected

[11] Imtiaz Ahmad, ed., *Caste and Social Stratification among Muslims* (Delhi: Manohar, 1973), chapter: Introduction.

[12] Abdus Sattar Dalvi, ed., *Hindustani Zaban* (Bombay: Khusru Number, Hindustani Prachar Sabha, Gandhi Memorial Research Centre, 1975), 37–38; Irfan Habib, *Essays in Indian History* (New Delhi: Tulika, 1995), 86; Eaton, *India in the Persianate Age*, 47.

in temple towns and cultural centres when people visited from across the regions and kingdoms.[13] These Indic literature, dance and music were always evolving, receptive, considerate, assimilative, creative and accepting different elements of social life coming from different parts of the world across the centuries. The Indian literature comprised of both the specifics and the universal. One can refer to the oldest literature of the world, the Rigveda, which has 21 textual variations; five of which still exist, 2 in full and 3 in fragments. Each surviving text has different number of *shlokas*, which are arranged in different orders. Possibly, as people migrated across the regions, their texts and the ordering of the *richain* changed or the number of *mandalams* (chapters) changed with different contents. Despite this, the Rigveda was universal and reflected a social bliss, an unalienated life where nature and society were supreme and in harmony.[14] Similarly, there are wide numbers of epics, puranas, smritis and shastras written by different authors or adapted in different regions that are both universal and specific in nature. Ramayana or its adapted versions in different languages by different authors are more than 300 in number; puranas are 18 in number, the regional–linguistic variations are still larger. Then, there are 20 smritis and 18 types of shastras. These numbers can further change depending on one's acceptance or rejection of text such as epics, puranas and smritis. The argument here is to emphasize the diversities and their celebrations that existed for centuries and kept on adding as the population expanded and settled down in new areas. Each new territory and its segment of population adopted, adapted and created its new literature, generated its new smritis. This literature reflected the intellectual and academic prowess of the people and their freedom of identity. The generic problem, however, with some of these texts is to fix

---

[13] For details, see M. P. Singh, 'Introduction' in *Indian Political Thought*, 3rd ed., ed., Himanshu Roy and M. P. Singh (New Delhi: Pearson, 2020).

[14] For details, see Himanshu Roy, 'Conclusion' in *Indian Political Thought*; Ram Vilas Sharma, *Itihas Darshan* (Hindi; New Delhi: Vani Prakashan, 1995), Bhumika and Chapter 1.

their dates contexts and, in many cases, even their authors. We do not know who wrote many of these texts, when and where were these written. Since these were written in Devanagari script, Sanskrit language and poetic form, Ambedkar had argued that many of these texts were written in the post-Buddha time as there was no script earlier. The earliest script, hitherto, discovered and deciphered was Brahmi. The Devanagari script had developed after the 8th century AD.[15] The second major generic problem of these texts is the absence of historical–social contextualization and the style of writings, which is poetry in stanzas, not prose. In the Greco-Roman or in the Chinese, Islamic civilizations, these problems were less in extent. Therefore, history known to us through foreign travellers, such as Chinese, Arabs or Europeans, is better recorded, more descriptive and factual, contextualized in time and space. Even the history known to us about the period of Muslim rulers in India is better recorded. The absence of paper technology in pre-Islamic India might have been one of the factors for such shortcomings. In terms of numbers of manuscripts written at different times, there is no shortage of it; rather, there is a massive number of manuscripts that are yet to be translated for public reading. But we do not find any historical descriptions in the manuscripts that have been translated; however, after all of these texts are fully translated, we will be able to analyse them better. The government and society in post-Independence India have yet to achieve this goal.

Islam

The Islamic history, territorially in the Indic region, began incrementally with the conquest of Baluchistan, Sindh and Multan by Muhammad bin Qasim in the 8th century CE which gradually expanded to whole of India after a few interruptions in between the 9th century and the 11th century. From the 12th century onwards till the 18th century, the political Islam—the Muslim

---

[15] For details, see note 14.

rulers—reigned over the whole of India. The last effective ruler to an extent was Shah Alam who finally lost his political sovereignty to the British. Their imprints on different facets of life are well recorded. Beginning from the Islamic chronicler Suleiman, Al-Biruni, Ibn Battuta, Amir Khusro, Isami, Ferishta, Firdaus, Badauni, Zia Barani, Abul Fazl to Mirza Itesamuddin and many more, or their works such as *Chachnama* to *Shiqurf Namah-i-Velaet*, the history of Indic civilization has been well documented from the elite Islamic perspective; or it may be argued that it was the dominant view of the time to look at the history as the Muslim rulers, who constituted of 75 per cent of the Arab Muslims (Turks, Iranians, Uzbeks, Arabs, Africans, etc.) in the elite structure, had acquired the political power. The Hindus were less than 30 per cent in the elite power structure. This was during the time of Shahjahan and Aurangzeb, when the Muslim rule was at its peak.[16] In the earlier stage of the Islamic rule, the Hindu composition of the *durbar* was far less and was subordinate to the new victors.[17]

As the Islamic rule expanded, it actuated disruptions in the pre-Islamic polity and culture that generated social tension over the centuries. The sovereign pre-Islamic Indic rulers were either destroyed or subordinated to Muslim rulers, whose first preference was the eligible Muslims who can fit into the required jobs. In their absence, since they were few in numbers and were mostly in the urban–administrative centres, the Hindus were assigned the tasks particularly in the rural areas where, initially, Muslims, particularly Saiyyads, were absent. The administrative, judicial and cultural transformations brought in by the Arabic–Persian–Turkish rulers changed the culture of urban Indic natives who came in touch with them and, subsequently, it impacted the rural natives among whom this culture percolated over the centuries. This was a passive revolution. At the top, they brought in their military, judicial, administrative systems from the

---

[16] For details, see Eaton, *India in the Persianate* Age, 331.
[17] Ibid., 42–43, 48.

Arab–Persian–Mongol–Uzbeks–Turkish world with which they were familiar, but which was subsequently new for India. It was the revolution from top. The pre-Islamic Indic system adopted itself with substantial modification.[18] There were internal conflicts among the Muslim elite, both political and cultural; but as the Muslim ruling elite of different sects and homelands settled down in India and expanded their territories to Delhi and beyond over generations, they acquired political independence from the Arabic–Persian rulers, of whom, in the initial years, they were their vassals.[19]

Polity

The first major change that was visible at the top in the polity once they settled down in Delhi as the monarchs was the formation of an elaborate system of 'ranked and salaried bureaucracy tied to the state's land revenue and military system', the system of slaves owned by the Arabic–Persian elite, their presence in the army, the office of Sultan and the structure of the military and the judicial administration. It had come from Iraq and Iran, where it had evolved over the centuries for different reasons. In the hierarchy, the Sultan was the absolute monarch, the rulership of whose was hereditary and he was to be acceptable to the nobility. There was a contest for being Sultan; but there was no division of power among caliphs, judicial heads or nobility. The Sultan was the final authority in every domain, temporal, judicial or divine. For, there was no episcopal order in India headed by a caliph. Only few symbols of natal relations continued in the initial centuries. The most lasting impact was the cultural legacy, religious symbols and inheritance of judicial taxation and military administration.

The social structure that developed over the centuries was dominated by the Muslim elite, monarchs and nobles who arrived

---

[18] Muzaffar Alam, *The Language of Political Islam in India* (New Delhi: Permanent Black, 2004), 3–4.

[19] For details, see Eaton, *India in the Persianate Age*, Chapter 1, 30–61.

as invaders and political rulers. The immigrants joined this hierarchy of elite as they arrived in India in search of jobs. This new political elite co-opted upper caste Hindus who converted to Islam for administrative and political needs. The Hindu nobility who accepted their suzerainty of the new political rulers were also co-opted in. The elite structure was fluid and in flux due to constant inflow of immigrants from across non-Indic regions. The Indic caste structure, however, remained intact despite the conversion of residents of different castes to Islam.

Culture

The conversion itself happened due to the combined powers of force of sword, the coercive state apparatus, the taxation and the ideological state apparatus, the Sufi, the Madrasa and the Persian language. It has been well recorded by Muslim chroniclers and travellers over the centuries. In the 16th century, 'when Raja Silhadi (also known as Raja Shiladitya) was imprisoned and asked to accept Islam he would on no account agree, and it was with great difficulty that he did himself the honour of entering Islam.... Rajputs were compelled to convert under political pressure.' Even in the Varta literature of Vallabha Sampradaya, there is an unsympathetic portrayal of Muslims. Also the converts felt that the conversion will provide them with better opportunities and living conditions. Richard M. Eaton's works refers to it[20]; Aniruddha Ray also confirms it. The inflow of immigrants and conversion of Indic subjects who imitated their elite's religious and cultural practices grew in tandem with the growth and depth of their political rule. In turn, this created and deepened the 'ideological and emotional hostility between the Hindus and the Muslims'[21] as this brought in an alien culture into the

[20] Eaton, Ibid., 169, 329–331; also, see Vasudha Dalmia and Munis D. Faruqui, *Religious Ineractions in Mughal India* (Oxford: Oxford University Press, 2014), XIX, 31, 55, 67; Aniruddha Ray, *The Sultanate of Delhi* (New Delhi: Manohar, 2019), 25, 410–411.

[21] Al-Biruni, *India*, xx.

localities. Within moments, the conversion changed the names
of converts, their rituals, worships, books, alphabets, dress,
food and transformed them to behave like Arabs and Persians. It
uprooted them suddenly and made them aliens in their own villages and localities. They used to be Indic, but now they became
Arabs, Persians and Turks. The hostility was so deep that even in
the 17th century, when Dara Shikoh was contesting for the throne,
a section of the Muslim community felt that 'if he...obtains the
throne, and establishes his power, the foundations of the (Islamic)
faith would be in danger and the precepts of Islam would be
changed for the absurdity of infidelity.'[22] For, Dara Shikoh was
viewed as lenient and tolerant towards Hindus, the infidels. He
had got the Upanishad translated into Arabic and believed that
Vedantic Hinduism and Islam were distinct in name only, which
was rejected by most Muslims at that time.[23]

The social gap between the two religious communities was so
wide that David Lorenzen felt that medieval Hindus sought to
maintain a distance[24] which has been substituted by the Varta
literature and Aniruddha Ray's works as referred to earlier.
The unfortunate part of the Islamic praxis was that even the
Sufis welcomed the conversion either by force or by choice. It
depended on the circumstances and timings. In Kashmir, they
encouraged the demolition of temples while maintaining out-
wardly good relations with Hindus. In Bengal, they converted
people forcibly and destroyed the Hindu temple near Pandua to
construct a *khanqah*.[25] Tavernier was astonished to observe this
kind of situation in 1676[26]:

> Idolators of India are so numerous that for one Muhammadan
> there are five or six gentiles. It is astounding to see how this

[22] Dalmia and Faruqui, *Religious Interactions in Mughal India*, 31.
[23] Ibid., 37, 55.
[24] Ibid., xix.
[25] Ray, *The Sultanate of Delhi*, 410–411.
[26] Jean Baptiste Tavernier, *Travels of India*, Vol. II (trans, V. Ball;
London: Macmillan, 1889), 181.

enormous multitude of one has allowed itself to be subjected by so small a number of persons, and has bent readily under the yoke of Muhammadan princes.

The Sufi, nonetheless, was the midwife that facilitated the expansion of Islam by softening its brutality. It led to its acceptance among the poor. For, Sufism originated in Persia in the 9th century and expanded to India in the 11th century.[27] One of its exponents was Amir Khusro, who was born in India but whose father had migrated from Balkh. Khusro praised India as his motherland and paradise, placed Sanskrit above all other languages except Arabic and treated Hindavi as his mother tongue.[28] But, on many occasions, his writings were contemptuous of Hinduism and glorification of Islam. One example is his description of a scenario at Chidambaram in which he says that the women of the infidels rub their vaginas on the ling of Mahadeo; or his description of Somnath in which he says that the Mecca of the infidels became the Medina of Islam. At other places, he talked about the triumphal march of Islam and submission of idolators through the power of sword. It seems he was contemptuous of Hindus about whom he felt that they exist solely for the service of Turks.[29] Islam or death[30] has been a recurring theme of debate throughout the regimes of Muslim rulers.

Over the centuries, Hindus adopted a part of Islamic culture, particularly those who were part of the administration or who intended to be part of it. Equally important was the fact that the Arabic–Persian rulers translated some of the Hindu texts or adopted some of the food, dress, language, etc., as per the availability and requirements of the society and topography. This adaptation and adoption took place in the 17th and 18th

[27] Alam, *The Language of Political Islam in India*, 82.

[28] See Dalvi, *Hindustani Zaban*.

[29] Harsh Narain, *Myth of Composite Culture and Equality of Religion* (New Delhi: Voice of India, 1990), 17; Sita Ram Goel, *Hindu Temples*, Part II (New Delhi: Voice of India, 1991), 271; Carl W. Ernst, *Eternal Garden* (Albany, NY: State University of New York, 1992), 25.

[30] Alam, *The Language of Political Islam in India*, 83.

centuries, which was partly mediated by Sufis. A segmentary or sectional composite cum integrative culture did evolve at the bottom and at the top, which was reflected in the Mazaar, tehzib, Qawwal, Kebab, tezia, Hindavi culture, commonly referred to as the Ganga–Jamuni culture. But this did not lead to the integration of the two religious communities; rather, it was the dominant–subordinate religious category reflected in one-way conversion from Indic religions to Islam to expand their social base. The local converts were 'integrated' with the Arabs–Turks under the banner of Islam. The Arabs–Turks, however, never treated them, the local converts, as their own. Rather, they were treated as the service providers and foot soldiers to their rule. Even in the cultural domain, the literary works that emerged in Urdu, Hindavi and Hindustani were treated as substandard in comparison to Persian; and the Persian literary composition of Hind was not even taken note of in Iran.[31] Nonetheless, translation works, lexicography or studies of astronomy, geography, anatomy and philosophy were being done as India was the 'emporium (and) traffic of the world...a large country with lots of money (and) unlimited numbers of craftsmen and practitioners of every trade'.[32] Parallel to it, the Indic traditions of Shastrartha, knowledge production and social reforms continued despite Muslim rule and penetration of Islamic culture. It was moderate in scale and spirit. One visible development was the construction of astronomical observatories at Delhi, Benaras and Jaipur built by Raja Jai Singh, which facilitated the scientific study of calculations of time. But, in other branches of science such as medicine, veterinary and agriculture, the development was low in scale. Even in law, grammar and philosophy, textual production was less visible. Al-Biruni was accurate when he had noted that Hindu sciences had retreated after the arrival of Islam. The other important facet of this culture was the Bhakti movement, which reflected the Indic genius at their best and was substantively the

---

[31] Ibid., 180–183.
[32] Cited in Sheldon Pollock, *Forms of Knowledge in Early Modern Asia* (New Delhi: Manohar, 2011), 242–243, 264–265.

resultant of the Islamic encounter. Most of the Bhakti poets from Basava, Vemana, Janabai to Sankardev, Tukaram, Kabir and Tulsi wrote and spoke in their native vernacular languages and dialects. This was one branch which witnessed substantive production of literary works. The other was about rituals, wisdom, commentaries on classical texts, vrat, darshan, etc.[33] Even *riti'kal* literary works did contribute to an extent. Dance and music, both popular folk and classical, made equally important contributions. While Bhakti and Sufi added different forms and themes to popular music and dance, urban, classical dance of different regions more specialized with nuances, *mudra*, *bhava*, continued to add and refine themes and forms of their presentation. It was religious in theme. A third category of dance and its theme termed as *mujra*, *kotha* acquired prominence, particularly after the arrival of Arabic–Persian rulers. It was substantively focused on the sensuous female body and was primarily fostered by and linked with the ruling elite in urban and semi-urban centres.

The Muslim rule also brought in its burqa for their women, which was not present in Indic society. What was existing was *ghoonghat*; a light face cover which was applicable more prominently among the social elite. Working women, particularly of lower social order, were relatively free from it. It was not possible for them to cover their faces while working in the fields. The *ghoonghat* was more applicable to the married women, that too, in the presence of known elders in the family, as well as in villages and towns. It may also be added here that there were wide regional, sub-regional variations. The tribal areas were free from it. They were also free from Sati, which was mostly voluntary and partly coercive. Unfortunately, local Indic converts to Islam initiated this practice of burqa of Arabic Muslim women and applied it on their women. But then, they got rid of Sati which was more applicable to Hindu women. The lower order among them, once again, was relatively free from it. Their labour was more important for their families. It (Sati) was more applicable

---

[33] Ibid., 24–27.

to the elite section. Even here, it was more voluntary rather than coercive. Coercion was applied in many cases, but it was not the rule.[34] Sati was not mandatory; plus, there were wide regional variations. It was almost non-existent in Southern and North-eastern India. It may also be clarified here that Sati was not the same as *Jauhar*; these were two different social occurrences; the latter was purely applicable to princely Hindu women who killed themselves in fire to save their honour once their king/prince lost the battle and their honour was at stake. Foreign travellers, both Europeans and Arabs, who stayed in India in different capacities for years, have written widely on Sati, social status of women, the condition of subaltern rural poor, peasants and royalties.

Social Structure

The condition of the rural poor, peasants and labour, as per their reports, was not very comfortable; while the condition of the businessmen and the elite was exceedingly well. The middle segment who worked in the administration was in better condition than the poor—the peasants and the labour—and the crafts-men, who were in abundance, particularly working in urban and semi-urban centres, were regularly employed and were also in a better economic position.[35] The taxation was heavy; it was not uniform. From one-third to one-sixth part of the peasants' pro-duce was taxable. The administration was not much concerned for the agricultural productivity. Only the tax was relaxed in case of calamities. With high fertility of soil, productivity could have easily been increased with little support from the administration to peasants. In the absence of it, they were the worst lot in the social order.[36] It was a common notable point among foreign travellers in the medieval period.

[34] Neena Kumari, *Madhya Kalin Bhartiya Samaj Evam Sanskriti* (Hindi; New Delhi: Research India Press, 2019), Chapter 3.

[35] Ibid., Chapter 2, 93–96.

[36] Ibid., 91–92; Ram Vilas Sharma, *Itihas Darshan* (New Delhi: Vani Prakashan, 1995), 171.

The social hierarchy of caste and gender was defined. but it was not frozen in time. There was fluidity with wide regional variations, and also changes were notable in it over the centuries. Plus, there were wide gaps between the scriptures and the popular praxis, both in rural and urban areas. Physical distancing was maintained with a few castes who dealt with dead bodies, cleaning, etc. But, with most other castes, physical distancing was not practised; rather, in the routine social chores, there were cordial discourse as per the norms of the medieval times. For, as discussed earlier, there would not have been students of different castes in schools and in higher, professional studies. Coercive methods in everyday social relations were rarely deployed; the state apparatus did use it, if required, for tax collection. Social mobility existed for both groups (castes) and individuals. It was both vertical and horizontal. Many castes, in many regions, converted to Islam; then, migrations also provided opportunities for social mobility. Specialized skills kept the craftsmen engaged as India was the emporium of the world and one of the most prosperous regions. The trade kept the castes fluid and the population mobile by affecting the rigidity of segregated social relationships; and this has been the case for centuries, irrespective of changes of political rulers, as India was the centre of export in spices, silk, cotton, etc., until the seizure of state power by the British East India Company.

Conclusion

The Company, beginning from 1757, not only defeated medieval sovereigns and looted populations and resources under the new economic system of colonial capitalism, which had a catastrophic impact on the social relations of Indic people, but it also radically colonized their minds that changed their perspective on their own history. It was partly in the similar fashion that had happened after the invasion and expansion of the Muslim rule in India over the centuries who had destroyed the political sovereignty of the Hindu rulers. The Hindu rulers were either killed or co-opted as subordinates to Muslim rulers who had arrived from Arab,

Iran, Turkmenistan, Uzbekistan, etc., with different backdrops of religions, cultures, polities and world views. It was the political–cultural revolution at the top that had passively percolated downwards at the bottom over the centuries, enacting a passive social revolution in culture among the Indic subjects. It had generated a world view among a percentage of subjects that looked at Mecca and to Arabs as their role models. It was akin to the colonized minds of a section of Indians created by the British, who looked at Indian history and society with colonized minds.

The different chapters in this book have interpreted the different facets of Indic civilization with critical appreciation. It's a decolonized interpretation of Indic institutions, ideas, philosophy and history, unlike colonized minds, who have deployed Western academic tools and frameworks of their polity, society, economy and culture to interpret Indic history. While they had slave and serf societies, Catholic Christian theocratic states, episcopal orders and political conflicts for supremacy between popes and monarchs, we had the idea of *rashtra*, which was territorial and cultural; the Shastrartha was held to arrive at new social ideas that reflected civic freedom and pluralism of ideas; and men and women from the lower strata of society became saint poets. Science and medicine, technology and research were of high standard as the prosperity from trade percolated in other sectors. Education was more a societal responsibility rather than being state centric. Islam partly changed the culture and polity. The change that occurred at the top was enacted by the sword; the change that occurred at the bottom was more voluntary, and the sword played an occasional role. The incentive of a positional shift, if converted to Islam, or the potentiality of it was always lurking at the back of mind. More importantly, Islam brought the culture of writing history, which made it easier for future historians to develop their own interpretations with accuracy of time, space and personalities in comparison to the centuries preceding Islam in India. Therefore, there is more comprehensive history of the Islamic period than the centuries preceding it, in which it becomes difficult to identify the personalities and manuscripts in context of their time and space with authenticity. Also, there was no conflict or confusion about the scripts and languages, as history of Islamic period was mostly written in the Arabic script and in Persian language, unlike the centuries preceding it in which there was a diversity of scripts and languages.

We celebrated pluralism, remained culturally united despite being in different kingdoms and had a wide degree of civic freedom in a pre-political society. The two pan-Indian epics, Ramayana and Mahabharat, were celebrated with multiple inter-pretations and adaptations; the traditions of the Rigveda were the social ideals for centuries. We had no systems of slavery and serfdom as dominant mode of economy as it was in Europe; we had no theocratic states, neither was there any episcopal order or duality and conflict for political sovereignty as it was between church and monarch in Europe. The villages functioned as democratic collective, when required, despite practising physical distancing with a tiny group of castes. Education was open to all; the literary contribution was massive; trade and commerce was thriving; the business and political elite lived in luxury and the craftsmen were employed. It was this prosperity and economic stability that had attracted the pagans, Muslims and Europeans over the centuries until the Company destroyed it after it seized the power beginning from 1757.

1

Evolutionary Trajectory of *Rashtra*

Balaji Ranganathan

This is more an introspection into the construction of traditions and historiography in premodern India as it assumes crucial importance within the very nature of the discourses that it has engendered in present times. It is a matter of crucial importance that existing trends need to be investigated afresh not necessarily negated so as to posit an alternative mode of reading historiography, for after all plurality and diversity have been facets of the intellectual traditions within India. The continuation, amalgamation and consolidation within Indic thought have been a part of intellectual transmission across South and Far East Asia, and this has been less understood or interrogated within Indic traditions. If we assume that the colonialist historiographical exercise within the confines of colonial capitalism was correct in its interpretation, then the trajectory, expansion and development of traditions within India and Asia stand compromised, creating a history with all of its resulting problems of interpreting tradition. The conceptual problems begin within sociological indicators which go on with their teleological impetus to construct a society while ignoring its own liminality. The liminality is evident within the very nature of choice informed as it is within the larger debris of colonialism and its received historiography.

Premodern India and the Problems of Historiography

So how has premodern India been examined within early sociology, which still casts a long shadow over the nature of things, and moreover how does post-coloniality even examine a case where the nature of the object of enquiry is so contaminated with colonialist debris? Has the nature of 'progress' demarcating the colonial against the premodern within the Benjaminian sense actually become a catastrophe which makes the present individual and the collective self-incapable of ever articulating a sense of the past?

The reason for keeping the 19th- and the early 20th-century frames for interrogation has been the comprehensive sociological nature of the narrative, which goes on to impregnate the political narrative also going on to create a post-colonial crisis within globalization pressures. Let me briefly interrogate the sociological categories brought in by early sociologists such as Emile Durkheim and Max Weber on account of their influence on the interpretation of early cultures along with the early Orientalists within India. Modern-day sociology questions the premises of both these theorists, but their readings have continued within the questions of pre-capitalist societies and larger questions of caste and traditions within modern India. This has had a profound effect on understanding early India, largely being seen within the category of primitive societies, and I am sure you would all agree that modern scholarship has been very apologetic with any early India enquiry. Emile Durkheim in his book *The Division of Labour in Society* brings out the inherent problems that are a part of the colonialist enterprise. Caught up within the growth of the nascent industrial capitalism within the 19th century, he distinguishes early societies within the binaries of pre-colonial capital and colonial capital. In the reconstruction of early urbanity and social cultures which build traditions, it is the larger impetus of capital which decides the nature of the primitive and the marginalized. In fact, early urbanity and cultures in premodern India is discounted by Durkheim within the notion of the mechanical

largely incapable of ever maturing into developed societies. Here, Romila Thapar mentions:

> Mechanical solidarity is the social integration of members of a society who have common values and beliefs. These common values and beliefs constitute a 'collective conscience' that works internally in individual members to cause them to cooperate. Because, in Durkheim's view, the forces causing members of society to cooperate were much like the internal energies causing the molecules to cohere in a solid, he drew upon the terminology of physical science in coining the term mechanical solidarity. In contrast to mechanical solidarity, organic solidarity is social integration that arises out of the need of individuals for one another's services. In a society characterized by organic solidarity, there is relatively greater division of labour, with individuals functioning much like the interdependent but differentiated organs of a living body. Society relies less on imposing uniform rules on everyone and more on regulating the relations between different groups and persons, often through the greater use of contracts and laws.[1]

A point that will be contested by me later in the presentation is the idea of the division of labour as being the normative for urbanity and social constructions. The *Chaturvarna* categories of the Rigveda were the foundations around which Indian society was interpreted and this idea of caste still informs our understanding of the traditions within India. The problems of interpreting early India and its traditions are largely based on the sources and commentaries of the early Orientalists. The Orientalist and the Anglicist controversy in the 1830s also foreclosed on the material advances and traditions, for example, metallurgical and sculptural traditions within the Shilpa Shastras, and an understanding of early cosmology with the *Surya Siddhantha*, just to cite a few examples. The Organic idea of solidarity solely rests within industrial capitalism, which goes on to make all merchant enterprise and merchant capitalism redundant as a solidarity within early India, bringing out an eternal problem of having an early India

[1] Romila Thapar, *History and Beyond* (New Delhi: OUP, 2003), 28.

that cannot be seen within the light of an advanced urbanity with its associative traditions. These readings of Durkheim along with Weber make early India a problem as the basic premise continues into modern-day discourses, and the very ideal of the Indic is compromised through received frames of analysis. Durkheim, unlike Weber, does not bring out the notion of caste creating traditions. He does not even directly comment on India, but the structures of early societies that he creates negate the rich and vibrant traditions within early India as not being based as it is on the divisions of capitalist labour. On the other hand, through his studies on early religion within India, Weber negotiates early Indian cultures and traditions through the translations of the Orientalist project. The focus on the lack of the emergence of capitalism within early India brings out the nature of primitive society as well as the resultant problems of the problem of Orientalist despotism and superstition. The colonialist modernity with its focus on law and science as indicators of economic and social progress was seen by him as representative of developed capitalistic societies. This effectively brings the entire idea of literary historiography, performative traditions, sectarian cultures, early Indian science and urbanity advances into the realm of the speculative, not being informed by the ideal of colonial progress, progress here meaning a clear division of labour that defines classes and occupations which constitute social relations. Weber does examine the stages of the formation of the polis, but it is the Western city that represents the frames of progress and not the oriental cities. Archaeological excavations of a large number of *janapadas* such as Rajgriha, Kaushambi, Lumbini, Taxila and Amravati might contest the claim on a lack of a developed urbanity. According to Weber, traditions of thought was only possible with well-developed social relations. This meant that the urban space had to be well-planned, with fortifications, trade centres, association of traders and guilds along with a limited autonomy of the law. Somewhere, older ideas of kinship were replaced by legal structures, religion grew in its primacy and the idea of a contract was born. The Indian case, according to Weber, did not see the predominance of the guilds and mercantile structures within the larger structures of governance. Economic structures replace the older kinship patterns within Weber's idea of a modern urban space. One way to understand this is that an archaeological history of India is going to be very different from an idea of linear history. How does one explain it? The larger problem associated with Weber is his examination of only the Vedic, Buddhist and Jain cultures for his frames of analysis. He effectively ignores larger philosophical traditions such as the Vaisheshika, Charvaka, Ajivika and traditions within the larger Pali canon, and he does not even examine the sectarian traditions such as Shaivism and Vaishnavism in India.

The current debates, informed by these colonialist discourses, will be unable to examine the nature of traditions within India solely based on the idea of labour. For the first instance, the problem of time and space is ignored with the use of a modern-day debate of class and capital in early societies, which needs a different frame for analysis. One mode would be to debate mercantile capitalism instead of industrial capitalism keeping trade networks and procedures in mind. Mercantile capitalism in the early years of the millennium and the medieval period was robust and there are numerous readings testifying to the same. This way, the role of traditions gets liberated being informed by local indigenous practices. The second problem that needs examination is the notion of caste as a normative when examining the discourses and traditions within India. Can the monolithic nature of caste be questioned when most early historians on India, from Romila Thapar to Upinder Singh (I shall keep Sheldon Pollock out of this debate) believe that caste originated in early India? Can the smritis bearing the imprint of an early society which might have read a different form and nature of hierarchy as opposed to the colonialist one be read as the bearer of traditions? The idea of caste saw its formation within colonialist capitalism in a larger sense by bringing back an early social stratification and by associating it with class, thus creating a problem of huge dimensions. There is also a lack of interrogation and an understanding of *jati* cultures confused as it is with the ideas of caste. The Weber and Durkheimian frameworks were carried on by M. N. Shrinivas with the ideas of Sanskritization, thus creating a hierarchal mode of categories in modern sociology. His larger premise was to challenge the monolithic notion of caste and traditions by bringing in an idea of upward mobility, but the notion of a Brahminical normative, however convincing it might be, points to an earlier colonialist historiography of caste and hierarchies. The limitations of this are due to a reductionist idea of tradition, which assumes that there can only be a single approach to participate in caste hierarchies. The limitations of caste as a category for traditions begins and ends within its own liminal status. One as an idea of a hierarchy which is beyond the limits of recordable history precisely because there are no historical sources, and the other is within the received traditions of colonialism. Hence, an amnesia regarding the traditional aspects in early India is a recurrent motif within discourses. The period has been seen within the Weberian models to be outside the economic structures that define a modern society.

This is precisely the reason that a change in perceptions is necessary since there are a number of misconceptions regarding the manner by which early India needs to be re-evaluated and perceptional problems need to be reiterated. Traditions in India have evolved over time and, though they have been intimately connected with religion, there has to be a refocus on the structures of traditions. Part of the problem is the pedagogical procedures that have been inculcated within the educational systems and attempts to bring a change of perceptions is seen among revivalists. If this conservative approach is not addressed, there is a constant danger of being limited by critical frames that we have today. Traditions and critical thought if taken out of these frames will bring in a sense of the past that is more holistic in nature. Much of early Indic thought has been caught up within the early sociological frames that I outlined, and this prevents a realistic estimate from taking place.

Rashtra: A Historiographical and a Literary Understanding

Rashtra has an interesting history in the evolution of the idea of geographical space and with the political idea attached to it. Today, we have a very clear distinction between the idea of a state and the idea of a nation. This evolution happened after Westphalia brought out our modern-day notion of the state. What was the idea within the larger trajectories of Indian political history, especially with early Indian texts, is a subject of this short chapter.

This discussion examines Sanskrit and Tamil sources as both see their full development by the 4th century CE; this statement is being made by dividing the development of Sanskrit into two phases. One is the pre-Panini phase reflected in the old Sanskrit of the Rigveda and some of the early mandalas in the other Vedas, and the other is the post-Panini phase which sees the development of classical Sanskrit by the 6th century CE, which is reflected in the epics such as the Mahabharata and the Ramayana. Sanskrit language, literature and commentaries see a full systemization after Panini and the *Ashtadhyayi* which sets the rules, both syntactic and paradigmatic. A pioneering work that has been done in this area is by Dr Shiva Acharya where there was a study of nation constructions and nationalisms in the Vedic period.[2] Although the import of this research is admirable, it is limited by the fact that it is enumerative and the larger historiographical understanding of the term within the larger ambits of historical and cultural change is missing. *Rashtra* has been understood in the larger context of colonialism and has been perceived to be largely a post-Westphalian exercise. This term finds a mention in most of the early Indian texts, and its interpretation is fascinating as it displays an evolutionary standard as it metamorphoses into a larger 19th-century version of nation and national consciousness.

[2] Shiva Acharya, *Nation and Nationalism in the Vedic Literature: A Study* (Assam: Gauhati University, 2000).

The term *rashtra* in Sanskrit is derived from the root word *raj*, which means to shine, and *stram* is added to it as a suffix, resulting in three ideas by which it can be deliberated. In this sense, *rashtra* can be defined as (a) that which reveals all people, (b) that by which all are revealed everywhere and with grandeur and (c) that which shines over all the spheres.

Some later literary texts like the *Amarakosha* define *rashtra* as an important organ of the state.[3] The divisions of the state are as follows: (a) a master or a king, (b) ministers, (c) friends, (d) account of the military and (5) a fort.

Shankaracharya, in the 8th century, refers to *rashtra* as *desa*. With him, the *rashtra* takes on the meaning of a kingdom[4] of subjects[5] or a state of *desa* when he is present.[6] Various scholars have ascribed various ideas and meanings with the word *rashtra*. The *Shatapatha Brahmana* examines *rashtra* as something that helps people accrue wealth, which then goes on to symbolize property.[7]

One of the early tracts within the Rigveda looks at the term *rashtra* as being equal to the *Ashvamedha yagna*.[8] The track reads *Raje vai esa yagnanam asvamedhah* on the same section where it qualifies *Rastram vai asvamedhah*.

This is an interesting development so far as the word *rashtra* moves from being defined as the organ of the state to being defined as all-inclusive as it includes both the material and the spiritual well-being of people. This means that, at this stage, the

[3] *Amarkosha* with the Maniprabha Hindi commentary (Choukhamba: Varanasi, 1976), 36, see Kshtriya Varga.

[4] Rigveda, Griffith's commentary and translation. *The Hymns of the Rigveda* (New Delhi: Motilal Banarasidas, 1973). 10/11, 3/1 10/174/1–5.

[5] Rigveda, Sayana's commentary (Mumbai, 1810), 4/42/1.

[6] Shukla Yagurveda, with Ubata and Mahidhara's commentary, ed. Panduranga Javji Sresthi (Mumbai, 1929), 22/22.

[7] Ganga Prasad Upadhyaya, ed., *Shatapatha Brahmana*, with Ratnadipika Hindi commentary (New Delhi: Pracin Vaignanikadhyayan Anusandhan Sansthan, 1967), 6/7/3/7.

[8] Ibid., 13/2/2/1, SB 13/1/6/3.

word somewhere veers between the material and the spiritual side of all things.

The word *rashtra* appears very frequently in the Vedic *samhitas*, though the connotation will be very different from modernday context. It is mentioned 11 times in the Rigveda, 71 times in the Shukla Yajurveda and 59 times in the Atharva Veda. Being derived from the root word *raj*, the term carries a distinct material and spiritual dimension. Within the *matra samhitas*, *rashtra* was created by the oblations during the *yagnas* and the beneficial outcome of this was the conferring of *rashtra on the people*.[9] This meant that *rashtra* was a psychological state that was a result of the oblations performed, and that this word was carried in a dialectical relationship between the material and the spiritual. The Atharva Veda also carries the idea of geography around it. The passage says that sages walked on the earth surrounded by oceans and they called it *rashtra*.[10] The mantra goes on to say that the land is paved with *rashtra* to bring prosperity to the people.[11]

One singular idea of the *Rigvedic* families and the mandalas is the idea of an integrative force that permeates the mantras. The mantras move on from the notions of agriculture, ploughing, dairy husbandry, implement making, the idea of fire and its facets, weather, politics, heroes and valour, the discovery of new deities, the role of seasons, sacred geography and, through the idea of the *Purusha*, the role of cosmology and all creation. Coming through these mantras are some further indications that Adi Shankara brings out in the 8th century with the idea of *desa* or territory. The Vedic corpus brings out through the *Purusha Suktam* the idea of what a Kshatriya has to do. The Rigveda in the 10th mandala is also mentioned in the Atharva Veda which

[9] Rigveda, Griffith's commentary and translation. *The Hymns of the Rigveda* (New Delhi: Motilal Banarasidas, 1973), 10/174/1.

[10] Ibid.

[11] Atharva Veda (School of the Saunaka), Sayana's commentary and translation of R. C. Sharma (Moradabad: Sanatana Dharma Yantralaya, 1986), 12/1/8.

reads *Rastram gupitam Ksatriyasya*[12] and goes on to read in the Shukla Yajurveda as *Varyam Rastre Jagramaha Purothiya*. In this sense, a Kshatriya had to protect territory and the land from all debacles, and it was the job of the *purohit* to advise the king on the sanctity of *rashtra*. At this stage, I repeat that it is important to note that there is a lot of fluidity in the word, and it goes on to qualify all three qualities of *artha, kama and moksha*. The word also meant a well-organized society, and this is visible within the *samhitas* as everything from the sacrifices to the cosmos is being codified and segregated into systems.[13] This is mentioned in both Atharva Veda and *Aiatreya Brahmana*. It is read as *Rastrani Vai Visah*. In fact, the Atharva Veda goes on to state that the society had to be a conscious one.[14] And a strong administration was one of the singular traits of a good *rashtra*.

Every territory has a conscious and popular memory today, and this was true of the world within the *samhitas* also. The idea of culture and history is evident when the mantra invokes the idea of memory. It goes on to place an emphasis on the role of the past, present and future.[15]

With the emerging ideas of kingship, a *chakravartin* had to donate his entire *rashtra* as an oblation sacrifice, and he accepted it again as a by-product of the *yagna*. At this stage, I want to emphasize that there is something fluid about this term. It goes on to span the temporal and the corporeal. There is something magical about it being associated with the soma sacrifice and role of the *Maha Purusha* as a part of cosmology. Infact the Rigveda states that *rashtra* was a living entity which without the

[12] Rigveda. Griffith's commentary and translation. *The Hymns of the Rigveda* (New Delhi: Motilal Banarasidas, 1973), 10/109/3, AV/5/17/3.

[13] Atharva Veda (School of the Saunaka), Sayana's commentary and translation of R. C. Sharma, (Moradabad: Sanatana Dharma Yantralaya, 1986), 1/29/1, AB/8/26.

[14] Ibid., 3/19/2–5.

[15] Rigveda, Griffith's commentary and translation. *The Hymns of the Rigveda* (New Delhi: Motilal Banarasidas, 1973), 10/15/2.

Brahmana for the ritual sacrifice the ideas of *rta, tapa, rashtra, srama*, dharma and karma could not be achieved.[16]

So a territory with the *chakravartin* and the *purohit* had to look after the nature of well-being, and this would continue until the sanctity of *rashtra* was respected.[17] Keeping this in mind, the concept of *rashtra* talks about a geopolitical territory comprising everything in terms of *artha, kama* and *moksha*, and it signified an organic unity of land, mind, earth and cosmos. It was thought to be catastrophic if the *idea of the rashtra failed*. It meant the following could potentially damage a *rashtra*.[18] The Atharva Veda mentions the following:

1. If a comet fell, *rashtra* would have to be re-invoked.
2. If a Brahmani was kidnapped
3. When a cow was not allowed to roam freely. Remember that this was a society that measured wealth in terms of cattle owned.
4. Where the Brahmans were tortured, and this is visible in the epical tradition and the *puranas* where atrocities heaped upon people lead to the avatar formations from Matsya to Kalki.

The popular literature and the idea of territory and the role of a *chakravartin* are also visible in the epical tradition. For want of time, I shall specifically concentrate on the Valmiki Ramayana. The point of interest for me is to understand the idea of Rama as an individual who becomes a model of kingship and good governance. This is reflected within the entire Kshatriya tradition, taking this epical character as model. What was so specific of this character which inspired an epic and a memory? One way of understanding this is the emergence of the smritis, especially

---

[16] Ibid., 11/7/17–18.

[17] Ibid., 4/42/1.

[18] Atharva Veda (School of the Saunaka), Sayana's commentary and translation of R. C. Sharma (Moradabad: Sanatana Dharma Yantralaya, 1986), 12/1/38, AV 5/17/6, AV 5/17/12, AV 5/18.

the Manusmriti, which codified the duties of all the *varnas*. The character of Rama is an illustration of this, where justice, law, governance and propriety are held supreme, and this is illustrative in the Ramayana and the Mahabharata, where the ideals of kingship and governance have to be learnt by all characters, be it the *Shanti Parva* in the Mahabharata or the ending of the Ramayana where the lessons by Ravana have to be learnt. Both these epics reflect the Vedic concept of *rashtra* being transgressed and reworked.

In fact, the Ramayana brings out the actual extent of territorial knowledge within this ambit of the *rashtra*. In the space of travel across peninsular India the Ramayana[19] mentions names of villages, rivers and cities that are extent today. This does not point to the historicity of the epic, but the geography within cannot be faulted. The division below has the old location, the river and the urban space situated in the modern-day location. The epic mentions the following:

1. Ayodhya Sarayu Ayodhya
2. Kampilya Ganges Kampil
3. Kasi Ganges Varanasi
4. Girivarja Sumagadhi Rajgir
5. Prayaga Ganges Allahabad
6. Hastinapur Ganges Meerut
7. Madhura Yamuna Mathura
8. Mahodaya Ganges Kannauj
9. Rajgriha (Vasumati) Vikasta Jalalpur
10. Visala Ganga Vaishali
11. Takshashila Indus Taxila (Pakistan)
12. Pushkalavati Swat and the Kabul Charsadda (Pakistan)
13. Gaya Phalgu Gaya
14. Mahishmati Narmada Maheshwara

Somewhere, the transition from the Vedic *rashtra* to the idea of *rashtra* as being connected with territory is seen in both the

---

[19] Valmiki, Ramayana, 2 vols. (Gorakhpur: Gita Press).

Sanskrit and Tamil traditions. With the connection with territory, there is a notion of sanctity. The early Vedic *rashtra* was fluid and had multidimensional connotations, and this sees a connection between the concepts of monarchy, kingship, population and territory with the epical tradition due to the codification with the smritis. This is also reflected with a parallel literary tradition in Tamil, which reflects the same concepts with the idea of a *rashtra*, but with the nature of the feminine aspect of the *Kaumari*.

The earliest Tamil literature that reflects both inner and outer subjectivity is the literature of the Sangam period that was composed between 300 BCE and 300 CE. This is the third Sangam period as we can infer from the earliest codification of Tamil poetics, the *Tholkappiyam*, which were composed around 300 BCE. Sangam poetry is described in a collection collated together in the 10th century, namely *the eight anthologies* or *the Ettuttokai* and the *Pattuppattu* or the 10 songs. There are more than 1,000 poems within these anthologies. The *Tholkappiyam* brings out the two categories of early Sangam poetry, namely *Akam* and *Puram*, where *Akam* would reflect the inner subjectivity as it is connected with the nature of love and the erotic, while *Puram* is concerned with the outer world which consists of kings and governance, battle, heroics and land. I am not concerned here in this chapter with the idea of *Akam* poetry, but with the *Puram* poetry, which describes and codifies territory. Tamil poetics has an intimate connection with land, which is reflected in the category of the poems. These categories are called *Tinai*. The fivefold geography of this poetry is as follows:

1. Kurinchi or mountainous tracks
2. Mullai or forest tracks
3. Marutam or river valleys
4. Neytal or coastal tracks
5. Palai or deserts or barren lands

This fivefold geography is reflected in the *Puram* poems, which describe the might of kings, government and war. It is to be noted that Tamil belongs to a different school of languages, unlike Sanskrit, and Sangam poetry does not reflect the geography of the upper Ganga valley. Although, surprisingly, *Palai* or the desert is a category which is not a geographical feature of the South Indian peninsula, which might mean that there was an awareness of Western Indian geographical features in the early years of the millennium. The idea of the land and the attachment towards territory is actually South Indian as these poems and the Tamil epics such as the *Silappatikaram* and the *Manimekalai* talk about the Chera and the Pandian kingdoms. The idea of Tamil nationalism today is connected deeply with the idea of the *Kaumari Kandam*, which points to the huge Tamil continent that saw a submergence due to tectonic activity and sea ingress through the centuries. Archaeologically, the current underwater excavations around Poompuhar near Chennai testify to a possibility of this fact as numerous submerged fortifications and structures have been found within the continental shelf area. This on the western coast at Dwarka is testified with the same kind of submergence pointing to rising sea levels during the early years of the first millennium as brought out the undersea excavations of the Indian Oceanographic Institute survey under S. R. Rao. This is also mentioned within the anthologies of Sangam poetry, which talks about the many Madurais lost due to sea ingress and earlier Sangams. In this poetry, the idea of territory is deeply connected with the idea of Tamilhood and Tamil consciousness, though Tamil poetry does not mention *rashtra* which is Sanskrit in origin, but it connects this idea with *Kaumari*, something that is reflected with the term *Kanyakumari* or Cape Comorin.

The construction of Tamil identity is evident in the Śangam corpus of poetry and the two Tamil epics *Śilappatikāram* and the *Manimekalaï*, which are major works datable to the 2nd century CE. Within the literary historiography of Indian literature, these texts shift away from the larger *puranic* mythology of the Ramayana and the Mahabharata, which became a phenomenon in the post-Gupta period from the 6th century CE onwards, to introduce a different idiom of protagonists, ideas and concerns to further bring out a distinct non-*puranic* feel to the construction of literature in South India.

Scattered around the Tamil country are numerous sites of rock-cut caves, temples, *bastis* and stupas that attest to the archaeology of the period, heterodox and tolerant, a period that also saw the rise of epics, which point to a larger historiography of the epic tradition in India. To cite the material conditions that generated the two epics going back to reconstruct the epigraphical history is fruitful. The epigraphical materials bring out a fair idea as to the social conditions that engendered the age and caused the production of the literary output. The two inscriptions cited below are among the numerous inscriptions that are found in the areas of today's territorial limits of Karnataka and Tamil Nadu.

> Vikârin saṁvatsara—having gratified six female mendicants with gifts and honourable treatment, etc., (and) having of his own accord washed the feet of Nâgadêvapaṇḍita, the head of the holy Vadiyûr-Gaṇa has given, at Sûṇḍî, in the northern part (of the village), 60 nivartanas (of land), by the staff which is the royal measure, for the purpose of repairing anything that may become broken or torn, (and) for the performance of worship, and to provide food, to the chaityâlaya—built at Sûṇḍî, the city which is the chief (town) of the Suldhâṭavî seventy villages—of his wife, the glorious Dîvaḷâmbikâ, who is a manifest goddess through the purity of (her) accurate perception.

> The boundaries of it (are): On the east, the cultivated land called Mânasiṅga-keyi; on the south, the land called the land of the jack-fruit trees; on the west, the field called Keppara-pola; (and) on the north, the stream that comes from (the village of) Bâlugêri. The village gives three gadyânas as thearuvaṇa; (and) the village preserves the entire arrangement.

> (L. 80.)—'This general bridge of piety of kings should at all times be preserved by you,'—(thus) does Râmabhadra again and again make a request to all the future princes! The earth has been enjoyed by many kings, commencing with Sagara; whosoever for the time being possesses the earth, to him belongs, at that time, the reward (of this grant that is now made, if he continue it)!

(L. 83.)—At Sûṇḍî, the chief (town) of the Suldhâṭavî seventy, the glorious Dîvaḷâmbâ,—the one Rambhâ of the world,—celebrated the sacrificial rites of six female mendicants, and caused the famous Jaina temple to be built. Ôm! Ôm! Ôm![20]

There is a second inscription that needs to be looked at. The text is given below.

Amanan matirai attiran urai utayanasa

The abode (*urai*) of Attiran, the Jaina monk (*amanan*) of Madurai (*matirai*) (Gift of) of Udayana (*utayana*)[21]

The state of the Tamil country is testified to by the inscriptions that point to the nature of *praxis* where there is the practice of the lived experience and it shows with the layer contours of history. A larger part of the propagation of world religions is through a degree of patronage and the formation of the donors and merchant guilds played an important role in the propagation of Buddhism, Jainism and various sectarian Hindu cults and belief systems. The formation of the rock-cut caves, *viharas* and temples were the larger contribution to the various guilds which actively propagated the beliefs through an expression of an artistic ability, amply testified with the monuments of Sañci, Nagarjunakonda, Bharhut and Amravati.

With the rise of the *puranic* epics such as the Ramayana and the Mahabharata around the 4th century CE, and the subsequent spread of the story kernels and the numerous retellings that followed, the two Tamil epics *Śilappatikāram* and the *Manimekalaï* bring out an earlier period a time, and the two translations of the inscriptions cited above point to the larger materiality of the period where there had been rulers who patronized and promoted

---

[20] Lewis Rice, *Inscriptions at Śravana Belagola* (Mysore: Government Press, 1880), 26.

[21] A Tamil Brahmi inscription found by Emmanuel Jebarajan of the American College, Madurai at Mettupatti, Nilakottai Taluka, Madurai District. It is unpublished so far.

the two religions and within the subsequent change that followed after the 8th century, the entire Tamil country moved considerably away following the mysticism of the Alwars and the Nayanars in the Vaishnavite and the Shivite traditions with the Aryanization of South India. As Shastri mentions,[22] though the notion of the Aryan is used here not with the reference to race but to ideologies, religious texts and belief systems as modern scholarship has largely done away with the colonialist constructions of the Aryan invasion.

The Materiality of History and the Archaeology of Texts

Śravanabelagola in Karnataka is a site which has witnessed a major penetration of Jainism and Buddhism, and though Jainism predominates the site from the early years of the millennium, the entire site stretching into Tamil Nadu has seen a major intersection between the two faiths. The entire area is dotted by *bastis* (Jain temples) and Buddhist sites that testify to the larger presence of donor grants and land being allotted to the two faiths. The Tamil country covered extensive parts of Tamil Nadu, Karnataka and parts of Kerala within the medieval and the present areas divided on linguistic boundaries in post-Independence India do no justice to the older syncretic forms of belief systems that had existed in the period. The larger intervention of archaeology during the colonial period after the 18th century saw a systematic translation and transcription of the larger oral traditions around the two religions and the period also saw a systematic translation of inscriptions in the area pointing to a larger presence of the two religions. A combination of archaeological analysis along with the historiography of the textual tradition can be quite fruitful leading us to an understanding of the cultural paradigms of early India and its related problems with literary historiography.

---

[22] Nilakanta Sastri, *A History of South India: From Prehistoric Times to the Fall of Vijaynagar* (New Delhi: OUP, 2007), 3.

B. Lewis Rice[23] mentions that when passing through Hassan district and moving towards Channarayapatna in Karnataka state, one can see two large hills looming in the distance and, as one gets closer, one can find a colossal statue of a human being carved out of stone on the tallest one, with some of the oldest inscriptional records talking about a time that predates Asoka the Mauryan emperor. Among the oldest inscriptions that surround a small *basti*[24] constructed around the 9th century, one talks about a man called Bhadrabahu, who is also a subject of a small cave which has footprints carved out in stone and an object of deep veneration among Jains who visit the place. Today, with the bifurcation of Indian provinces on linguistic grounds after Independence, this area falls within the state of Karnataka, though around 400 BCE, it was largely a Tamil country. The site has two hills, a lake and a small town nestled between the two, and the place is named Shravanabelagola; where Shravana is the *Sramana* or the ascetics, a term loosely used in the early years of the first millennium to signify the followers of Jainism and Buddhism. The two hills, Vindhyagiri and Chandragiri, dominate the landscape sheer granite monolithic mounds jutting out of the ground at over 3,500 feet over sea level. The Chandragiri hill is of a greater antiquity as it has the largest number of inscriptions (271), and the Vindhyagiri hill having 172, and both point back to time to the earliest historically datable period of India, and they both follow a consistent theme recording the fasting until death, or *Sallekhana*, which resulted in the extreme purification of the body as it emptied off desire, accounts of kings and the hagiography associated with them, donations by pilgrims and the ritual installation of images. High up on the Vindhyagiri hill is a cave associated with Bhadrabahu Swamy, who had migrated down to Shravanabelagola along with the then Mauryan emperor. The cave is the holiest of holy places in the area, subject to a deep state of veneration, which commands a view from the small Jain *basti* situated on the Chandragiri hill. Hagiography in the area

[23] Rice, *Inscriptions at Śravana Belagola*, 14.
[24] A Jain site of worship in Kannada.

states that the original *basti* was built by the grandson of Asoka in honour of his grandfather Chandragupta Maurya, though the present one, built in the 9th century, faces this cave. Jain traditions maintain that this cave was the site where Bhadrabahu Swamy, a Digambar acetic, passed away and the Chandragupta *basti* points to this cave. Surrounding the *basti* are a larger number of inscriptions in old Kannada, which mention the traditions that surround this site and especially interesting is a perforated screen within the *basti* that chronicles the coming of Bhadrabahu and his entourage, including the Mauryan emperor Chandragupta. Dasoja, a sculptor from the Hoysala dynasty around the 12th century CE, had reportedly carved the screen, pointing to the old memories that surround the place and the building up of the hagiography and the *Sthala Puranas of Shravanabelagola*.

The story of Bhadrabahu Swamy is connected with a dream of Chandragupta Maurya on a full moon night in the month of Kartika, where he sees the following 16 dreams, and an inscription at Shravanabelagola records it[25]:

1. The sun setting
2. A branch of the Kalpavriksha breaks up and fall
3. A divine car descending from the sky and returning
4. The disk of the moon sundered
5. Black elephants fighting
6. Fireflies twinkling in the night
7. A dry lake
8. Smoke in the air
9. An ape sitting on a throne
10. A dog eating out of a golden bowl
11. Young bulls labouring
12. Kshatriya boys riding donkeys
13. Monkeys scaring away swans
14. Calves jumping into the sea
15. Foxes pursuing old oxen
16. A 12-headed serpent approaching

[25] Rice, *Inscriptions at Śravana Belagola*, 25.

Bhadrabahu Swamy interprets the dreams as the following, an interesting overview of the reasons behind the migration of people from the seat of Pataliputra, the site of the Mauryan empire in the north, to the small cave on Vindhyagiri hill. The hagiography surrounding the duo is connected with the interpretation of the dreams of Chandragupta Maurya and old memories being carved out in stone at the site. Bhadrabahu's response to the dream is as follows, and it points to the larger notions of patronage, geographical awareness and the institutionalization of Jainism around 350 BCE.

1. All knowledge will be darkened.
2. The Jain religion will decline, and your successors on the throne will not take *diksha*.
3. The heavenly beings will not henceforth visit the Bharatakshetra.
4. The Jains will be split into sects.
5. The clouds will not give seasonable rain and the crops will be poor.
6. True knowledge being lost, a few sparks will glimmer with a feeble light.
7. Aryakhanda will be destitute of Jain doctrine and falsehood increase.
8. The evil will prevail, and goodness be hidden.
9. The vile, the low-born and the wicked will acquire power.
10. Kings, not content with a sixth share, will introduce land rent and, demanding twice and thrice the amount, oppress their subjects.
11. The young will form religious purposes but forsake them when old.
12. Kings of high descent will associate with the base.
13. The low will torment the noble and try to reduce them to the same level.
14. Kings will assist in oppressing the people by levying custom duties and other unlawful taxes.
15. The low with hollow compliments will get rid of the noble, the good and the wise.
16. Twelve years of dearth and famine will come upon this land.

The interpretation of the dreams of Bhadrabahu Swamy of wide-spread chaos and the prospects of a massive famine adds to the discomfiture of the emperor and, taking the initiation or *diksha* and embracing Jainism, he proceeds with a large group of Jains to the site of the two hills that dominate the countryside around Shravanabelagola, where Bhadrabahu Swamy, perceiving his end is near, decides to pass away in the cave and is immortalized in a set of stone footprints worshipped till date by Digambar Jains in India.

With a couple of centuries, Buddhism follows in a big way with the advent of Aśoka and the large number of his edicts being found in the areas that are part of the two epics, *Śilappatikāram* and the *Manimekalaï*. The Jain Āgama traditions talk about the Śvetāmbara guru Kālakāchārya being received in the court of the Sātavāhana king around the 1st century BCE and the presence of the Jain Digambar monk Viśākhāchārya choosing to establish his areas of operations in the Choḷa and Pāndya territories. What is amply testified is that the two religions got their immense patronage within the Pallava courts of Kāñchīpuram and the Pāṇḍyan courts in Madurai. Kāñchīpuram is well known as one of the four Vidyāstānas, a seat of learning, mentioned in the Mahābhāshya of Patañjali, the others being Kolhāpur in Mahārāshṭra and Penukoṇda in Āndhra Pradesh.

The surprising heterodoxy of the texts following the Sangam period is not at odds with the earlier period, which followed the larger principles of *Akam* and *Puram*, as seen in the *Tolkāppiyam*, the treatise on grammar, and the two epics are situated firmly within religious traditions and the *Akam* and *Puram* traditions, though the *Śilappatikāram* on analysis does not appear to be in a fixed religious structure of Jainism but espouses a greater tolerance to the various beliefs around, unlike the *Maṇimekalaï* which is completely a Buddhist inspired work. The surrounding country and the politics of constructions, along with religious interpellations, construct literature, and the two epics testify as to the modifications of the basic Kōvalaṇ and the Kaṇṇaki stories, which should have been present within the orality of the region much before the entry of the two religions.

The author of the *Śilappatikāram* is Iḷaṅkō Aṭikaḷ and Aṭikaḷ means a Jain saint or an acetic, and an interesting legend is associated with the author of the *Maṇimekalaï* Śāttanar that he actually met Iḷaṅkō Aṭikaḷ to seek his permission to bring out the Buddhist version of the epic, which is quite acceptable within the politics of the period as there has never been a large-scale violence between the Buddhists and the Jains in history, unlike the heterodox sects and the Hindu ones.

The Buddhist presence is considerable in South India, and the Asókan edicts situated at Yerragudi, Siddapura and Suvarnagiri point to the southernmost sites of his influence, and one of his edicts mentions the Cēral, Cōḷa and Pāndya kingdoms, as well as a larger peaceful acceptance of Buddhism during his time in South India. The larger dialogical influences of ahimsa and karma with the two religions point to the common source of origins and the larger differentiation within Buddhism with the *Mahayana* traditions entering after the 3rd Buddhist council. The *Maṇimekalaï* displays a high influence of *Theravada* doctrines and is best exemplified by *Maṇimekalaï* the protagonist with the Boddhisattva attributes. Makkâli Gosâla, the Ajivika teacher of Ajivika traditions of the 4th and 5th centuries BCE was the teacher of both Mahavira and the Buddha and the role of karma with the repeated births and transmigrations are concepts that both Jainism and Buddhism have borrowed from the Ājīvika philosophy that grew and flourished before the advent of both the religions.

The setting of the epics within the cities of Puhâr and Kâñci within the Tamil domains is significant as two Greek works *The Periplus of the Erythraean Sea* dated at 1st century CE and Ptolemy's *Geography* dated at 2nd century CE mention Puhâr as the town Khaberis and Kaveris *Emporium* and the flourishing Roman trade with the Tamil kingdoms, and both epics describe at length the markets in the two towns providing a setting which is common place and with common men within the larger urban set-up, unlike the larger North Indian epics the Ramayana and the Mahabharata. Situated within the larger Jain and Buddhist themes are the mercantile communities and the guilds and the role of trade and its contribution to urbanity with courtesans, palaces, the common man and the religious institutions and individuals who populate the epics. This points to the larger dimensions of sovereignty, trade and a cross-national and international framework of geopolitical awareness.

Chronotopes and Interpellation in the *Śilappatikāram* and the *Manimekalaï*

Situated within *Puhâr*, the epics develop a kernel of the Kōvalan and the Kaṇṇaki and the Kaṇṇaki story that, as mentioned earlier, was present in the oral form and, probably as the details are unknown to us today, the kernel of the story might not have been within the larger Jain and Buddhist traditions and being adapted later as a representation for a larger audience which followed the two religions as seen with the larger Sanskrit epics the Ramayana and the Mahabharata and the spread of Vaishnaivism.

Mikhail Bakhtin in his essay 'Forms of Time and Chronotope in the Novel'[26] talks about the *chronotope* as an intrinsic connection between time, space and the development of literary genres. The chronotopic Kōvalan and Kaṇṇaki story is ahistorical in the sense that all good stories are permitting the gaze across time to shift and re-alter components in a discursive framework I shall term as *Interpellative Textual Signatures*. The *Interpellative Textual Signatures* permits the story to be told, retold and altered within an epistemic violence of ideologies where the violence is sublimated by the very nature of the plasticity of the *Signature*, leading to multiple versions and retellings of the same story existing in a peaceful symbiotic existence cannibalistic and nurturing at times within history and its chronotopic existence. The *Signature* functions through the function of *metonym* an epistemic space

---

[26] Mikhail Bakhtin, 'Forms of Time and Chronotope in the Novel' (1851); V. B. Leitch, *The Norton Anthology of Theory and Criticism* (New York, NY: W. W. Norton, 2001).

where there exists a Manichean duality, the potentialities of a binary clash appealing to the primordial instinct of mankind as it resolves the spaces within the world within a conceptual violence of the Manichean battle for order and resolution. The notional idea of the Manichean battle of the fight between the forces of light and darkness gets interpellated within characters such as *Manimekalaï* and *Kaṇṇaki* as they make sense of the world order around them across time within different sectarian ideologies. It is this Manichean quality that the chronotopes permit the *Textual Signatures* to be interpellated. The Kōvalaṇ and Kaṇṇaki story precisely within its ahistorical positioning is able to gather its chronotopic existence in history across time, getting appropriated within sects and coexisting and competitive ideologies.

The story centres on Kōvalaṇ and his affair with Mātavi, a courtesan who dominates the relationship and with whom Kōvalaṇ has a daughter called Manimekalaï. This is unknown to him and she is the subject of the sequel of the *Śilappatikāram*, the *Manimekalaï*. Kaṇṇaki, who is distraught, reunites with her husband after the affair with Mātavi breaks down due to a misunderstanding and, to recoup their losses, the two migrate to *Maturai*, the kingdom of the Pāṇṭian king Neṭunceḷiyaṇ. Seeking to sell the anklet belonging to Kaṇṇaki, Kōvalaṇ is cheated by a jeweller and is accused of stealing the queen's anklet and is executed. Kaṇṇaki is distraught and going to the kings court she breaks her anklet to prove that her anklet has diamonds and not pearls inside and in her distraught state she tears off her breast and flings it at the city of *Maturai* which burns to cinders before she ascends to heaven. Interestingly, there is a presence of the Jain nun Kavunti in the epic and the entire demise of Kōvalaṇ being attributed to the misdeeds of an earlier birth bringing in the entire Jain ethos of transmigration of the soul.

Manimekalaï, the daughter born out of Kōvalaṇ and Mātavi's relationship, continues the tale within a Buddhist setting as she proceeds on her way to becoming an *arhat* and, in the process, articulates the entire central beliefs within the *Mahayana* scriptures with its emphasis on the nature of the Bodhisattva. The larger *Interpellative Textual Signatures* in the story permits this entire overturning of religious ideologies and belief systems. The dialogical influence of language can be seen in a variety of discursive forms such as governance, monarchy, religion and the grotesque as the interpellative effects of the author Iḷaṅkō Aṭikaḷ plays out in his search for the precise Manichaean duality, and the historical present constructing the Tamil land permits a Jain retelling of the text.

The *Śilappatikāram* abounds with Jain themes and the idea of expiation is a major theme within Jainism. There are spaces within the text that show the Jain themes but still the text cannot be bracketed or is completely interpellated by the *Interpellating Textual Signifiers* to term it as completely Jain. The larger Jain observance that occupies the *Śilappatikāram* is the idea of *Sallekhana, Kuvanti*, the Jain Sadhvi who is the spiritual preceptor of Kaṇṇaki and Kōvalaṉ, ritually practises this extreme Jain austerity where the body is slowly starved to death, a classic example and practice of practising complete nonaction within the body and mind.

> And she moaned: 'Was this the fate of those Who were my companions?' She vowed to starve herself to death.
>
> So ended her life.[27]

The *Vipāka śrutam*, or the *Oral Traditions of Karmic Life*, one of the 60 Jain Āgamas (canonical texts) in Jainism that divides the life of the individual into the sentient and the non-sentient, the *Jīva* and the *Ajīva*,[28] and it is the world of karma that creates the non-sentient. The state of *Ajīva* brings out the notion of illusion and the notion of doer, the primordial mover of the self and ego. There is a sage's conversation to *Kuvanti* at *Śrīraṅkam* where he explains to her the transience of life and the problems of reigning in karma. It is also connected to the basic Jain belief that

---

[27] Iḷaṅkō Aṭikaḷ, *The Śilappatikāram* (New Delhi: Penguin, 1939), 238.
[28] Ibid., 336.

an *arhat*, or an evolved one, has to intervene to help a devotee and seeker of truth on the path of salvation, an idea that is not far removed from Buddhism and the notion of the Boddhisattva, especially when one sees how the two religions share common roots and are symbiotic with their root ideas.

> No one can escape the prison house
> Of the body's rebirth unless he is blessed
> With the light of the revealed Āgamas.[29]

The Jain traditions mention that Chandragupta Maurya, while settling down at Shravanabelagola and beginning the long-scale institutionalizing of the Jain faith in South India, had taken to the *Sallekhana* as a final mode of liberation. The Jain history in South India has shown a widespread practice of *Sallekhana* or ritual starving to death and Buddhism moves away from this with its emphasis on the middle path as a major distinguishing mark with its sister religion. Although having a Jain structure, there is no prescriptive ideology or a fundamental belief system in the *Śilappatikāram* as a text goes on to admit that there can be a movement away from its own belief systems, pointing to the larger ideologies and religious sects that had been coexisting in Tamil country. What can be inferred from both texts is the state of the province where the epics are situated. It points to a larger shift in the literary imagination away from the Sangam corpus, with its emphasis on the five *tiṇais*, the bifurcation of experience with emotion and land within the *Tolkāppiyam*, where the land decides the corresponding emotion. The *Śilappatikāram* and the *Manimekalaï*, though incorporating the basic *Akām* and *Purām* divisions, is able to take the epic to accommodating new traditions that are coming in from North India, which suggests a slow but sure homogenization of Indian literary traditions with the various tellings and retellings of the versions of the epical traditions.

---

[29] Ibid., 258–260.

The Buddhist doctrines are firmly fixed in the *Manimekalaï* and this points to the gradual building up of the Buddhist doctrine in South India. The fact that this expansion was not predatory is attested to in the epic as *Manimekalaï* has a dialogue with all the other faiths that have been around with the gradual entry of Sanskrit and the larger Vedic principles from the 4th century CE onwards. *Arvana Adigal* brings out the basic tenets of Buddhism, which sets *Manimekalaï* to the path of Arhatwood. *Arvana Adigal* explains the larger Buddhist doctrines comprising *Shuttunarvu* or perception, *anumâna* or deduction, along with the larger logics of argument, the 12 *nidhanas* or fetters that bind us to life and the four noble truths. The text mentions:

> It was through these four stages that Arvana Adigal led Manimekhalaï towards the truth, by his exposition of the dharma, free from all inconsistency, and lit for her the bright light of knowledge.

> Manimekhalaï, as beautiful as a doll, having put on her monastic habit henceforth led the life of austerity that is indispensable for attaining wisdom and being free of the burdens of faults that bind us to the interminable cycle of birth.[30]

The larger dialogic impulses present in both epics seek some common grounds for the human soul, though the matters of doctrine and modes of achieving it differ. The formation of the Chronotopes engendering human experience and literary genres along with the *Interpellative Textual Signatures* seek out the subject within a given historicity and the material conditions that engender it. The historical formation creates the literary experience and is an indicator of the linguistic signs and the ideologies of the period. Within the stupas at Nagarjunakonda and Amravati and the Jain *bastis* present in Tamil Nadu and Karnataka, as well as the rock-cut caves of the early years of the 1st century, both these epics point to a period in South India where a transition was in the making, of a period from the earlier

---

[30] Sâttanār, *Manimekalaï* (New York, NY: New Directions, 1989), 172.

imaginations that engendered the *Sangam* poetry to a new fresher import from the heart of the Indian subcontinent.

There is a huge difference between the Vedic imagination, which is in a state of formation regarding the notions of sovereignty and landownership, especially with the notions of *rashtra*, while the Tamil literary corpus points to a full-fledged development of identity connected with land, especially with the idea of the Kaumari Kandam, though one must examine the time gap between the Rigveda and the third Sangam corpus as the latter is later by nearly 1500 to 1800 years. We currently have no historical evidence of the first two sangams.

The notion of the *rashtra* evolves through time and is intimately connected with religion and ideological formations. One important thing to note is that the role of the nation, though intimately connected with the imagination, still has a material foundation. The term *rashtra*, through its evolution across time, finds its colonial articulation in terms of nation, nationhood and nationalisms and it's this ability of ideas and language to reach across time to find its articulation. The idea of the *rashtra* does not emanate just from the colonial period but it evolves to the latter stage through a complex interaction of history, materiality and an idea of a personal self.

2

Hindu, Hinduism and Hindutva

Bhuwan Kumar Jha

In contemporary Indian social and political life, the terms—Hindu, Hinduism and Hindutva—have been posited with fascinating arguments about their origins, meanings and consequently political implications. In the sense and context of its signifying a religious community, the word Hindu, in contrast to the nomenclature of other religious groups, is often seen as a term of relatively recent origin. It is claimed to be a British creation, or at best emerging specifically during the British era. The diversity of the Hindus, reflected in the multiplicity of their beliefs, customs and rituals, is paradoxically made to support the argument of their lacking a coherent religious identity before the 19th century and, therefore, the British colonial government is credited with the agency to impart to the Hindus a religious identity. This chapter would be tracing the origins, meanings and the historical context of the term Hindu—its identification with the culture and way of life of people living in a particular geographical area; changes in its being used in a territorial sense to being shifted to the sense of religious practices; oriental and colonial identification and connotation; the Indian response, etc. The increasing use of the term 'Hinduism', how Hindutva came to be used and defined,

Savarkar's use of the term and, finally, how Gandhi looked at Hindu and Hinduism, shall also be discussed and analysed.

Bhārat and Hindu: Interconnections

The term Hindu emerged in the larger context of signifying the territory within certain geographical boundaries identified with rivers and mountains, and concomitantly and consequently with people inhabiting these regions. At a different level, it would seem to overlap with the cultural traits of people and their unique ways of life so different from those arriving from outside. It may be worthwhile to trace the beginning of its usage and the context therein. Such an exercise takes us to other similar terms having a huge bearing on our enquiry. In the ancient Indian literature, the term Bhārat is often used in the context of describing the Bharat tribe or signifying a specific geographical region. It is used in many other contexts and with different meanings too. In fact, in the *puranic* and Vedic literature, at least four different meanings of the term can be traced. In one set of *puranic* literature (*Markendaya Purana, Vishnu Purana* and *Skanda Purana*), Bharat appears as the son of Rishabh, who in turn was the son of Nabhi, and it was after him that the land was referred to as Bhāratavarsha. *Skanda Purana* clearly mentions Bhāratavarsha as Nabhivarsha (Nabhi for navel or the centre). However, in *Agni Purana*, Bharat after whom this land is called Bhāratavarsha is the son of Dushyant and Shakuntala. *Shatapatha Brahmana* records this Bharata as having performed *Ashvamedha yagna* and achieving the exalted status of *chakravartin*. However, the Mahabharata interprets it differently. The *Adi Parva* of the great epic calls the descendants of Bharat or those born in his clan as Bhārat, and both were shown as expanding the glory of Bhāratavarsha throughout the world.[1]

---

[1] Pandit Madhusudan Ojha, *Bharatavarsha the Indian Narrative: As Told in Indravijayah* (translated by Kapil Kapoor, edited by Wilson John; New Delhi: Rupa, 2017), 13–22. Mahabharata mentions the term Bhārat as many

Further, the larger understanding or co-relation of the term with the area under coverage itself underwent change from time to time. Panini's *Ashtadhyayi* (500 BCE) mentions Prāchya Bhārat as a *janapada* lying between the north and the east. However, in the Mahabharata, Bhārat is seen as a much larger territorial zone. *Puranic* texts frequently use the term Bhāratavarsha with slight variation in the texts as regards the area or the region. The *Vishnu Purana* for the first time provides a vivid and somewhat precise description of what constitutes Bhārat: 'the land that lies north of the ocean and the south of the snowy mountains is called Bharata, and there dwell the progenies of Bharata.'[2] It is in the context of the usage of these terms to connote the geographical and cultural zone that the origin of the term 'Hindu' may be located. Madhusudan Ojha in his *Indravijayah*, written during the early 20th century, made a strong point here. He argued that the part which is addressed by the word Hindu or Hindustan is only half of Bhāratavarsha—

Hindupaden ca hindustānpaden ca yadāhurdyatanāḥ
Bhāratavarshaṃ tat khalu nāmārdhasyāsya jāniyāt

And it was in this sense, he underlines, that the word 'Hind' was used for the first time to signify the eastern part of Bhāratavarsha in the book of the Parsis called *Dasatir* compiled during the 6th century BCE[3]:

Api Pārasīkajāterasti Dasātīrnāme granthe
Paurastyabhāratārth Hindapadaṃ sarvataḥ pūrvaṃ

---

as 725 times. See http://sanskrit.jnu.ac.in/mb/ibasic.jsp?searchtype<hig>=</hig>direct&itext (accessed on 22 June 2021).

[2] D. D. Pattanaik, *Cultural Nationalism in Indian Perspective* (New Delhi: Social Publications, 2016), 40. Some *puranas* describe Bhāratavarsha as being divided into nine *dvipas* or islands. In many texts, Bhārat is shown as part of Jambūdvīpa.

[3] Ojha, *Bharatavarsha the Indian Narrative*, 23; he informs that the 65th verse (or *aayat*) of the book *Zarathustra* (known as *Jaradasati* in the Vedas) mentions that Vyasa came from Hindustan—'The Brahmin named Vyasa came from the country, Hind. Here no one was equal to his wisdom.'

In this interpretation, the area referred to as 'Hind' became only a part or subset of the larger geo-cultural zone called Bhāratavarsha. The entire country would therefore consist of land on both parts of the river Indus. The Achaemenid Empire of ancient Persia (6th century–4th century BCE) also referred to the frontier region of Indus as Hi(n)du in its inscriptions.[4] Etymologically, the term 'Hindu' has its similarity with the term 'Sindhu' used in *Zend Avesta* of the 3rd century BCE.[5]

Usage of Hindu in a More 'Religious' Sense

According to Arvind Sharma, the Chinese traveller Hiuen Tsang (7th century CE) used Shin-tu or In-tu or Indu or moon. And it was at this point, he argues, that the connotation of the term overflowed into religion.[6] When the country came into first widespread contact with Islam after the Arab invasion of Sind in 712 CE, the process of systematic conversion to Islam began. This was the first time that the need to define the people in this part of the world in a 'religious' sense arose. If people were to be converted, then it meant a change in their religion and, hence, the existing connotation was sought to be defined in such a religious sense. The Arab invaders frequently used the term Hindu. *Chach Nama*, or the history of Sind, uses the term Hinduwan and Hindawi, denoting Indians in general and their language in particular.

Carl Ernst argued that the beginning of the concept of Hindu religions could be located in the Persian literature of the

[4] Arvind Sharma calls reference to the word Hi(n)du in the inscription of Darius-I, dating back to 518–516 BCE as the earliest datable use of the term. Sharma argues: 'Sindhu becomes "India" in Greek, acquiring a purely territorial reference never compromised once acquired, but in the east it becomes Indu in Chinese, in the process acquiring a religious ambience.' See Arvind Sharma, 'On Hindu, Hindustan, Hinduism and Hindutva', *Numen* 49, no. 1 (2002): 1–36.

[5] Zend Avesta mentions Hapta Hindu (seven rivers) which may be identical with the *Rigvedic* term *Sapta Sindhav*.

[6] Sharma, 'On Hindu'.

Ghazanavid period in India starting 990 CE. It was deployed with a more precise formulation by Al-Biruni in his Arabic works. He used Indian texts such as Gita, *Yoga Sutra* and *Vishnu Purana* among others and deployed the phrase 'Hind' in different ways to show a distinction between the people of this part of the world in geographical and in religious sense.[7] In *Kitab-ul-Hind*, he used the term 'Hind' to distinguish Hindus from Buddhists, and also between Brahmanas and Sramanas. *Futuh-us-Salatin*, a Persian work of Abdul Malik Isami, compiled in the Deccan in 1350, used the term 'Hindi' to mean Indian in an ethno-geographical sense and 'Hindu' for followers of religious belief.[8] *Tarikh-i-Firuzshahi* of Ziauddin Barani, compiled in 1357, frequently uses the terms Hunud and Hinduwan in both religious and political sense. *Dabestan-e Mazaheb*, a famous Persian work of the mid-17th century, while providing description about various religious sects, devotes one chapter to Hindus but ends up being a vague description only. The text has two closely related versions available, where major descriptions are similar but there are important differences too. There are sub-chapters on *Mimansa*, *Vedanta*, *Tark*, Yoga, Vaishnavites, etc.[9] Among the Indian rulers referring to the word Hindu in the context of asserting their monarchical legitimacy, Bukka Raya-I (rule 1356–1377), the second ruler of the Vijayanagara empire, appears to be the earliest example when he described himself as *Hinduraya Suratran* (or the king among Hindu kings). This description was continued to be used by his successors. In the north, Rana Kumbha, who came a century later, described himself as *Hindu Suratran* while celebrating his victory over Delhi and Gujarat.

[7] David Lorenzen, *Who Invented Hinduism* (New Delhi: Yoda Press, 2006), 34.

[8] Ibid., 34.

[9] Irfan Habib, 'A Fragmentary Exploration of an Indian Text on Religions and Sects: Notes on the Earlier Version of the *Dabistan-I Mazahib*', *Proceedings of the Indian History Congress* 61, no. 1: Millennium (2000–2001): 474–491.

Hinduism: British Creation or Merely an English Nomenclature?

Wendy Doniger is a firm supporter of the view that perceives Hindus' identification as a religious group to be a direct result of the British colonial imperative. While focusing on diversity within Hinduism, she argues that Hindus did not develop a strong sense of religion until there were other religions against which they needed to define themselves.[10] She categorically states that till the 17th century, the identities of Hindus in India were 'segmented on the basis of locality, language, caste, occupation, and sect' and it was only after the British began the practice of defining communities by their religion, and when foreigners in India tended to 'put people of different religions into different ideological boxes, did many Indians follow suit, ignoring the diversity of their own thoughts and asking themselves which of the boxes they belonged in'.[11] This line of argument, ironically, puts the diversity of Hindus, which is considered as a unique and essential feature of the community, in direct opposition to their categorization as a religious category.

Brian Pennington presents a slightly divergent, though not entirely contrary, view of how and when 'modern Hinduism' came to be counted as a world religion, comparable to major faiths such as Christianity, Buddhism and Islam. The period from 1789 to 1832, he argues, was decisive in this development, and it was in the process of adapting to the colonial milieu that 'Hindus themselves entered a dialectic space in which they endorsed and promoted the British publication of ancient texts and translations, resisted missionary polemic, and experimented with modifications, alterations, and innovations in Hindu religious forms.'[12] He agrees that the word 'Hindu' has signified

[10] Wendy Doniger, *The Hindus: An Alternative History* (New Delhi: Penguin Viking, 2009), 24.

[11] Ibid., 25.

[12] Brian K. Pennington, *Was Hinduism Invented? Britons, Indians and the Colonial Construction of Religion* (New Delhi: OUP, 2005), 4.

regional, religious or cultural identifications at least since the 6th century BCE, but argues, at the same time, that Hinduism of our conception is 'indeed the creation of the 19th century'. However, he sees this 'creation' as part of a global phenomenon where many other modern religious and social institutions emerged. The construction of an 'essentialized Hinduism' with a stable catalogue of laws, sects, rituals, etc., he argues, was furthered by the requirement of the colonial administration during the 19th century.[13] He makes another valid point that the trend in the Western historiography to paint a picture of competing groups as 'reformers' (like the Brahmo Samaj) versus orthodox (like the Dharma Sabha) obscures their mutually shared goals, interests and strategies, and more importantly, their common passion for preserving and embodying the ancient past.[14] Pennington thus makes a distinction between how Hindus were seen prior to the 19th century and afterwards, agreeing to the existence of a religious and cultural identity since ages and construction of an 'essentialized Hinduism' afterwards. However, the idea of an 'essentialized Hinduism' that Pennington is talking about was limited to the official perception or colonial cataloguing of the subject people and, therefore, at the level of people and the community, the diversity of traditions and rituals continued unabated. The idea of a 'modern Hinduism' that he is referring to is again contestable since it indirectly links the idea of modernity in India with the British colonial rule and its policies.

David Lorenzen draws our attention to the earliest use of the term Hindu with English suffix 'ism' by Rammohun Roy during 1816–1817. Roy made the first clear use of the term in 1816 when he pointed to the peculiar mode of diet as among the theory and practice of 'Hindooism', but a year later, he underlined a more nuanced basis: 'The doctrine of the unity of God are real Hinduism, as that religion was practiced by our ancestors, and as it is well known at the present day to many learned

---

[13] Ibid., 168–170.
[14] Ibid., 171.

Brahmins.'[15] The more common usage of the term emerged only in the latter half of the 19th century with M. Monier-Williams' *Hinduism* published in 1877 and reprinted later in several revised editions. Monier-Williams found unity in two historical factors: first, origin of Hinduism lay in a simple, pantheistic doctrine but which eventually branched out into an endless variety of polytheistic beliefs and superstitions; and second, Sanskrit was the only sacred language and only sacred literature which was accepted and revered by all adherents alike. The founding principle of Hinduism, he concluded, was the often-quoted Sanskrit shloka—*ekam eva advitīyam*—which means there is but one Being, without a second.[16]

Contrary to the commonly held belief of Hinduism being invented during the 19th century, Lorenzen concludes that it was during the 13th–15th centuries, and through the rivalry between Muslims and Hindus, that a Hindu religion, which had been theologically and devotionally grounded in texts such as the Bhagavad Gita and the *puranas*, acquired a sharp self-conscious identity.[17] In other words, Hinduism as a religion had existed since ages, and sharpening of identity took place during the 13th–15th centuries. In any case, to impart any agency to the 19th-century British rule for 'inventing' Hinduism would be highly misplaced, the misunderstanding arising largely through the attempt to find an English equivalent and attaching suffix 'ism' to the word Hindu.

Heinrich von Stietencron draws a distinction between the usage of the word Hindu as occurring in the early Persian inscriptions and in the *Avesta* in singular and in plural. While in singular, the usage meant the river Indus and region around it, in plural,

---

[15] Lorenzen, *Who Invented Hinduism*, 3–4. Lorenzen also notes another use of the term in a letter published in a volume of *The Asiatic Journal and Monthly Register* published from London in 1818.

[16] Ibid., 11–13.

[17] David Lorenzen, 'Who Invented Hinduism?' *Comparative Studies in Society and History* 41, no. 4 (1999), 630–659.

it referred to the population of the region.[18] By the 13th century when Islam was well-entrenched in many parts of India, the word Hindu came to designate all non-Muslims in the administrative lexicon. Thus, when the Portuguese traders settled in the early 16th century, followed by the English and the Dutch a century later, it was this Islamic understanding that they encountered. While the Portuguese used the term 'Gentoo' (from 'Gentio', meaning heathen), the East India Company drew the term 'Hindoo' from the Persian-speaking Mughal nobility.[19] Although this new usage recognized Hindus as having a religion of their own, it also led, as Stietencron argues, to a new 'misunderstanding' since the word 'Hindu' is equivalent in origin and meaning to the word 'Indian'—the latter deriving from the Greek name for the same river Indus (*Indos* in Greek):

> Thus it was not primarily the name of a religion, but of a people—even if the Muslims in the seventeenth century did not call themselves Hindus, but applied to themselves the names of their respective regions of ethnic origin. This misunderstanding continued to have its effect later, so that in the nineteenth century the new term 'Hinduism' in the sense of 'religion of the Hindus' was coined, which is still used today, but whose meaning is debatable.[20]

Stietencron also draws attention to two popular reports by the 18th-century travellers: John Holwell's *Interesting Historical Events Relative to the Province of Bengal and the Empire of Indostan* (London, 1767) and Alexander Dow's *A Dissertation Concerning the Customs, Manners, Language, Religion and Philosophy of the Hindoos* (London, 1768).[21] Both of these books became sources of information for Voltaire (1694–1778)

---

[18] Heinrich von Stietencron, *Hindu Myth, Hindu History: Religion, Art, and Politics* (New Delhi: Permanent Black, 2005), 200; the word

[19] Ibid., 202.

[20] Ibid., 202–203.

[21] Holwell's book appeared in German the same year and in French next year. Dow's work appeared in French next year.

and then Herder (1774–1803), who felt that world's most primal religious thinking was to be found in India.[22] It was the age of Enlightenment with its search for pre-Christian intellectual and theological roots, argues Jyoti Mohan, that provided the context for Voltaire's hypothesis. Voltaire opposed the view that the Biblical revelation was the most ancient when he argued that religions of China and India had preceded it. From this vantage point, he underlined that the teaching and theology of Church were derivative of Hinduism, and that, apart from the Indian influence on Greece, there were many similarities between Hindu and Catholic customs.[23] In a letter to the Frederick the Great, Voltaire even claimed that the Christian religion was based on the old religion of Brahma.[24] Commending the early Indians for their 'mildness' and for high moral values as compared to 'ours', Voltaire characterized Hindus with most ancient form of worship: 'As India supplies the wants of all the world but is herself dependent for nothing, she must for that reason have been the most early civilized of any country, and by a like consequence necessarily have had the most ancient form of worship.'[25] A century later, the great German philosopher and sociologist, Max Weber, also expressed his opinion on how Hinduism ought to be seen. Unhappy with the way Hinduism was being compared to existing religions of the world, Weber suggested that Hinduism is something other than a 'religion' in 'our sense of the word'. Further, in the Hindu terminology, he argued that the term

---

[22] Stietencron, *Hindu Myth*, 211.

[23] Jyoti Mohan, 'La Civilisation La Plus Antique: Voltaire's Images of India', *Journal of World History* 16, no. 2 (2005): 173–185. Voltaire felt that the notion of monotheism originated with the Brahmans, and similarly 'Adimo', the earliest Hindu man and Brahma were appropriated as 'Adam' and 'Abraham' in *Old Testament*.

[24] In his 'Letters d'Amabed à Shastasid, Grand Brame de Maduré' (1769), Voltaire compared what he called the degenerated forms of Christianity with the ancient and humane religious tradition of India. See Stietencron, *Hindu Myth*, 211.

[25] Mohan, 'La Civilisation La Plus Antique'.

'sampradāya' came closest to the Occidental term 'religion'.[26] Stietencron agrees with Weber's views, underlining that Hinduism is not one of the religions but 'a civilization or culture containing several religions' or a sociocultural unit or civilization containing a plurality of distinct religions. The precise overlapping of terms Hindu and Indian, Stietencron argues, was ignored with the result that the term Hindu came to designate the followers of a particular religion in India.

> This was a fundamental misunderstanding of the term. And from the Hindu the term 'Hinduism' was derived by way of abstraction, denoting an imagined religion of the vast majority of the population—something that had never existed as a 'religion' (in the Western sense) in the consciousness of the Indian people themselves.[27]

An analysis of these thoughts and trends in contemporary Western scholarship on India studies shows a wide variation on how the history of the word Hinduism needs to be understood. It ranges from judging Hinduism, and by implication Hindu religion, in its current form as an 'invention' by the colonial system beginning in the early 19th century to the idea of imparting most ancient and primal form to Hindu, which could be signified by different names. Central to the debate here is the way the vantage point has been chosen and how complimentary ideas about Hindu religion and Indian nationhood have evolved. The urge to push the 'invention' theory is complimented by the idea of divesting Hindu religion or Hinduism of any progressive or modern thinking unless the British rule happened. While the view about its primal origin is matched by the emphasis on philosophical, moral and spiritual underpinnings to the extent that it ought not to be kept on the same pedestal as many other major religious systems of the world.

[26] Stietencron, *Hindu Myth*, 225.
[27] Ibid., 226, 228–229.

The Colonial Context: British and Indian Constructs

During the onset of the East India Company's rule in India and through its initial effort (roughly from the 1770s to the 1830s) to gather knowledge about India—its history and its institutions—attempts were made to define Hindu, besides describing its attributes. This period, known as the era of Orientalists, was characterized by an evocation of the Aryan golden age, chiefly through the efforts of William Jones, Wellesley and Jonathan Duncan. This effort attempted to entrench an ethno-geographical–religious identity which was shown to be different from Christianity, Islam or Buddhism or Jainism. Parallel to this effort was the official–administrative project of finding precise Hindu and Islamic laws in India. An important milestone was the publication of *A Code of Gentoo Laws* (1776). These laws, originally in Sanskrit, were translated by pandits to Persian from which Nathaniel Halhed, a grammarian with the East India Company, translated them into English. This project was funded by Warren Hastings, the governor general. Along with the Orientalists' attempt to know and define Hindu and describe its attributes came the Evangelical missionaries, who set up their initial base in Serampore in Bengal, where they started a printing press in 1800. Led by William Carey and William Ward, this press published more than 2 lakh books by 1832. The *Bible* was translated to 25 Indian languages. These missionary leaders also created pressure on the British Parliament. Consequently, the Charter Act of 1813 allowed Christian missionaries to set up their base and operate in India. The missionaries interpreted Hindu and Hinduism in ways which would suit their agenda of propagation of Christianity and attract conversion. Another attempt to define Hindu and its attributes came from the Liberal–Utilitarian–Anglicist group from the beginning of the 19th century. James Mill in his *History of British India* (1818) divided Indian history into three parts: Hindu–Muslim–British and strengthened the idea of a British civilizing mission.

The second part of the discourse emerged through the reform movements and literary works of the 19th century where appeals to ancient Indian scriptures to justify reforms formed an indispensable part. Whether it was Ram Mohan Roy, Ishwar Chandra Vidyasagar or Dayananda Saraswati—none referred to the ideas of European Enlightenment to justify their scheme for reforms of the Hindu society. This created an impression of an inward-looking approach where the idea was to carve out a modern Hindu reformist identity based on scriptures whose prescriptions, it was claimed, had been contaminated over a period of time. In other words, the modern reform agenda built the image of a progressive Hindu society in the past. The Sanatani Movement, which developed during the late 1880s with the formation of the Bharat Dharma Mahamandal under the patronage of the Maharaja of Darbhanga, with Din Dayalu Sharma as the founder and Madan Mohan Malaviya as an important preacher, further developed the idea of an inclusive Hindu society and positioned itself in opposition to those teachings of the Brahmo Samajists and the Arya Samajists which were critical of the *shastric–puranic* world of Hindu culture and dharma.

It was within this Hindu reformist trend that a search for finding overlapping characteristics between those of Hindu history and culture on the one hand and India as a nation on the other began towards the end of the 19th century. Bankim's later writings bear a testimony to this trend. In his *Ananda Math*, which had a fair bearing on the growth of early nationalism, he consistently treated the term 'Hindu' and 'Indian' as synonyms and used them interchangeably without any discrimination.[28] Although the immediate effect of Bankim's later writings was only psychological, as there was no commensurate programme for a nationalist campaign, they nonetheless evoked in the people of Bengal a 'rising consciousness of power, of pride in their language, in

[28] For an analysis of how Bankim's writings affected the growth of 'Hindu' nationalism, see T. W. Clarke, 'The Role of Bankimcandra in the Development of Nationalism', in *Historians of India, Pakistan and Ceylon*, ed. C. H. Philips (London: OUP, 1961), 429–445.

their literature, in their religion, and most of all in themselves'.[29] Similarly, M. G. Ranade's vision of Indian history, though in a milder way, also contained this Hindu element. He saw Indian history as a movement of upward synthesis in which Hinduism and Islam interacted in a 'mutually fecundating' manner. This process, he felt, was arrested by Aurangzeb, bringing the Marathas to power.[30] Ranade was quite conscious of the history of the region and evinced a lot of early interest in the history of Shivaji and of the Bhakti Movement, culminating in his book *Rise of Maratha Power*, in which he saw the rise of Marathas as a national uprising. Both Bhandarkar and Ranade were eager to challenge the rigid orthodox practices but, at the same time, insisted on revitalizing Hinduism from within.[31] Vivekananda, with his unflinching faith in Hindu religion and spirituality, felt that the difference between the worlds of two religions was more apparent than real and prayed therefore that the country might manifest the twofold ideal of an Islamic body and a Vedantic heart.[32] However, more significant ideological contribution of the Swami was the revitalization of Hindu dharma, invoking the idea of selfless service as its essential constituent and generating a lot of positive curiosity in the Western mind about what Hinduism actually preached and stood for. In his celebrated address in the Parliament of Religions in 1893, he thanked his audience 'in the name of the mother of all religions', highlighting pluralism and universality of India's spiritual traditions and denouncing religious narrow-mindedness and fanaticism.[33] Through his

---

[29] Ibid.

[30] Arvind Sharma, *Modern Hindu Thought: The Essential Texts* (New Delhi: OUP, 2002), 157–158.

[31] See Richard Tucker, 'Hindu Traditionalism and Nationalist Ideologies in Nineteenth-Century Maharashtra', *Modern Asian Studies* 10, no. 3 (1976), 321–348. Also see Richard Tucker, *Ranade and the Roots of Indian Nationalism* (Bombay: Popular Prakashan, 1977; 1st published in 1972).

[32] Tapan Raychaudhuri, *Europe Reconsidered: Perceptions of the West in Nineteenth-Century Bengal* (New Delhi: OUP, 1989), 244.

[33] Makarand Paranjape, *Swami Vivekananda: Hinduism and India's Road to Modernity* (Noida: HarperCollins, 2020), 8–9.

reinterpretation of Hinduism in the West, Makarand Paranjape points out, Vivekananda 'globalized it for the first time in modern history' transmitting views about Hinduism and India on their own terms.[34]

The third part of the discourse which talked directly or indirectly about Hindu and Hinduism moved, in addition to the talk of Hindu unity, towards the political implications of this identity. The latter emphasis was in response to the changing political context of the early 20th century. In this discourse, which espoused a strong social and political identity for Hindus, the Arya Samajists and the Sanatanist elements converged on a common cause. The all-India census operations starting from 1881 had religion as a category to be enumerated. This posed serious difficulties both for the officials and the people. The colonial system of mapping Indian people, though facing multiple hiccups, pushed not only the contesting claims but also made available, for the first time, ready figures of population of communities in specific areas as well as over a period of time relative increase or decrease in such figures. These figures became the primary source for raising the issue of demographic imbalance as well as that of conversion. The Census reports of 1901 and 1911 illustrate quite well the unique difficulties faced by the officials in enumerating Indian religions and also furthered the belief that Hindus should not have been seen in the same way as other religious groups. The 1901 report underlined a 'grave' difficulty that the 'dividing line between Hinduism and Animism is uncertain. Hinduism does not, like Christianity and Islam demand of its votary the rejection of all other religious beliefs.'[35] Greater wisdom dawned on the officials during the 1911 census operations, as the report noted:

> In this country, no one has any objection to stating his religion, and if all the creeds were clear, definite and mutually exclusive, there would have been no difficulty whatsoever in the way of

[34] Ibid., 10.
[35] Quoted in Rakesh Sinha, ed., *Is Hindu a Dying Race* (New Delhi: Kautilya Books, 2017), 11–12.

obtaining an accurate return. With the exception of the exotic religions, such as Christianity and Islam, there is no such thing as a definite creed.... The Hindu word 'dharma', which corresponds most closely to our word 'religion', connotes conduct more than creed.[36]

The introduction of representative principles through the Indian Councils Act of 1892, which received a second wind through the Morley–Minto Reforms of 1909, also sharpened identities along the lines of communities. This process moved hand in hand with attempts to define Hindu and Hinduism further and consequently bringing to the fore the idea of political Hinduism. Lajpat Rai claimed that the Arya Samaj worked as a progeny of Hinduism, brought the Hindu society out of the 'abysmal pit of decadent Hinduism' and endowed it with a spirit of 'self-respect' and 'self-confidence'.

Before the advent of the Arya Samaj the Hindu community believed that it was a helpless and insignificant lot which was getting a drabbing from all sides. Whoever came from outside gave it a blow with impunity and went away. Due to constant religious and communal onslaughts the Hindu religion became rotten to the core.[37]

On 22 October 1909, speaking at the DAV School compound in Lahore, immediately following the first Punjab Hindu Conference, Lajpat Rai sought to bring solidarity in the ranks of the Hindus.

In the existing condition of the country the first business of the Hindus is to strengthen themselves and bring about a sense of solidarity and unity in their ranks. This is what to me seems to be the highest patriotism even from the Indian point of view. In the

---

[36] Quoted in Ibid.

[37] 'Arya Samaj and Politics', article written by Lajpat Rai under the pseudonym of Izzat Rai, 30 September 1907, published in *Zamana* (December 1907), translated from Urdu, *The Collected Works of Lala Lajpat Rai*, Vol. III (Delhi: Manohar, 2004), 76, 78.

present struggle between Indian communities, I will be a Hindu first and an Indian afterwards; but outside India or even in India as against non-Indians, I am and shall ever be an Indian first and a Hindu afterwards.[38]

A prominent leader of the Arya Samaj and the Punjab Hindu Sabha, Lal Chand published a book in 1909, *Self-abnegation in Politics*, in which he accused the Congress of overlooking the communal interests of Hindus, though majority of its members were Hindus. He equated self-abnegation in politics with a 'misplaced and ill-timed' *sanyasa* that was suicidal when it implied 'the displacement of one community by other to the ruin of the community practicing self-abnegation'.[39] An important part and parcel of this discourse of political Hinduism was the concern raised about the demographic imbalance. U. N. Mukherjee's book *Dying Hindus* (1909) inspired a host of Arya Samaj and Hindu Sabha leaders like Shraddhanand. Speaking as chairman of the reception committee of the first Punjab Hindu Conference at Lahore in October 1909, Lal Chand referred to the writings of U. N. Mukherjee and said that awakening among Hindus was not limited to Punjab alone. He welcomed official efforts to count number of different communities as it awakened them about their immediate concerns: 'The counting of numbers has commenced as a distinct community and this is the first elementary but very essential step towards self-assertion.'[40] The numerical strength of a community became an important yardstick to measure its progress as it became a vital barometer for judging various parameters of the group:

Numbers carry great weight in this age as they have done in preceding times and help materially in deciding the fate in any struggle.

[38] Weekly report of the Director of Criminal Intelligence (30 October 1909), Home (Political Files), National Archives of India (NAI) (November 1909), no. 32–41, B, 48–49.

[39] R. B. Lal Chand, *Self-abnegation in Politics*, 2nd ed. (Lahore: The Central Yuvak Sabha, 1938), 61.

[40] *Tribune* (22 October 1909).

The progress of a community is now as much measured by its numerical strength as by its moral and economic achievements. A community dwindling in numbers is on the death path and no wonder that European nations exhibit their utmost anxiety not merely to maintain but to increase their numbers.[41]

When Shraddhanand sought financial support for his *Shuddhi* campaign in 1923, he also referred to the issue of declining numbers of Hindus and a lack of solidarity.

The great Arya nation is said at the present moment to be a dying race, not only because its numbers are dwindling but because it is completely disorganized. Individually man to man second to no nation on the earth in intellect and physique, possessing a code of morality unapproachable by any other race of humanity, it is still helpless on account of its divisions and selfishness. Lakhs upon lakhs of the best in the race have been obliged to profess Mahomedanism and thousands have been enticed away to accept Christianity without the least effort on the part of their brethren to retain or reclaim them.[42]

A patron of the Bharat Dharma Mahamandal, the Maharaja of Darbhanga maintained that Hindus were uniquely positioned in India vis-à-vis other communities in the sense that India was the only country which they could call their own.

The Hindus are tied to the soil of India in such a way as people of no other race or religion can be. By reason of their religion and the constitution of their society, they would not leave this country, under any circumstances whatsoever. There is no country in the world other than India that the Hindus can ever call his own. A people such as this cannot but feel inseparably attached to their rulers as they are tied to their country...[43]

[41] Ibid.

[42] Quoted in J. T. F. Jordens, *Swami Shraddhanand: His Life and* Causes (New Delhi: OUP, 1981), 132.

[43] Presidential speech of the Maharaja of Darbhanga, Calcutta Convention of the Bharat Dharma Mahamandal (28 December 1906), *Tribune* (30 December 1906).

How 'Hindutva' Originated?

The first significant use of the word Hindutva is from the Bengali book of the same name, *Hindutva: Hindur Prakrita Itihas*, written by Chandranath Basu (1844–1910) in 1892. Having written *Shakuntala Tattva* earlier in 1881, he used the same suffix (meaning reality or essence) in his construction of the term Hindutva and, moving beyond the debates where one set of doctrines was shown to be superior to another set of doctrines, he emphasized upon the fundamentals or essentials of Hindu.[44] The long reference to the book that appeared in the *Calcutta Review* of July 1894 appreciated Basu's ideas on such lines.

> The Hindus are notorious for the diversity of their transcendental doctrines, every individual school having a complete set of doctrines of its own. Babu Chandranath has selected the noblest doctrines of Hinduism, but he has not followed any one of the ancient schools of Hinduism. Yet he does not aim at establishing a school of doctrines himself. His sole object is to compare, so far as lies in his power, the leading doctrines of Hindu faith with those of other religions.[45]

Amiya Sen underlines that Chandranath Basu, who invented the term Hindutva in 1892, saw it as constituting the vital and defining qualities of 'Hinduness', evaluating social ideas and practices of Hindus in a comparative scale of civilizations.[46]

---

[44] A man of letters, Chandranath Basu had been the principal of Jaipur College in Calcutta and as a respectable translator in the government service. Later on, in 1901, he published another book with suffix *tattva*—*Savitri Tattva*. Andersen and Damle think that Savarkar built on the early use of the term employed by Chandranath Basu in his book *Old Hindu's Hope: Proposal for Establishment of a Hindu National Congress* (1888). See Walter K. Andersen and Sridhar D. Damle, *The RSS: A View to the Inside* (Gurgaon: Penguin Viking, 2018), 79, 327–328.

[45] Quoted in Makarand Paranjape, 'Hindutva before Savarkar: Chandranath Basu's Contribution' (2017). Available at https://www. dnaindia.com/analysis/column-hindutva-before-savarkar-chandranath-basus-contribution-2411145 (accessed on 30 October 2018).

[46] Amiya P. Sen, 'A Hindu Conservative Negotiates Modernity: Chandranath Basu (1844–1910) and Reflections on the Self and Culture in

Savarkar's Hindutva

Although the term Hindutva had been used earlier, it is Vinayak Damodar Savarkar who is widely identified as the leader who propounded the theory of Hindutva. A leading revolutionary of his time, founder of Abhinav Bharat (a secret society of revolutionaries), author of the first nationalist interpretation of the revolt of 1857, undergoing a decade-long imprisonment in the dreaded Cellular Jail, Savarkar had come full circle by the time he landed at Ratnagiri in the early 1920s. Introducing his seminal book on 1857, though emphasizing the importance of consciousness of the past, Savarkar advised against using the animosities of history.

> The nation ought to be the master and not the slave of its own history. For, it is absolutely unwise to try to do certain things, simply because they had once been acted in the past. The feeling of hatred against the Mahomedans was just and necessary in the times of Shivaji—but such a feeling would be unjust and foolish if nursed now, simply because it was the dominant feeling of the Hindus then.[47]

After his transfer to Ratnagiri Jail in 1922 and after subsequent release in 1924 with many restrictions imposed on his movement and activities, he now displayed his Hindu reformist agenda, fighting against untouchability, calling for temple entry and encouraging inter-caste dining.

> From today I shall not believe in highness or lowness of caste. I shall not oppose the intermarriage between the highest and lowest castes. I shall eat with any Hindu irrespective of castes. I shall not believe in caste by birth or by profession and henceforth I shall call myself a Hindu only—not Brahmin, Vaishya, etc.[48]

Colonial Bengal', in *Her Story. Historical Scholarship between South Asia and Europe. Festscrift in Honour of Gita Dharampal Frick*, eds., Rafael Klober and Manu Ludwig (Heidelberg: Cross Asia Books, 2018), 175–188.

[47] V. D. Savarkar, *The Indian War of Independence of 1857* (London: Abhishek Publications, 1909), vii–viii.

[48] Andersen and Damle, *The RSS*, 80.

It was here in Ratnagiri Jail in 1923 that he finalized his *Hindutva or Who Is a Hindu?* It had been preceded at the political level by the incorporation of the Khilafat issue within the nationalist agitation led by Mahatma Gandhi. Although it worked to unite Hindus and Muslims temporarily in a common cause, fierce communal riots were witnessed in Malabar and some other regions after the suspension of the Non-cooperation Movement. The Khilafat issue, used as an anti-imperialist device, also worked to enhance the power of the Islamic clergy among common Muslims. Recalling later in 1966, Acharya Kripalani felt that the Ali brothers had joined the movement because they thought more in terms of Khilafat than in terms of the Independence of India.[49] Sentimentality reigned supreme as Maulanas would weep in the Khilafat meetings and staunch nationalists such as Ansari and Syed Mahmud grew beard because 'they would not be allowed to speak if they were without beard and moustache.'[50]

The riots in Malabar which witnessed large-scale conversions of Hindus enraged, among others, many prominent Marathi leaders. B. S. Moonje, a leader of the Congress and later a frontline Hindu Mahasabha leader, made on-the-spot assessment and concluded that the Hindus of Malabar were 'mild and docile' in sharp contrast to the Moplahs who were 'domineering in spirit and ferocious'.[51] M. R. Jayakar, a liberal and a Hindu Sabha leader, called the Moplah riots one of the 'darkest chapters' in Indian nationalism which, nonetheless, he felt, had taught the Hindus to 'organize themselves'.[52]

[49] Oral transcript of J. B. Kripalani, Nehru Memorial Museum & Library, Acc. no. 403, 53.

[50] Ibid., 163–164, 172–173.

[51] Moonje's report on 'Forcible conversions in Malabar' (4 August 1923), *Moonje Papers* (New Delhi: Nehru Memorial Museum & Library), subject file no. 12.

[52] Oral evidence of M. R. Jayakar (President, Bombay Presidency Hindu Sabha) before the Bombay Riots Enquiry Committee (New Delhi: Jayakar Papers, National Archives of India, 1929), file no. 437.

Through his *Hindutva*, Savarkar attempted to articulate a uniform definition of 'Hindu' and identified the agenda that lay before the community under its peculiar historical circumstances. The publisher of the second edition hailed Savarkar's definition of Hindutva, Hindu and Hinduism as a remarkable 'scientific discovery' amounting to a 'veritable revelation'.[53] The book fashioned 'an organic order' out of the 'chaos of castes and creeds', and the definition itself was hailed as having provided a basic broad foundation for a mighty and consolidated Hindu nation standing effectively against heavy odds.[54] Savarkar thus provided the Hindu Mahasabha and its fraternal organizations with 'a platform, a slogan, a Bible, and a banner'.[55] Shraddhanand exclaimed: 'It must have been one of those Vedic dawns indeed which inspired our seers with new truths, that revealed to the author of Hindutva this "Mantra", this definition of Hindutva!'[56] N. C. Kelkar felt it provided a 'new scientific analysis' unseen before.[57]

The very first entry to the book evinced Savarkar's categorical assertion: 'A Hindu means a person who regards this land of *Bharatvarsha* from the Indus to the Seas as his Fatherland as well as his Holy-Land that is the cradle land of his religion.'[58] Briefly summed up, it read: 'He is a Hindu to whom *Sindhustan* is not

[53] V. D. Savarkar, *Hindutva: Who Is a Hindu?*, 6th ed. (Bombay: Veer Savarkar Prakashan, 1989, 1st published in 1923), p. vii. In addition, the book revealed to the Indian leaders 'their real national self, in which and through which consciously or unconsciously they lived and moved and had their organic Being'.

[54] Ibid., vii.

[55] Dhananjay Keer, *Savarkar and His Times* (Bombay: Popular Prakashan, 1950), 203.

[56] Ibid., 147.

[57] Ibid., 148.

[58] Savarkar, *Hindutva* (lines just below the title). In his presidential address at the Nagpur session of the Hindu Mahasabha in 1938, Savarkar proclaimed that 'the land which extends from the Indus to the southern seas is Hindusthan—the land of the Hindus and we Hindus are the nation that owns it'. V. D. Savarkar, *Hindu Rashtra Darshan: A Collection of the Presidential Speeches Delivered from the Hindu Mahasabha Platform* (Bombay: Laxman Ganesh Khare, 1949), 63–64.

only a *Pitribhu*, but also a *Punyabhu*.'[59] Through this definition, he attempted to bring all non-Muslim and non-Christian groups under the ambit of Hindu, a description which becomes clearer as one progresses through the book. Savarkar identified three essentials of Hindutva: *rashtra* (a common nation), *jati* (a common race) and *sanskriti* (a common civilization).[60] The term Bhāratiya or Hindi was seen as a synonym of the term Indian but, in order to get incorporated into the Hindu fold, Savarkar made it clear that one should fulfil some other conditions as well. He should adopt Indian culture and history, and inherit Indian blood and must worship the land because Hindus were united not only by the bonds of a common motherland but also by the bonds of love to a 'common blood' because 'they are not only a nation (*rashtra*) but also a race (*jati*).[61] Moonje, a frontline leader espousing militarization of the Hindus during the 1930s and 1940s, echoed Savarkar when he asserted that the system of caste had not affected the 'common flow of blood into our race'.[62]

Hindutva is 'history', announced Savarkar, and therefore it embraces all the departments of thought and activity of 'the whole being of our race'.[63] The 'contests' and 'conflicts' of the medieval period, he suggested, had made Hindus conscious of

[59] Savarkar, *Hindutva*, 116. This definition of a Hindu, which excluded religious groups such as Muslims and Christians but included other groups such as Sikhs, Jains or Buddhists in its ambit, was repeated by Golwalkar as well, thus denoting its acceptance by the RSS.

[60] Ibid.

[61] Ibid., 84.

[62] See Christophe Jaffrelot, *The Hindu Nationalist Movement and Indian Politics, Strategy of Identity Building, Implantation and Mobilisation with Special Reference to Central India* (London: Hurst & Company, 1996), 28. For details about the idea of militarization espoused by the Hindu Mahasabha during the late colonial period and in particular the effort made by Moonje to start the Bhonsala Military School at Nasik in the mid-1930s, see Bhuwan Kumar Jha, 'Militarizing the Community: Hindu Mahasabha's Initiative (1915–1940)', *Studies in History* 29, no. 1 (February 2013): 119–146.

[63] Savarkar, *Hindutva*, 3–4.

themselves helping to weld them into a nation. And, consequently, it was a 'common progress' of the Hindu movement as
a whole because 'Sanatanists, Satnamis, Sikhs, Aryas, Anaryas,
Marathas and Madrasis, Brahmins and Panchams—all suffered
as Hindus and triumphed as Hindus'.[64] And at this juncture in
history, as a consequence of 'enemies' hating the community
'as Hindus', the term Hindustan became an eloquent expression to the main political and cultural point at issue and more
expressive than the terms such as Āryāvarta, Dakśiṇapatha,
Jambūdwīpa or Bhāratavarsha.[65] Moonje took this definition
further and clarified that the followers of different sects in
India were not different from the Hindus of Hindustan and,
therefore, the Hindu Mahasabha had been going about the task
of exposing 'these false and mischievous cults of separatism so
that the people of India may be welded into one solid nation of
the Hindus of *Hindustan*':

> Differences in religion or religious sects do not lead to the group-
> ing of people or of a nation elsewhere into so many communi-
> ties different and separate from one another. Then why in India
> alone should any countenance be given to those who preach that
> because a group of Hindus profess Islam or Christianity, they are
> separate in essence from the Hindus of Hindusthan. [66]

Savarkar located the essence of Hindutva in the commonality of
inheritance and experience. Therefore, in reality, a Hindu is one
who has 'inherited and claims as his own the Hindu *Sanskriti*, the
Hindu civilization, as represented in a common history, common
heroes, a common literature, common art, a common law and
a common jurisprudence, common fairs and festivals, rites and
rituals, ceremonies and sacraments'.[67] An absolute overlapping

[64] Ibid., 44–45.
[65] Ibid., 45.
[66] Presidential address, Andhra Hindu Sabha Conference, Bezwada,
7 November 1929, *Indian Quarterly Register* (July–December 1929),
340–341.
[67] Savarkar, *Hindutva*, 100.

of these features was not mandatory but a Hindu 'has more of it common with his Hindu brothers than with, say, an Arab or Englishman.'[68] Thus, according to Savarkar, Hinduism is the 'ism' of the Hindus and must necessarily mean the religion or the religions that are 'peculiar and native to this land and these people'.[69] As a corollary, he clarified that the term Hinduism must not denote the religion of the majority but 'the religion of all Hindus'.[70] In other words, while the religion of the majority could be denoted by the Sanatan, the *shruti*–smriti–*puranokta* or Vedic dharma, rest of the Hindus could be denoted by Sikh, Arya, Jain or Buddha dharma.[71] Therefore, Hinduism or Hindu dharma became the generic term to denote 'these *Dharmas* as a whole'.[72]

Coming in the specific political and historical circumstances, Savarkar's Hindutva defined Hindu, Hinduism and Hindustan in categorical terms. For him, the very word Hindutva (or essence of Hindu or Hinduness) was about defining Hindu or, in other words, finding out who precisely constituted a Hindu. In this endeavour to discover Hindutva's essential constituents, he made *rashtra*, *jati* and *sanskriti* as the fulcrum around which it revolved. At one level, he expanded the ambit of Hinduism as the 'ism' of all religions native to this land and, at another, he made loyalty to the land (fatherland) a precondition for being considered a Hindu.

Gandhi's Interpretation

Gandhi was firmly grounded in everything good that Hinduism had to preach. His constant reference to Bhagavad Gita and Tulsi's 'Ramcharitmanas', and invoking Hindu gods and

[68] Ibid.
[69] Ibid., 104.
[70] Ibid., 107.
[71] Ibid.
[72] Ibid.

goddesses to instil confidence in his followers in order also to draw the lines of morality, made his leadership stand out. Some of his debates with the priestly class on the question of temple entry for outcaste groups saw him firmly quoting from the Hindu shastras to advance arguments against discrimination of any kind. In his umpteen writings and speeches, he was never tired of calling himself a Sanatani Hindu or a Hindu who believed in the eternity of its existence, since it actually meant dharma or way of life or a higher moral order. Although a firm believer in the Vedas, Upanishads and the *puranas*, he rejected everything that contradicted the fundamental principle of morality and did not feel bound to accept 'the ipse dixit or the interpretations of pundits'. Asked to define a Hindu, he wrote:

> In a concrete manner he is a Hindu who believes in God, immortality of the soul, transmigration, the laws of Karma and Moksha, and who tries to practise Truth and Ahimsa in daily life, and therefore practises cow-protection in its widest sense and understands and tries to act to act according to the law of varnashram.[73]

Having been born a Hindu, Gandhi wrote that he had remained as such simply because he had never found it inconsistent with his moral sense or spiritual growth. He declared that he had found Hinduism to be most tolerant of all religions known to him and, in particular, its freedom from dogma held special appeal for him because it provided largest scope for self-expression. He did not regard Jainism and Buddhism as separate from Hinduism and felt that the concept of ahimsa or non-violence found highest expression and application in Hinduism: 'Hinduism believes in the oneness not of merely all human life but in the oneness of all that lives.'[74] Finally, given his profound love for civilizational ethos and selfless and frugal living, Gandhi found in the first verse of Ishopanishad the ultimate pearl of wisdom, one, which even if used alone, could characterize the very essence of Hinduism: 'if

[73] *Young India* (14 October 1926).
[74] *Young India* (20 October 1927).

all the Hindu scriptures were turned to ashes and only this one verse remained, there would be no loss'[75]:

Īśāvāsyamidaṃ sarvaṃ yatkiṃca jagatyāṃ jagata
Tena tyaktena bhuṃjīthāḥ mā gṛdaḥ kasyasviddhanam[76]

Concluding Remarks

The argument supporting the 'invention' of the Hindu religion in the 19th century, while displaying a somewhat superficial understanding of the cultural ethos and history that define a Hindu, is shaped primarily by the eagerness to see the religions of the world in a specific sense of one God, one scripture, one belief, etc. It may be argued that the term Hindu with suffix 'ism' (Hinduism) is in all probability a term put to use first in the early 19th century in the context of a religious group or in deference to its identification in contrast to other groups like Christianity or Islam. But the very idea of 'invention' starts and ends with this English nomenclature. It is pretty clear that, centuries preceding this age, the word Hindu was widely used to refer to the people inhabiting this land and later to those who were not Muslims and Christians. On such occasions, they were believed to be following some specific rituals, customs and beliefs which were different from those of others. The overt reference or categorical implication that the community signifier emerged during the colonial rule or was invented by the colonial rulers is historically untrue and misplaced.

The terms Hindu, Hinduism and Hindutva have travelled a long history with these nouns or, at times, with different names,

[75] *Harijan* (30 Januar 1937; from his speech at Quilon and Haripad). The verse means that everything that moves in this world is enveloped by the Lord. One should enjoy by renouncing these and never covet the possessions of others.

[76] All this—whatsoever exists in the universe—should be covered by the Lord. Having renounced (the unreal), protect (yourself) through that detachment, and enjoy (the real). Do not covet anybody's wealth.

very much like the often-quoted shloka from Upanishads *Ekam Sat Vipra Bahudhā Vadanti*, meaning 'Truth (or that which exists) is One but Sages or learned people call it by different names.' It is pretty clear that the project of calling Hindu religion or Hinduism a colonial invention has more to do with English equivalents and, at times, a tendency to impart agency to the colonial instruments for 'homogenizing' India's traditions. The idea of treating Hindu and this land as overlapping in ancient period and continuing through to the contemporary times depends on how expansive is the interpretation of the term Hindu itself. The dharmic and cultural interpretation of the term, which focuses on universality and plurality of character would enable it to be all-embracing in its outlook. Similarly, Hindutva—when seen as Hinduness or essence of Hindu—puts it on a higher pedestal. That Hindu (the word and/or the community) has origins going back to the most ancient times is amply reflected in the word *Sanatan* or eternal. Most problems in interpretation also appear to have arisen due to the misunderstandings about communities or groups within Hinduism with varying traditions, rituals, customs and languages which ironically, for a common Hindu, constitutes its very uniqueness.

3

Manusmrti and Social Marginals

Nandini Bhattacharyya Panda

In the context of India's classical tradition, Manusmrti is the oldest and most popular text in the genre of smriti literature. It is considered as the repository of tradition of the Hindus. Manusmrti is situated as a normative text indexing India's moral, ethical and social evolution; it is the culmination of the work of several authors who defined 'custom'. The text comprehensively deals with spiritual, temporal, moral, ethical, social, economic and familial matters ranging from cosmogony to conjugality. This chapter deals with the textual analysis of Manusmrti in the context of social margins such as Shudras, Chandalas and women, and its varied interpretations and appropriations in different periods of time and political contexts in India and the West.

The chapter is divided into three sub themes. The first sub theme undertakes a textual analysis of Manusmrti to understand and unfold the nature and content of the text, especially in relation to social hierarchy and patriarchal agenda. It focuses on two aspects. The textual analysis in this chapter would reflect upon how women and marginal communities are situated within an enigmatic framework in the text. Another sub theme analyses colonial appropriation of Manusmrti by the Orientalist ideologues and colonial rulers. The text emerged as the signifier of values embodied in Indian classical *shastric* tradition in colonial representation to vindicate certain policies, especially in relation to women. The next sub theme analyses the evaluation, reflection and appropriation of the text by two Western scholars, Friedrich Nietzsche and Indologist such as Wendy Doniger. Both produced their view about primacy of this text in the *shastric* genre in similar vein of colonial ideologues/rulers, but in different periods of time.

The Background: *Shastric* Tradition and Manusmrti

Manu is believed to be the first among the writers on the vast corpus of literature on Dharmashastras/smritis. P. V. Kane and other scholars hold the tentative date for Manu as 500 to 400 BC. Scholars are sharply divided over there was one Manu or several Manus. The text attributes divine origin of Manu in the introductory verses in the text to invoke the infallibility of the dictums. The assertion of divine origin of Manu is intriguing. Presumably, the attribution of divinity had been carried out with an ideological or a social agenda. On the basis of close reading of the text, one can identify several verses that say: Manu *abrabit* (Manu stated) or Manu *Kalpayet* (Manu imagined). It suggests that many anonymous writers in different periods and regions interpolated or extrapolated their verses and thereby their views and ideologies in the text. The extrapolations do indicate that Manusmrti enjoyed prime status in certain period of time. The interpolators/extrapolators attributed divinity to 'Manu' to appropriate the textual space for expressing their own ideology, mostly on women.

A few paragraphs should be added to situate Manusmrti as a text within the vast corpus of Dharmashastra tradition. The origin and development of the Dharmashastras are shrouded in uncertainty and myth. There is no definite historical explanation as yet of the actual origin of the texts. The ultimate source, however, is known to be the Vedas. The word Veda did not strictly refer to the Vedic texts but to the totality of knowledge, the sum total of understanding of all religious and moral truths, whether revealed or not. Smritis are held to be indirect perceptions founded on memory (a literal translation of the word smriti), on the basis of which dharma grew into a discipline or science known as Dharmashastras. A definite date for their beginning has not been identified. It is generally believed that the original smritis—Manusmrti, Yajnavalkyasmrti, Naradasmrti and many others—were written approximately between 500–400 BC and 800 AD. Manu is popularly believed as the first among the compilers. The text enjoyed a paramount status among the early British rulers as representing the most 'authentic' and 'ancient' laws of the Hindus.

The Process of evolution, to which this millennium-old tradition responded so well, demonstrates that it was not a static tradition. It may be observed that the durability and dynamic of this tradition gathered through the emerging traditions of *Tikas* or commentaries and *Nibandhas* or treatises from the 8th or 9th century onwards. *Tika* was the commentary by the authors on the original smritis. But the illustrations and interpretations of each author varied covering specific issues relevant to a certain region. For example, Medhatithi's *Manubhasya* and Kullukabhatta's *Manavarthamuktavali* did not offer the same interpretation on specific issues/verses. About the *Nibandhas* dwelling upon certain texts, the authors used to make a choice by offering a critique of others and writing a discourse. The basic principle was to extract the rules of dharma from the vast mass of authoritative texts and put forward author's independent views.

Around the 10th or 11th century onwards, the tradition was bifurcated into two broad intellectual schools of thought: *Mitaksara* and *Dayabhaga*. The original propounder was Vijnanesvara, the ninth commentator from Mithila or Benaras. Further ramifications within this tradition emerged along geographical boundaries—Maharashtra or western India and Deccan and South India—in addition to Benaras or Mithila tradition.

Jimutavahana, the 10th/11th-century commentator from Bengal, produced his discourse on *Dayabhaga* (division of property) that marked a break from earlier discourses on social and moral codes of conduct. These two traditions differed on certain fundamental issues. For example, regarding appropriate time of generation of ownership in ancestral property, *Mitaksara* tradition held that ownership is generated immediately after birth—*Janamasvatva vada*—whereas *Dayabhaga* propounded that ownership rights devolved after the death of both parents—*Uparamsvatva vada*. Among other differences, a very significant difference occurred over widow's rights to property. The *Dayabhaga* tradition held that even in an undivided family, the widow could inherit her husband's share, whereas widows were not entitled to such rights in such a situation according to *Mitaksara* tradition. Again, *Dayabhaga* prescribed an equal share of the unmarried daughter/s and son/s over ancestral property after father's death. *Mitaksara* had no such provision for unmarried daughters. There were other fundamental differences as well.

The proliferation of *Nibandhas* and *Tikas* indicate a buoyant environment for the tradition to be flourished over centuries and millennia. In fact, the unabated growth of such discourses till the beginning of colonial rule strongly suggests that the Islamic power in India accepted or accommodated the parallel existence of the *shastric* tradition. The pre-eminence and dominant influence of the Brahmans as reflected in the writings of early British ideologues and officials also indicate that even the Mughal rulers did not attempt to integrate this tradition within the state hierarchy of command and control, instead respecting the autonomous domain of the shastras. There was a virtual decline of this tradition during the colonial period despite the patronage of Sanskritic learning. But Indian participation in this new enterprise was minimal. The tradition of writing *Tika* and *Nibandha* became either insignificant or extinct immediately after the consolidation of British rule. The colonial interest in this tradition was reflected in their translation enterprise of selective texts which they deemed important and necessary.

Three plausible explanations may be given for the unusual and uninterrupted survival of the tradition over millennia. First, this tradition survived, evolved and flourished through discussions, debates and interpretations, and such periodic interpretations were necessitated by social changes. Second, the expounders enjoyed considerable autonomy to pursue their intellectual exercises. Third, no evidence suggests that the state could exercise dominating influence either to reinterpret or to incorporate the ruling ideology within the discourses. Rather, various *Nibandhas* were produced to highlight the essential features of dharma concerning community, social, moral, religious, familial, conjugal and legal behaviour of the people. The issues ranged from *Dayabhaga* (division of property), *vyavahara* (principles of jurisprudence), *prayaschitta* (penance), *shuddhi* (purification), *vivaha* (marriage) and various other issues. The internal dynamics of the tradition was reflected in the regional variation in *Dayabhaga* and *Mitaksara*.

Extant pre-colonial evidence suggests that shastras evolved as a tradition of intellectual and philosophical knowledge rather than one integral to administration. Perhaps, for that reason, pandits were not merely concentrated around centres of administration, but in different localities including remote villages. There were eminent centres of learnings such as Nabadwip, Kalna, Bhatpara, Kumarhatta, Bansberia and various others. Nabadwip produced innumerable scholars and their reputation reached far beyond geographical boundaries of Bengal. Sri Chaitanya, Gadadhara, Vasudeva Sarvabhauma and Raghunatha Siromani were some of the luminaries from Nabadwip.

The community of scholars ran academics known as *Tols* and *Chatuspathis*. Adam's Third Report, Dines Chandra Bhattacharya's seminal work Vange Navya-Nyaya Charcha and Ponchanon Mondal's Chithipatre Samajchitra provide a long list of such institutions. There are prolific accounts on the relation between teachers and students, which was not confined to academic instructions only. They were a part of guru's household.

The students received title from the preceptor depending on the merit, quality and originality such as *Sastri, Nyayalankar, Kavyalankara* and *Vyakaran Tirtha.* The students opened their own academic after successfully obtaining the degree.

The extant evidence does not indicate at all that such institutions were controlled or managed by the state. However, the tradition of knowledge received both appreciation and, at times, material support from local and regional authorities: zamindars and rajas. In some instances, rent-free lands were granted to such academia and the authorities organized debates and discussions in the court—*Tarka Sabha.* The rajas of Burdwan and Nadia were famous for their enthusiastic support and encouragement towards such intellectual activities.

It is intriguing why Manusmrti has been perceived as the key text that embodied the morality, ethics and most importantly *the laws* of the Hindus by the colonial rulers and Western Indologists and philosophers. Indeed, the perception had been integrally linked with civilizational, political, ideological and patriarchal agenda. The present author elaborately discussed colonial appropriation of the *shastric* tradition to reconstitute the landownership pattern and women's rights in the book *Appropriation and Invention of Tradition: The East India Company and Hindu Law in Early Colonial Bengal.*[1] Manusmrti did play a crucial role in the scheme of colonial appropriation of the classical tradition of the Dharmashastras, especially to facilitate the patriarchal agenda. It will be discussed in the coming pages with selective focus on the textual contexts of Manusmrti which had/have been drawn under appropriations as well as social debates.

---

[1] Nandini Bhattacharyya Panda, *Appropriation and Invention of Tradition: The East India Company and Hindu Law in Early Colonial Bengal* (New Delhi: Oxford University Press, 2008), paperback and electronic edition in 2012.

Textual Analysis of 'Margins' in Manusmrti:
Shudras, Chandalas and Women[2]

As is well known, the most significant component of Manusmrti is the classification of social hierarchy in the caste order: Brahman (the priestly caste), Kshatriya (the warrior caste), Vaishya (the merchant and agricultural caste) and Shudra (the menial/servile caste). Commentators such as Medhatithi and Kullukabhatta produced several commentaries over the ages on this text. Manusmrti has been translated in numerous foreign languages as well as every Indian language, needless to mention. Despite the primacy that it enjoyed as the most important text within the vast corpus of Dharmashastra tradition, Manusmrti is also a much-maligned text. The design of the social hierarchy in the text is also looked at as an embodiment of an edifice that created 'Indian women'. The text created controversies (at times condemned) insofar as the structural design of social layers within the power structure, Manusmrti is more famous or infamous for being the epitome of Indian patriarchy. The notion of 'margin' in the text broadly relates to the Shudras, Chandalas and women. This section will gaze at the structuring and label-ling of marginality in the text by analysing both ideological enunciations and exclusionary practices.

The essence of Manusmrti is about Brahmanical control over society and the higher orders living on the lower—the Shudras, Chandalas and Antaja. The textual design to invoke Brahmanical supremacy has been vigorously criticized in the past continues to be criticized till date. Manusmrti designed a marginal corner for women in a problematic space which is also a site of casti-gation and debates. In this context, this section focuses on the problematic and intriguing framework of Manusmrti to evaluate

---

[2] The verses quoted in this chapter are based on the compilations of smriti and *samhitas* in two volumes under the title Aryashastra. Manusmrti is the first text to be analysed and translated in the first volume. The volumes were first published in 1965 in Calcutta with further editions.

the consistency and stance in relation to women. The following section shall briefly deal with schematic structure relating to Shudra or even lower orders, which reduced the text as one of site of Brahmanical voice.

Shudras

The reductive verses on Shudras proliferate in the text and those are espoused with a view to create a servile and menial caste devoted to the command of higher orders, especially the Brahmans. As is well known, such enunciations are sites of resistance, debates and resistance towards conceiving a visionary 'post-Hindu' India. Briefly, the text says that a dependent Shudra should eat remains of a meal, wear torn clothes and sleep on worn-out bed.

Uchhistamannam databyam jirnani basanani ca
Pulascaiva dhanyanam jirnascaiva parichhadah.[3]

Translation: Shudras should eat the leftover of food left in the plate of the Brahman and wear torn cloth. Brahman shall offer (to the Shudras) straw for sleeping and worn-out cloth as dress (translation mine).

They are not allowed to cook in the household of a higher caste. They would be appreciated if they act piously in a religion function without the right to chant holy verses. Shudras are able to earn money but cannot save and become wealthy. A wealthy Shudra who has no access to knowledge (Vedic knowledge) may become arrogant and undermine and belittle a Brahman from vanity.

Saktenapi hi sudrena n karyo dhanasanchayah
Sudro hi dhanamasadya brahmanameva vadhate.[4]

---

[3] Manusmrti, Chapter 9, verse 125.
[4] Ibid., verse 130.

Translation: Shudras may earn money by being engaged in other profession, but they should not be allowed to save money because a rich Shudra may insult a Brahman from his pride for wealth (translation mine).

The agenda of creating a servile class is repeatedly emphasized in the text. For example:

Ekameva tu sudrasya prabhuh karma samadisat
Etesameva varnanam susrusamanasua.[5]

Translation: Almighty has determined only one task for the Shudras, that is, to offer selfless services to the three higher castes without any ill feeling/vengeance (translation mine).

In Manusmrti, Chandala (a mixed race born from inter-caste marriages of lower and mixed castes) has no social space. The dictates for the Chandalas are more stringent and revealing. For example, the Chandalas should live outside the boundary of a village and should not be offered food in a plate/bowl. They can only rear dogs and donkeys. They will wear corpse's clothes, eat in tottered utensil, adorn iron jewellery and should not settle in a fixed place.

Candalasyapacanam tu vahirgramat pratisrayah
Apapatrasca kartvya dhanamesam svagardhavam
Vasangsi mrtacelani bhinnabhandesu bhojanam
Karsnayasamalankara paribrjya ca nityasa.[6]

Translation: The clothes of dead people should be the worn by the Chandala; they should eat in broken utensils; iron ornaments should adorn their body; dog and donkey should be their pet and they should live outside the village and roam around in different places (without having a fixed habitation; translation mine).

[5] Ibid., Chapter 1, verse 91.
[6] Ibid., Chapter 9, verses 51–52.

The text further added:

Diva careyuh karyartham cihnita rajasasaneih
Avandhavam sabncaiva nirhareyuriti sthitih.[7]

Translation: The Chandalas should bear special signs in their body to be marked by the king. They should come in the habited areas only in the daytime for their work (for livelihood/buy or sale of commodities). They should cremate the corpses of those who had no friend and relative (translation mine).

The Chandalas should not enter the town or village at night as asserted in the text:

Ratrou na vicarayestu gramesu nagaresu ca.[8]

Translation: The Chandalas should not enter the village or town at night (translation mine).

The verses quoted above are self-explanatory with well-demarcated boundaries of segregation within given social groups. Here, one finds the sole agenda of excluding the Chandalas from mainstream life. Labelling was necessary to distinguish the untouchables in their own bodies, which is repeatedly emphasized in the text. Labelling should be ensured through their entire existence, for example, in dress, ornament, movement, livelihood and even pets. But the exclusion was designed in a more vital aspect. Chandalas should not be allowed to own land. It has already been mentioned that the Shudras were restricted from accumulating wealth. The embargo on landholding is not clearly stated in the text. The embargo on accumulating wealth and holding land, respectively, by the Shudras and Chandalas was designed to ensure exclusion for the marginal order.

The section ends with some questions and observations. Kane assumed that the original Manusmrti contained not less than

[7] Ibid., verse 55.
[8] Ibid., verse 55.

100,000 verses. Many verses have been lost through the passage of millennia and the text in present form contains 2,765 verses. Another interesting feature of the text is that the chapters (*adhyaya*) are not evenly structured. For example, Chapters 8 and 9 contain maximum number of verses, 420 and 326, respectively. Primarily, the longer chapters incorporated interpolations/extrapolations, though other chapters also revealed this trend, especially Chapter 5, which partly reflected on the status and character of women. Kane did not explicitly mention that Manusmrti became the site of interpolations and extrapolations over millennia leading to the distortion of the original text. This aspect is evident from close reading of the text. The exclusionary structure in caste hierarchy is a part of Chapter 10 (of 12 chapters) and that very chapter is described as the part of the Manusamhita narrated by Bhrigu (Bhrigu Kathita Manusamhita). The text therefore leaves many twilight zones or riddles that are not possible to resolve in the present day, even relating to the exclusionary enunciations regarding the lower orders. In view of the contradictions and inconsistencies in text, one may raise the question regarding the original contents of the text and the subsequent distortions. The enigmatic framework regarding women in Manusmrti is situated in this context.

Women

In Manusmrti, women are situated in the most contested and problematic margin or edge within the socio-familial structure. It is rather intriguing how the text had been read as the epitome of Indian patriarchy given the contradictory and inconsistent nature of the text. In certain verses, Manusmrti offers liberal and generous space for women that the following verses withdraw through enunciations by inserting strictures and vulgar patriarchy. The textual inconsistencies make it difficult to ascertain the actual stance in favour or against women. Certain verses make it evident how the textual space for women in Manusmrti had been subjected to ideological shifts through interpolations and extrapolations over passages of time. Strange contradictions situate women within the binary of subject and object, good and evil.

Bad woman are portrayed beyond redemption through prolific definition of their character. For example, women are lustful with insatiable sexual desire, frivolous, arrogant, jealous and greedy with excessive fondness for jewellery, luxury and inclination towards men, irrespective of their age, as is invoked in the following verses:

> *Naita rupam pariksante nasam vayasi samsthitih*
> *Surupam va birupam va pumanityeva bhunjate.*
> *Pounscalyaccalacittacca naihsnhyacca svabatah*
> *Raksita yatnato(a)piha bhatrsvata bikurbate.*[9]

Translation: Women do not look for beauty and care for age, young or old; they would enjoy with any man, handsome or ugly. By nature, women are lustful, frivolous and merciless. Therefore, men should take good care of them (translation mine).

The good women in these types of verses are also subjected to social/familial subjugation. They should be obedient to the husband and elder members of the family and perform her household duties impeccably. As a good wife, she should remain servile to her lord/master (husband) and ready to comply with all his inflictions without protest.

> *Yasmai dadyat pita tvenam bhrata vanumate pituh*
> *Tam susrset jivantam samsthiamca na langayet.*[10]

Translation: The woman has been offered to the husband by the father or, in his absence, by the brother. The woman should take care and nurse her as long as he lives. It is her duty not to disobey the dictum even after the death of her husband (translation mine).

---

[9] Ibid., verses 13–14.
[10] Ibid., Chapter 5, verse 151.

A good widow should live on starvation diet (roots, some categories of vegetable without fish, meat and pulses) and carefully stay away from male company.

Kamantu kshapayeddaham puspumulaphalaih subhaih
Na tu grhniyat patyou prete parasya tu.[11]

Translation: After the death of the husband, the widow should survive on auspicious fruits, roots and flowers, and spend the rest of her life. She should never think of other men (translation mine).

The following verses may be subjected to various interpretations. The verses however assigned a respectful status for women with the family, as cited below:

Yatra naryastu pujyante ramante tatra devatah
Yatrai na pujyante sarbbastraphalah kriah.
Socanti jamayo yatra vinasyatyasu tat kulam
Na socanti tu yatraita varddhate taddhi sarvada.
Jamayo yani gehani sapantyapratipujitah
Tani krtyahataniva vinasyanti samantatah.
Tasmadetah sada pujya bhusanachchhadanasnaih
Bhutikarmairnarairnityam satkaresutsavesu.
Santusto bharya bharta bhartra bharya tathaiva ca
Yasminneva kule nitya kalyanam tatra vai dhruvam.[12]

Translation: God prevails in those places where women are respected. The rituals yield no blessings unless women are respected in a family. Families get destroyed in which women are tortured and remain sorrowful. Those families prosper in which women remain happy. The families lose their prosperity and wealth being cursed by women due to disrespect and torture inflicted upon them. It is therefore the duty of the members of the families, those who aspire prosperity and wealth, to honour women and always provide them with food, cloth and ornaments

---

[11] Ibid., verse 157.
[12] Ibid., verses 56–60.

during auspicious and festive occasions. Those families are definitely blessed in which the husband and wife are satisfied with each other (translation mine).

The discussion above thus offers a glimpse on the ambivalent domain of women in the textual space in Manusmrti.

The ambivalence or inconsistencies or ideological shifts through extrapolations while one analyses the alternative space for women in terms of economic rights by which they could inherit property as mothers, widows (in the absence of son/grandson and great grandson) and unmarried daughters along with their claim over *Stridhana*. It is rather intriguing that the discussion on the economic/property rights for women is preceded by the insertion of the most popular, infamous and oft-quoted enunciation about women, which invokes an image of liminal and subordinate status of Indian women.

Pita raksati koumare bharta raksati youbane
Raksanti sthabibe putra na srti svatantramarhati.[13]

Translation: Women are protected by their father in their childhood, by the husband in their youth and by their son in their old age. Women are never independent.

Such enunciations are inserted in the text in different chapters as well. For example, Chapter 5 invoked the morality of a respectful and harmonious space for women. That chapter invariably added:

Nasti strinam kriya mantrairiti dharma vyavasthitih
Nirindriya hyamantrasca striyo(a)nrtamiti sthitih.[14]

Translation: Women have no right to religious act and sacred chanting according to prevalent views. They have no capability/access to the Vedic learning. They are vain and useless (translation mine).

[13] Ibid., Chapter 9, verse 3.
[14] Ibid., Chapter 5, verse 115.

Chapter 9 of Manusmrti elaborately deals with the prescriptive norms relating to property and inheritance of both men and women. Manusmrti mentioned at least seven categories of *Stridhana*: *Adhyagni* or *Youtuka* (gained during marriage), *Adhyavahanika* (property received from parents while going to husband's house), *Anvadheya* (property given by parents, parents-in-law, husband and other members of the family during marriage), *Pitrdatta, Matrdatta, Bhratrdatta* (respectively given by father, mother and brother at any time).[15] *Stridhana* is devolved in the female line, starting from daughters and ending with a long list of female successors.[16] The text also underscores the point that the king would be a person in case of usurpation of *Stridhana*. A woman could even take punitive action against a person who would usurp her *Stridhana* property.[17]

However, margins were drawn in other vital aspects, as is already pointed out, to restrict autonomy of women. Therefore, the economic space became constricted in the textual frame making the text ambivalent and contradictory. This aspect of Manusmrti in relation to women is glaringly evident in the case of *Putrika*. Manusmrti originally prescribed a special category of female heir called *Putrika* (son designate). *Putrika*'s rights had been prescribed similar to a son's rights:

> *Yathaivatma tatha putrah putrena duhitasama*
> *Tasyamatmani tisthantyam kathamanyo dhanam haret.*[18]

Translation: A son is like a soul to a person. Daughter is also the same. How can others receive the wealth of a person if soul of a person exists in the world? (translation mine)

This autonomous right, as prescribed for women, had been drastically altered by adding complex statements about women's rights to property inheritance. The verses propose complex lists of

[15] Ibid., Chapter 9, verse 194.
[16] Ibid., verses 195–199.
[17] Ibid., Chapter 3, verse 52.
[18] Ibid., Chapter 9, verse 30.

heirs to *Putrika*'s property which does not convey any meaningful statements other than advocating male heirs by replacing the female. The right of *Putrika* has been finally reduced to merely becoming the begetter of a male heir, as is invoked in the following verse:

Douhitra eva ca haredputrasyakhiam dhanam
Douhitra hyakhilam rkthamputrasya piturharet.[19]

Translation: Grandson (son of daughter) should inherit the wealth of the grandfather. The grandson should inherit the wealth of a sonless person (translation mine).

The above verses demonstrate how the margins for women had been frequently violated and subverted through continuous extrapolations by anonymous authors showing vulgar faces of Indian patriarchy.

Interestingly, Manusmrti contained many prescriptive strictures on men, such as the issue of adultery. Contrary to the extant understanding about the high pitch of patriarchy in the text that absolved men from misdemeanour, Manusmrti contains elaborates strictures on male behaviour. The text elaborates on the acts of adultery and prescribes in Chapter 7, *shloka* 352: 'The king would impose harshest punishment on those men who are adulterous having extramarital affairs with other men's wives. Those men should be expelled from the land leaving a stigmatizing mark on the body.' Again, one may observe striking inconsistency in the same chapter, verse 361, in which the text recommends that men should pay in gold as punishment for the same act. The strictures on men for violation of familial norms and moral conduct, especially in relation to women, are obliterated from popular imagination.

The textual analysis would briefly add two important points. First, there is no reference to Sati in the text. Indeed, the text contains several verses advocating ideal widowhood on starvation

[19] Ibid., Chapter 10, verses 131–132.

diet and deprivation of self, as is already mentioned. Again, there was a twist. Manusmrti mentioned 12 categories of sons accepted in the society: *Aurasa, Kshetraja, Dattaka/Datrima, Apabiddha, Gudotpanna, Kanina, Krtrma, Sahoda, Krta, Svayamdatta, Soudra* and *Pounarbhaba*. Apart from *Aurasa*, all other categories of sons were begotten a person other than the husband. Here, *Pounarbhaba* sons would be briefly defined. The original *shloka* explained *Pounarbhaba* as follows: if a woman who is deserted by her husband or a widow wants to beget a son by her own choice or will is called *Pounrbhaba*.[20] This category of son contradicts the dictum for a widow to follow austere widowhood and stricture against having sexual contact with men. That definition was subsequently abrogated through a new definition in Chapter 9, *shloka* 176[21]: 'If a married virgin once after leaving her husband come back again, then that that husband would accept her by performing certain rituals. The son born out of that couple would be called *Pounarbhaba*'. By contradicting the earlier *shloka*, the new definition definitely imposed strictures on women to have sexual contact with men other than the husband. This attempt to subvert the connotation and meaning of *Pounarbhaba* son, however, was not completely successful. Presumably, an original *shloka* still remained in the text to corroborate the original meaning of *Pounarbhaba*, as is evident in the following verse:

> *Samsthitasyanpatasya sagotrat putramaharet*
> *Tatra yad rkthajatam syat tasmin pratipadayet.*
> *Dvou tu you dvabhyam jatou striya dhane*
> *Tayoryad yasya pitryam syat tat sa grhnita netarah.*[22]

Translation: The wife of a sonless person should beget a son by engaging a male from the same caste and bestow the property to that son. If any dispute arises between a son begotten by the

---

[20] Ibid., verse 175.
[21] Ibid., verse 176.
[22] Ibid., verses 190–191.

husband (*Aurasa*) and *Pounarbhaba* during the lifetime of a mother, the mother should bestow the property to that son whose father owned the property (translation mine).

One may find numerous examples of negative/positive–positive/negative binary in the prescriptive verses on rights, status and entitlements of women. And such aspects make Manusmrti a problematic text. Given the nature of the textual space of Manusmrti in terms of the contradictions and inconsistencies, it is difficult to define textual space as an unambiguous domain of the epitome of Indian patriarchy and also a space in which women dwell within a uniformly structural ideology.

There are some unsolved mysteries. The colonial rulers perceived Manusmrti as *the authentic law* of the Hindus. It is difficult to explain why William Jones, the early juridical ideologue of the British Empire despite finding the text as 'partial and fanciful' as well as 'absurd and ridiculous', pioneered the translation of this text into English under the title 'Institutes of Hindu Law' or Ordinations of Menu.[23] By this translation, he initiated the trend and popular perception of Manusmrti as the 'law' of the Hindus. Manusmrti literally means 'memories or heard perceptions from Manu'. Jones transformed the mnemonic tradition into a legal text *per se* by ascribing unauthorized attributes in the title. The next few pages analyse the colonial appropriation of Manusmrti to subvert women's rights to property and inheritance.

The Colonial Rulers and Appropriation of Manusmrti

Manusmrti was found to be an extremely popular text among the early administrators and Orientalist scholars and the popularity remained throughout British rule. The text was represented as

---

[23] William Jones, *Institutes of Hindu Law, Or, the Ordination of MENU, According to the Gloss of Culluca* (London: Lawbook Exchange, 1794).

the 'the most ancient' and 'authentic' laws of the Hindus. This popularity survived throughout the entire period of colonial rule in India, which is evident in numerous translations of this text. In fact, Manusmrti is popularly considered as the authentic traditional laws of the Hindus as well as the epitome of Indian patriarchy even today despite the inconsistencies as is evident from the above analysis.

The serious anomalies however did not reduce the veneration of the early rulers of the East India Company. The British rulers in India, especially the early rulers in Bengal, rather dwelled upon the ambivalence and marginal/negative image of 'Indian woman', further marginalizing the image of 'Indian woman' in global parlance. The principal instrument for them was Manusmrti. The primary motive was to subvert existing property rights for women as prescribed in *Dayabhaga* tradition and customary practices.[24]

As is already mentioned, William Jones, the early juridical ideologue of the British Empire, pioneered the translation of this text into English under the title 'Institutes of Hindu Law'. By this translation, he initiated the trend and popular perception of Manusmrti as the 'law' of the Hindus. Manusmrti literally means 'memories or heard perceptions from Manu'. Jones transformed the mnemonic tradition into a legal text *per se* by ascribing unauthorized attributes in the title, though he himself projected the text as 'partial and fanciful' as well as 'absurd and ridiculous'.[25] The 'moral' theory of social gradation and caste hierarchy in Manusmrti found a new dynamic with this metamorphosis. It must be mentioned in this context that Jones offered an interpretative translation of the text while translating the relevant portions relating to women's rights to property. For example, it has been specifically mentioned in a verse that the ancestral property should be divided after the death of both father and

---

[24] The śāstras or Dharmaśāstras did not represent a static tradition as has been discussed in the text.

[25] Jones, *Institute of Hindu Law*, xvii.

mother. The son/s would not have any right over the property while either parent lives.

> *Urddham pitusca matusca sametya bhrataram samam*
> *Bhajeran paitrkam rkthamanisaste hi jibotoh.*[26]

Translation: After the demise of both father and mother, the brothers would assemble to divide the property. They are not the owners of the property during the lifetime of both father and mother (translation mine).

Jones extended the meaning of the verse in his book and added his own interpretation: 'unless the father chooses to distribute it'.[27] One may observe the marginalization of women's right in such attempts. Jones' *Institute* is full of such interpretative translations to reduce women's claims over property. It is difficult to proliferate the examples within the contour of a single essay.

The extant historiography on British imperialism and multiple layers of patriarchy in India deals with women's issues from varied perspectives. It includes intervention within the sphere of social reforms and the process of modernization of culture and society. Such studies however hardly deal with the colonial attitude and policy in the sphere of economic entitlements of women, mainly property and inheritance; though the colonial knowledge about Indian women was initially generated through administrative experiences and gradual evolution of colonial governance relating to revenue and judicial matters. *Manusmrti* was appropriated as an infallible guide in dealing with women's entitlement to property even in revenue governance.

The book written by the present author however unfolds the history of 'invention' of 'Hindu law' through codifications in Sanskrit and subsequent rendering into English.[28] The book further shows how the selective use of shastras, including

---

[26] Manusmrti, Chapter 9, verse 104.
[27] Jones, *Institute of Hindu Law*, 258.
[28] Panda, *Appropriation and Invention of Tradition*.

Manusmrti, became the prime instrument to marginalize extant residual and substantive rights of women, especially widows in land and property, prescribed in the *Dayabhaga* texts and customized through practices, had been marginalized and subverted through codifications and courtroom deliberations. The colonial rulers came in India with an ideology that sustained inhibitions against the property rights of women. In contemporary England, women had no right to inherit and hold property. The vast corpus of *shastric* literature contained varied and contradictory principles in relation to status and entitlements of women.

The contemporary colonial documents recorded that the early British rulers in Bengal had to encounter a large number of big and small female proprietors in the initial era. It is also evident from the documents that they were reluctant to accord necessary sanction to such rights. In short, they expressed their reservation to accept women as revenue payers in their treasury. Their reluctance was subsequently reflected their policies towards women's rights to property and inheritance. There was a systematic attempt to suppress women's rights in the colonial courts, as evident in the extant records. The rulers tried to replace female proprietors by male counterparts on several occasions as recorded in the revenue papers.[29] For example, John Shore, the second Governor-General of the Company's government during the 1780s in Bengal, systematically emphasized the lack of agency of the native women in managing their estates. He put forward an argument about the malevolent proxy role of male servants or the relatives and defined every woman as 'passive instruments' in their hands.[30] To substantiate his argument, he invoked the oft-quoted dictum from Manusmrti that 'women remain under the guardianship of the father during childhood, under the husband during youth and under the son in the old

[29] Ibid.

[30] W. K. Firminger, ed., *The Fifth Report from the Select Committee of the House of Commons on the Affairs of the East India Company 1812*, vol. 2 (Calcutta: R. Cambray & Co., 1817), 72.

age as women can never be independent'. On the basis of this citation, he argued that women in Bengal 'by the laws of their religion and customs [were] secluded from the public society'.[31] He asserted that, as proprietors, women were incapable of managing such 'a situation of so much importance and responsibility, as the management of the settlement and collection'. Hence, he declared female proprietors as 'disqualified landholders'. In this context, the recommendation of Philip Francis, an important member in the Governor-General's Council, may be cited. Francis recommended that 'A Court of Ward might be established for the care of estates, of which the incumbents are *minor*, *idiots* and *female*' (emphasis mine).[32] The above is a significant example of how Manusmrti was economically and strategically appropriated in order to subvert women's property in the official sphere.

It is also quite significant that the early rulers appropriated Manusmrti to undermine women's rights to property. John Shore (the second Governor-General of Bengal) officially declared women as 'disqualified landholders' by citing the oft-quoted dictum from Manusmrti that stated: 'women should live under their father when they are young, under the husband in youth and under the son/s in old age as women should not be independent' (Manusmrti, Chapter 9, verse iii). William Jones, the erudite Orientalist and the sitting judge in the Supreme Court towards the end of the 18th century, who translated Manusmrti for the first time in English, frequently inserted his own views from his translated text, especially when women's status rights and entitlements were concerned. Jones' translation of Manusmrti in essence turned out to be more of an interpretation than a translation of the text.

[31] Ibid., 78.
[32] *Original Minutes of the Governor-General and Council* of Fort William on the Settlement and Collection of Revenues of Bengal with a Plan of Settlement Recommended to the Court of Directors in January 1776 (London, 1782), 30.

Manusmrti in Select Western Discourses

As is briefly mentioned, over the ages, Manusmrti is an extremely popular *albeit* a controversial and debated text throughout the world. One may also say that the world came to know about the 'predominant' aspect of Indian culture, Hindu society, ethics and morality through translation of Manusmrti. William Jones, the erudite Orientalist and juridical ideologue of the British Empire, is the pioneer in this trajectory. It was followed by myriad translations, both in Indian and non-Indian languages. As for the colonial period was concerned, mention should be made to the translation of A. C. Burnell who commenced the translation but finished by Edward Hopkins and was published in 1891. The translation by George Buhler published in 1886 in the *Sacred Books of the East* collection received critical acclaim. Ganganath Jha translated the text into English and published the work from Calcutta between 1921 and 1929. Huttner translated the text in German language and published in 1797. Julius Jolly also translated the text in German, and it was further translated into English. A. Loiseleur-Deslongchamps, the first holder of the chair in Sanskrit in College de France, translated the text in French under the title *Lois De Manu* and published in 1833. G. Stretchly also produced a new translation in French in 1893. The above are only a few examples amid an elaborate list of translation of Manusmrti in English and other European languages. In recent time, Wendy Doniger's translation of Manusmrti under the title *The Laws of Manu* received popular acclaim.[33] This section will briefly refer to two authors—Friedrich Nietzsche and Wendy Doniger—in order to understand how the caste theory and social scheme in Manusmrti had been projected in Western world in different perspectives.

Jones' attempt to add a new dynamic to the text with the attribute of 'law' is already discussed in the chapter. He represented Manusmrti as the iconic symbol of moral, social and

---

[33] For further details, see Wendy Doniger and Brian K. Smith, *The Laws of Manu* (Gurugram: Penguin Books India, 1991), xix.

philosophical code of the Hindus. He stated: 'To use the words of the most venerable text in the Indian Scripture, which illuminates all, delights all, from which all proceed, which all must return, and which alone can irradiate *not our visual organs merely but our souls and* our intellects.'[34]

Jones' translation of Manusmrti created a profound but differential impact on European imagination. A large number of scholars, such as Max Muller, found curious but scholarly attraction to study and understand Indian tradition through Hindu classical texts. For Fredrich Nietzsche, the eminent 19th-century German philosopher, Manusmrti brought a new meaning in nourishing his theory on race and civilization. He found the supreme dictum of a moral society in the 'law of Manu'[35] compared to the Bible. Nietzsche derived a powerful instrument in his propagation of race theory. He expressed his delight over the creation of four castes by Manu's Law: 'This law sets the task of breeding no fewer than four races at once: a priestly race, a warrior race, a merchant and agricultural race, and finally a servant race, the Sudras.'[36]

Nietzsche considered the creation of four castes as 'the protective measures of Indian morality'.[37] To him, '*Caste-order*, the most supreme, domineering law, is just the sanction of *natural order*, natural lawfulness par excellence'.[38] He asserted:

> Nature, not Manu, separates out predominantly spiritual people from people characterized by muscular and temperamental strength from a third group of people who are not distinguished in either way, the mediocre—the latter being the great number, the first being the exceptions. The highest caste—which I call *the*

[34] Ibid.

[35] Fredrich Nietzsche, *The Anti-Christ, Ecce Homo, Twilight of the Idols*, ed. Aaron Ridley and Judith Norman (Cambridge: Cambridge University Press, 2005), 184.

[36] Ibid.

[37] Ibid.

[38] Nietzsche, *The Anti-Christ*, 58.

few—being the perfect caste, also has the privilege of the few: this includes representing happiness, beauty, goodness on earth.[39]

Nietzsche's theory on race and civilization thrived on the concept of exclusion of the Chandalas and also the Shudras. He found in the set of dictums in Manusmrti a shield to protect the privileges of the higher orders and to contain the 'low' and the 'mediocre' from revolting against the 'high' and 'superior'. To him, Chandala was a symbol of racial impurity and social disorder. While endorsing Manu's dictums by saying 'Indignation is the privilege of the Chandala,'[40] he explained: 'the Chandalas are the fruits of adultery, incest and crime.'[41]

Nietzsche found that the dictums in Manusmrti in relation to women were commendable and supreme. He said, 'I do not know any book that says as many kind and delicate things to female as the law book of Manu.'[42]

The text of Manu—the most 'high' and 'venerable' as invoked by Jones, the text containing 'duty', 'justice' and 'principle' as attributed by Doniger—provided the most powerful instrument to Nietzsche's theory of racial purity and exclusionary practices in structuring social hierarchy. In other words, Manusmrti fostered rationale to a reactionary philosophical theory in Europe that sustained fascism and a highly classified social order.

Wendy Doniger observed that 'Nietzsche continues to use Manu as a stick with which to beat Christianity which he characterizes as "the victory of Chandala values...the underlying Chandala revenge as the *religion of love*."' Nietzsche added that the 'religious legislation' of Manu was set with a 'goal to "eternalize" the supreme condition for a thriving life, a great organization of society'.[43]

---

[39] Ibid.
[40] Ibid., 58.
[41] Ibid., 185.
[42] Ibid., 57.
[43] Ibid., 60.

Manusmrti still intrigues the imagination of scholars and thinkers on a global level. For example, Wendy Doniger described Manusmrti as 'a pivotal text of the dominant form' of Hindu philosophy and 'most influential construction of the Hindu religion and Indic society as a whole'.[44] She feels that 'Manu is an attempt at consolidation and unity'.[45] The text, in Doniger's view, is 'an encompassing representation of life in the world—how it is, and how it should be lived'.[46] Doniger believes that Manusmrti is about dharma, 'which subsumes the English concepts "religion", "duty", "law", "right", "justice", "practice", and principle'.[47] For 'social and religious duties' tied to class and stages life (the *Varnasrama Dharma*), she emphasizes that 'Manu has become, and remained, the standard source of authority in the orthodox tradition for that centerpiece of Hinduism'.[48] Regarding the social gradation of caste order, Doniger sums up: 'In particular, it is evident that Manu is speaking not of an individual occupying a certain social function, let alone a particular profession, but rather of a class that may be constituted ritually, socially, and ethnically, as well as professionally.'[49]

There are myriad texts in India, other Asian countries, and the West that offered varied views and interpretations of the contents, significance and primacy of Manusmrti to understand Hindu civilization and the Brahmanical social order. This chapter only cited two authors who offered their interpretations in different periods of time and contexts.

To sum up, Manusmrti allowed narrow but ambivalent margins for Shudras and women; as it appears, for the Chandalas, the margin had no ambivalence. Interestingly, Manusmrti became a political tool both in India and the West. For the

---

[44] Doniger and Smith, *The Laws of Manu*, 17
[45] Ibid., 35.
[46] Ibid., 17.
[47] Ibid.
[48] Ibid.
[49] Ibid., 24.

colonial rulers, the hierarchical model and ambivalent stance for women in the text had been appropriated to create a sub-ject–ruler paradigm and an instrument to subvert residual but substantive property rights for women. In post-colonial India, Manusmrti is a fierce site of political debate about caste hier-archy and the privilege pattern. The debate in India lies beyond the scope of the chapter. In the West, the text became an instru-ment to create the civilizational binary in the lines of superiority, rationality and moral society.

The textual analysis of Manusmrti in this chapter and the varied interpretations have been undertaken to point out that Manusmrti should be read through a new window. The text should be re-read and re-analysed not as 'authentic law' or 'moral codes' for Hindus. The British rulers introduced 'law' in the Indian soil within the paradigms of 'equity' and 'rule of law'. British 'law' was structured within the coercive and punitive domain of 'justice'. The textual design and contents in Manusmrti do not fall within this structure. The text does not contain any notion of punitive measures other than 'curses for going to hell or to be born as an animal'. Moreover, the entire corpus of *shastric* literature does not contain a synonym for 'law' as the 18th-century Englishmen understood the term. The Western concept of 'law' is a new attribute on the text leaving aside the value judgement either as a divine precept or as a much-maligned monster.

Manusmrti as a text should be viewed as a repository of knowledge that surfaces the dilemma and ideological shifts on various issues, most importantly, women's status and entitle-ments. The textual analysis in this chapters tries to argue that the text accommodated and internalized varied ideologies over passage of millennia, including the interpretative and lopsided intervention of the colonial rulers in the textual space through translation. In the long run, it turned out to be a textual space combining contradictory and inconsistent index of 'moral' code for the caste Hindus in India. It is not possible to ascertain how the textual space morphed within historical time frames. Notwithstanding the absence of historical time frame from the original compilation and its reduction into contradictions and ambivalence, Manusmrti is still a significant site of history. It indicated gradual degeneration of women's status and entitlements, perhaps over a long span of historical time from a constitutive, if not liberal space to vulgar face of 'Indian patriarchy'. The significance of Manusmrti as a moral code or 'law' is questioned by various social and gender groups. A fresh reading of Manusmrti however is necessary to situate the text as a site of history while keeping the term 'history' in a democratic space—the way oral history and literature have found place in historical writings.

4

Jurisprudence in Pre-colonial India

Balaji Ranganathan

Introduction

This chapter seeks to understand the formulation of laws, and the manner in which it was received in pre-colonial India. It will be brief in terms of analysis. But it will try to bring out the salient features of the law that existed in pre-colonial India. The subject of these ancient texts has been much commented upon. I shall not be discussing this in my chapter as the focus is on to have an understanding of this early society which created the corpus.

Hindu Laws

There were many sources of the law with the Shruti, which consisted of the four Vedas, namely the Rigveda, Sam Veda, Yajur Veda and Atharva Veda. The Vedas deal with religious and liturgical duties, practices and customs, and the smriti refers to tradition and codices written to codify cultural practice. The other texts were the Dharmashastras which were equated with laws. Some of the prominent Dharmashastras were Manusmrti (200 BC–200 CE), Yajnavalkya Smriti (200–500 CE), Naradasmriti

(100 BC–400 CE), Visnusmriti (700–1000 CE), Brihaspatismriti (200–400 CE) and Katyayanasmriti (300–600 CE).

The Codes of Apastamba, Gautama, Baudhayana and Vashistha are the earlier sutras which preceded the Dharmashastras. These texts have been used for legal opinion and judgements. It needs to be made clear that these normative texts were mostly meant for Brahmans who were also the authorial interpreters. These texts discussed the rules of the ashram, studenthood, domestic householders' duties, renunciation, diet, the duties of the various ashram's systems, daily sacrifices and funeral practices. The Dharmashastras focus on the *achara*, *vyavahara* and *prayaschitta*. The *achara* provided rules of daily rituals, life cycles, specific duties of the four ashrams and proper conduct. *Vyavahara* dealt mainly with laws and legal procedures which included the duties of a king, the idea of *rajdharma*, examining witnesses and to enforce punitive punishment for any criminal activity. In fact, legal procedures including that of filing a case were called *vyavahara*. The equivalent of modern lawsuit was called *purvapaksha*, and that of written statement as *uttar*. The trial was called *kriya* and verdict as *nirnaya*. The Brihaspatismriti has description of legal systems. If I can use the modern-day term, there were four kinds of tribunals, namely stationary and movable courts, the royal signet, in the absence of the king, and commissions under the king's presidency[1] and a hierarchy of courts. In villages, the village councils (*kulani*) dealt with simple civil and criminal cases. At a higher level, in towns and districts, the courts were presided over by government officers under the authority of the king to administer justice.[2] In order to deal with problems among members of artisanal class, traders, etc., trade guilds were authorized to exercise an effective jurisdiction over their members. Family courts were also established. Puga assemblies made up of groups of families in the same village decided civil disputes among

[1] P. V. Kane, *History of Dharmasastra*, Vol. 3 (Pune: Bhandarkar Oriental Research Institute, 1973), Chapter 11, 288–289.

[2] Ibid.

family members. Minor criminal cases were dealt with by judicial assemblies in villages, whereas criminal cases of a serious nature were presented before the central court usually held under the king or royal authority. The appeal system was practised, and the king was the highest body of appeal. Another notable feature was that a bench of two or more judges was always preferred to administer justice rather than a single individual being the sole administrator of justice.[3] The *Arthashastra* and *Nitishastra* of Chanakya, which are again early Mauryan texts that predate the smritis, had a structured content that picked up the idea of the Vedic dharma in content but was largely secular in the focus of statecraft. The texts focused on numerous subjects from the focus on the nature of the state to the ideas of agriculture and taxation. This is at much variance with the nature of the content of the Dharmashastras. One way of understanding this is to look at these normative texts as being individualistic in its application, while the *Arthashastra* was a treatise on statecraft.

Coming to the nature of dharma, the word poses a dilemma as it is not quantifiable within the Vedic corpus. Dharma is not an action here, but an idea that constitutes a 'support'. So any action had to be virtuous only if it was supported by dharma. Patrick Olivelle on the Dharmasutras mentions that the term

> dharma may be translated as 'Law' if we do not limit ourselves to its narrow modern definition as civil and criminal statutes but take it to include all the rules of behaviour, including moral and religious behaviour, that a community recognizes as binding on its members.[4]

The sections below will briefly examine the four sutras and their concerns. The Apastamba Sutra mentions in the section on the nature of social stratification and the nature of kinships constructed

---

[3] Ibid.

[4] Patrick Olivelle, *The Law Codes of Āpastamba, Gautama, Baudhāyana, and Vasistha* (annotated text and translation; New Delhi: Motilal Banarasidas, 2000), 21.

where a Brahman could have four marriages, a Kshatriya three, the Vaishya two and the Shudra who could only have one wife. There is also a mention of mixed communities of people. [5]

The text also mentions many communities that are extinct today or have merged into other communities. The text also clearly mentions the nature of authority with the birth of the sons of these communities. The blood lines are clearly outlined and the marriage within any of these communities directly was connected to the right of the son to the nature of the sacrifice. This hierarchy points to the importance of genealogy, especially within early India, which had a high degree of migration and intermarriage.[6]

This is interesting because most of the categories mentioned here are extinct today. What could be the broad reason for this social arrangement and its specific emphasis on genealogy and

[5] Baudhayana, 231; Olivelle, *The Law Codes of Āpastamba*, 231.
Also see E. Hultzsch, ed., Baudhayana Dharmasutra, 1st ed. Abhandlungen für die Kunde des Morgenlandes, 8 (Leipzig, 1884). 2nd ed. Abhandlungen für die Kunde des Morgenlandes, 16. Leipzig, 1922. ed. with Govinda's commentary by L. Srinivasacharya. Government Oriental Library Series, Bibliotheca Sanskrita, 34. Mysore, 1907. ed. with Govinda's commentary by U. C. Pandeya. Kashi Sanskrit Séries, 104 Varanasi: Chowkhamba Sanskrit Series Office, 1972; Tr. in Buhler 1879–1882).
L. Srinivasachar and R. Shama Sastri, eds., *Baudhayana Grhyasutra*, 3rd ed. (Mysore: Oriental Research Institute, 1983).
W. Caland, ed. *Baudhayana Srautasutra*, 3 vols. (Reprint; New Delhi: Munshiram Manoharlal, 1982).
[6] Baudhayana, 231; Olivelle, *The Law Codes of Āpastamba*, 231.
Also see Hultzsch, Baudhayana Dharmasütra. *Abhandlungen für die Kunde des Morgenlandes*, 8. Leipzig, 1884. 2nd ed. Abhandlungen für die Kunde des Morgenlandes, 16. Leipzig, 1922. Ed. with Govinda's commentary by L. Srinivasacharya. Government Oriental Library Series, Bibliotheca Sanskrita, 34. Mysore, 1907. Ed. with Govinda's commentary by U. C. Pandeya. Kashi Sanskrit Series, 104 (Varanasi: Chowkhamba Sanskrit Series Office, 1972; Tr. in Buhler 1879–1882).
Srinivasachar and Sastri, *Baudhayana Grhyasutra*.
Caland, *Baudhayana Srautasütra*.

birth. As I understand it, early India was a fluid dynamic space of various communities that migrated into the Gangetic valley; some of it being by conquest such as the White Huns, the Greeks and Central Asian communities like the Kushans. They had brought in different cultural codes and this made it necessary to make a differential status in terms of birth. It can be taken as a protectionist exercise which led to the formation of these codes, which later become normative, especially during the colonial period. Speaking on the legal system, the Apastamba Sutra has a very clear idea on the nature of jurisprudence. The legal sources are the Vedas, and it mentions the nature of the legal assembly, where one needed four men who had a hold on the four Vedas, including all the supplements. Within this gathering, there had to be a minimum number of 10 people with three Brahmans who represented the three stages of life, though the law was flexible to say that even one man of a sound scholarship could instead represent the law.[7]

The legal assembly has been an integral part of ancient India legal systems. Within monarchical system, there had been a federal outlook on the administration of the law. It was a participatory form of legal administration of jurisprudence. This was to be seen in the colonial period again, but it was within the unitary system, contrary to the federal system displayed in these early jurisprudence systems.

The sutra goes on to mention the difficulty of the law where it states that the path is not very easy to negotiate and there was a general impossibility for a single person to articulate on the law.[8]

---

[7] Vasistha Sutra, 365; Olivelle, *The Law Codes of Apastamba*, 365.
Also see Kane, *History of Dharmasastra*, Vol. 5; A. A. Führer, ed., *Vasistha Dharmasutra*, 1st ed. (Bombay: Government Central Book Depot, 1883; Bombay Sanskrit and Prakrit Series, 23; Poona: Bhandarkar Oriental Research Institute, 1930. Ed. with Krsnapandita's commentary Vidvanmodin Benares, 1878. Tr. in Buhler 1879–1882).
[8] *Baudhayana Sutra*, 197; Olivelle, *The Law Codes of Apastamba*, 197.

The law is a reflection on the nature and form of society. A multitude of smritis and Dharmashastras with their commentaries and the law being geared on *varna* meant that there was a need for a democratic interpretation of the law. Being very federalist in terms of the assembly composition, the legal systems were extremely specialized at this time which led to a representative group of people administering the law. This was a singular feature of the early legal systems.

The Gautama Sutra mentions that the larger administration of justice had to be based on the Vedic texts and the *puranas*. It was democratic enough to mention that if the law was not running contrary to the shastras, then even the subsidiary laws of different regions could be considered.[9]

The anxiety of this early society is extremely evident where the text goes on to examine the nature of geography and the inhabitants that live in it. This is important to understand that the idea of purity, which later becomes a law, is more to do with the influx of communities that have migrated through and settled within the various parts of India. The codes here become a safeguard to construct and maintain cultural practices which are clearly in threat as early Indian society stabilized with the acceptance of various communities. The text mentions the distinction between the south and the north of India. It mentions five areas where cultural practices differ, and the nature of the law is also different. It is largely related to the dietary habits where there is a prohibition of eating with any person who has not been initiated. It goes on to include the practices of eating with one's wife, a prohibition on eating stale meals and, in terms of kinship, there was a prohibition of intermarrying into ones *gotra*,

[9] Gautama Sutra; Olivelle, *The Law Codes of Apastamba*, 147.
Also see A. F. Stenzler, ed., *Gautama Dharmasutra* (London: Trubner, 1876) with Haradatta's commentary by N. Talekar, 61. Poona, 1966. Ed. With Maskarin's commentary by L. Srinivasacharya. Government Oriental Library Series, Bibliotheca Sanskrita, 50. Mysore, 1917. Ed. with Maskarin's commentary by Veda Mitra (New Delhi: Veda Mitra and Sons, 1969. Tr. in Buhler 1879–1882).

especially close kinship ties like marrying the daughter of the mothers brother or the sister of the father.[10] The text also goes on to describe the cultural practices and customs connected with the people in these places. The people living in the north of the country were largely connected to the practices of selling wool and animal husbandry. The professions were proscribed to the particular community which, if neglected, could lead to the ideal of being excommunicated and it was subject to the authority of the regions mentioned.[11]

There is an interesting corollary to ancient Indian texts which gives a geographical understanding of the idea of a state and also an understanding of the subjects towards which the law is administered. Apart from geographical awareness, there is also a space within which the law has to be administered, which points to a multitude of legal systems, some of which were existing in the south of India as legal traditions but have been lost now with the advent of time and changes within history.

The text clearly mentions the geographical nature of the law being administered. On the Land of the Aryas, the text mentions

[10] *Baudhayana Sutra*, 199; Olivelle, *The Law Codes of Apastamba*, 199.
Also see Hultzsch, *Baudhayana Dharmasutra*. Abhandlungen fur die Kunde des Morgenlandes, 8. Leipzig, 1884. 2nd ed. Abhandlungen für die Kunde des Morgenlandes, 16. Leipzig, 1922. Ed. with Govinda's commentary by L. Srinivasacharya. Government Oriental Library Series, *Bibliotheca Sanskrita*, 34. Mysore, 1907. Ed. with Govinda's commentary by U. C. Pandeya. Kashi Sanskrit Series, 104 (Varanasi: Chowkhamba Sanskrit Series Office, 1972. Tr. in Buhler 1879–1882).
Srinivasachar and Sastri, *Baudhayana Grhyasutra*.
Caland, *Baudhayana Srautasutra*.
[11] *Baudhayana Sutra*, 199; Olivelle, *The Law Codes of Apastamba*, 199.
Also see Hultzsch, *Baudhayana Dharmasutra*. Abhandlungen für die Kunde des Morgenlandes, 8. Leipzig, 1884. 2nd ed. Abhandlungen für die Kunde des Morgenlandes, 16. Leipzig, 1922. Ed. with Govinda's commentary by L. Srinivasacharya. Government Oriental Library Series, Bibliotheca Sanskrita, 34. Mysore, 1907. Ed. with Govinda's commentary by U. C. Pandeya. Kashi Sanskrit Series, 104 (Varanasi: Chowkhamba Sanskrit Series Office, 1972. Tr. in Buhler 1879–1882).
Srinivasachar and Sastri, *Baudhayana Grhyasutra*.

that the land surrounding the river Saraswati, which had disappeared, and the areas around south of the Himalayas near the *Kalaka* forest are the areas that are composed of the Arya people, and their cultural practices were in the keeping with the Arya ethnology.[12]

The Vashistha Sutra also mentions geography and the physical delimitation of land to illustrate the area in which the law needs to be administered, pointing to the fact that the law was not of a homogeneous kind and different forms of the law might have existed in early India. The law was intimately connected with the flow of the River Saraswati and its disappearance, and it intimately delineates the geography in which the law is administered and recognized. Hence, the law was recognized to be authoritative if it was bound within the areas covered by the Saraswati in the west, the Himalayas in the north and the Vindhyas in the south. This was supposed to be land of the Aryas, and the sutra very clearly delimits the authority of the law of the forest dwellers.[13]

The Apastamba Sutra text mentions that inheritance could be a problem without heirs and that if this was the case then the property could devolve to somebody from somebody within the same lineage or could be passed down to relatives within the family.

[12] *Apasthamba Sutra*, 199; Olivelle, *The Law Codes of Apastamba*, 199.
  Also see G. Buhler, *Apastambha Dharmasutra*, 1st ed (Bombay: Education Society's Press, 1868). 2nd ed. Bombay: Government Central Book Depot. Part I, 1892; Part II, 1894. 3rd. ed. Bombay Sanskrit and Prakrit Series, 44, 50. Poona: Bhandarkar Oriental Research Institute, 1932. Ed. with Haradatta's commentary Ujjvala by U. C. Pandeya. Kashi Sanskrit Series, 93 (Varanasi: Chowkhamba Sanskrit Series Office, 1969. Tr. in Buhler 1879).
  R. Garbe, *Apastambha Srautasutra* (Reprint, 3 vols.; New Delhi: Munshiram Manoharlal, 1983).
[13] *Vasistha Sutra*, 351; Olivelle, *The Law Codes of Apastamba*, 351.
  Also see Kane, *History of Dharmasastra*, Vol. 5. Führer, *Vasistha Dharmasutra*. 1st ed (Bombay: Government Central Book Depot, 1883; 3rd ed.) Bombay Sanskrit and Prakrit Series, 23. Poona: Bhandarkar Oriental Research Institute, 1930 (with Krsnapandita's commentary VidvanmodinL Benares, 1878. Tr. in Buhler 1879–1982).

In case this was a problem, then it could move to the teacher, a student or the priest. The king had a condition that he could not enjoy the inheritance but had to distribute the same to the practitioners of the three Vedic systems. There was an injunction against the property of the Brahman where the king was advised not to acquire the property of a Brahman, which was akin to poisoning.[14]

Of all the *varnas*, the Brahman was free from the process of taxation. This was a singular feature in most of the law codes examined. The Vashistha Sutra mentions on the issue of taxation, where the king could hold one-sixth of the wealth but not the wealth of a Brahman.[15]

Keeping with this notion of hierarchy, the Gautama Sutra mentions a singular idea of women inheriting property, which is modern and emanates with the modern nation state and is linked with the issues of emancipation. This also brings to question the larger discourse of women and their subjugation within Hindu law, especially with the dichotomy of duties and the laws of succession. The law displays an emancipatory attitude towards gender as the entire notion of offering of oblations was inadvertently misinterpreted as being overtly patriarchal. The sutra is clear on the role of the daughter as being able to offer the oblation within the

---

[14] *Baudhayana Sutra*, 221; Olivelle, *The Law Codes of Apastamba*, 221.
Also see Hultzsch, *Baudhāyana Dharmasutra*. 1st ed. Abhandlungen für die Kunde des Morgenlandes, 8. Leipzig, 1884. 2nd ed. Abhandlungen für die Kunde des Morgenlandes, 16. Leipzig, 1922. Ed. with Govinda's commentary by L. Srinivasacharya. Government Oriental Library Series, Bibliotheca Sanskrita, 34. Mysore, 1907; Ed. with Govinda's commentary by U. C. Pandeya. Kashi Sanskrit Series, 104 (Varanasi: Chowkhamba Sanskrit Series Office, 1972; Tr. in Buhler 1879–1882).
Srinivasachar and Sastri, *Baudhayana Grhyasutra*.
Caland, *Baudhayana Srautasutra*.
[15] Vasista Sutra, 355; Olivelle, *The Law Codes of Āpastamba*, 355.
Also see Kane, *History of Dharmasastra*, Vol. 5. Führer, *Vasistha Dharmasutra*, 1st ed. (Bombay: Government Central Book Depot, 1883). Bombay Sanskrit and Prakrit Series, 23. Poona: Bhandarkar Oriental Research Institute, 1930. Ed. with Krsnapandita's commentary Vidvanmod in Benares, 1878. Tr. in Buhler 1879–1882.

fire ceremony if the person in question had no son. This brings in a major change within the interpretation of the shastras with respect to gender and especially the role of the daughter as being able to participate within rituals.[16]

Regarding the idea of inheritance and the division of property, the Gautama Sutra is more elaborate than the Apastamba Sutra. The text mentions a range of categories where inheritance can be problematized and regularized. The text mentions the question of inheritance in the absence of a son. Here, the widow is authorized to adopt a new son and, if there was a close relation like the brother-in-law, then his son could be the legal heir, though there is a clause that states that an heir has to be through a blood relation and not through a conjugal right with any man. Hence, property and inheritance were seen to be a very close kinship ritual.[17]

On the question of women's property and the right to hold the same, the sutra mentions that the property of the wife would go to the daughters and the dowry was supposed to go to the brothers after the death of the mother.[18] This notion of kinship inheritance is an emancipatory idea. Here, a notion of fairness with relation

---

[16] Gautama Sutra, 187; Olivelle, *The Law Codes of Apastamba*, 187.
Stenzler· *Gautama Dharmasutra*, with Haradatta's commentary by N. Talekar, 61 (Poona, 1966). Ed. With Maskarin's commentary by L. Srinivasacharya. Government Oriental Library Series, Bibliotheca Sanskrita, 50. Mysore, 1917. Ed. with Maskarin's commentary by Veda Mitra (New Delhi: Veda Mitra and Sons, 1969. Tr. in Buhler 1879–1882).

[17] Gautama Sutra, 187; Olivelle, *The Law Codes of Apastamba*, 187.
Stenzler· Gautama Dharmasutra (with Haradatta's commentary by N. Talekar, 61; Poona, 1966); Ed. with Maskarin's commentary by L. Srinivasacharya. Government Oriental Library Series, Bibliotheca Sanskrita, 50 (Mysore, 1917); ed. with Maskarin's commentary by Veda Mitra (New Delhi: Veda Mitra and Sons, 1969. Tr. in Buhler 1879–1882).

[18] Gautama Sutra, 187; Olivelle, *The Law Codes of Apastamba*, 187.
Stenzler, Gautama Dharmasutra (with Haradatta's commentary by N. Talekar, 61; Poona, 1966); Ed. with Maskarin's commentary by L. Srinivasacharya. Government Oriental Library Series, Bibliotheca Sanskrita, 50 (Mysore, 1917); Ed. with Maskarin's commentary by Veda Mitra (New Delhi: Veda Mitra and Sons, 1969. Tr. in Buhler 1879–1882).

to property is maintained where the nature of kinship–relationship is crucial to property distribution. Hence, a wife's property was at a liberty of being proportioned off within the gender itself. It did not entail the male to be a sole recipient of the property. Speaking about the property, the sutra mentions that if the family unit had disputes and had been divided, then the property could move to the elder brother. In case the family united again and the brother died, then the coparcener inherited the property and, if there was a son who was born after the portioning, then he was the sole inheritor of the estate.[19]

Here, the notion of joint family as a structure is crucial to an understanding. Although there is a very clear division between male and female personal property, the sutras do not preclude the idea of nuclear family arrangements. On the question of defining legal heirs, there is an astonishing modernity that got subverted during the colonial period with the introduction of the English common law. The sutra mentions the idea of legal heirs that a biological natural child or a son who has been adopted or a child born out of wedlock would be the sole inheritor of the property. An unmarried woman who had a child or a son was born to a woman who had remarried could also inherit the property. The same was the law for a son born to a daughter who had been recognized as a family head or a son who had offered himself for adoption. Here, the law stated that, in the absence of a natural son, they could receive the share of one-sixth of the property.[20]

---

[19] Gautama Sutra, 187; Olivelle, *The Law Codes of Apastamba*, 187.
Also see Stenzler, Gautama Dharmasutra (with Haradatta's commentary by N. Talekar, 61; Poona, 1966) with Maskarin's commentary by L. Srinivasacharya. Government Oriental Library Series, Bibliotheca Sanskrita, 50. Mysore, 1917 (with Maskarin's commentary by Veda Mitra; New Delhi: Veda Mitra and Sons, 1969. Tr. in Buhler 1879–1882).

[20] Gautama Sutra, 187; Olivelle, *The Law Codes of Apastamba*, 187.
Also see Stenzler, Gautama Dharmasutra (with Haradatta's commentary by N. Talekar, 61; Poona, 1966; with Maskarin's commentary by L. Srinivasacharya. Government Oriental Library Series, Bibliotheca Sanskrita, 50. Mysore, 1917. Ed. with Maskarin's commentary by Veda Mitra (Delhi: Veda Mitra and Sons, 1969. Tr. in Buhler 1879–1882).

There is an openness regarding the definitions of conjugal relationships and the resulting property issues here. In a larger sense, there is a great deal of democratization in the definition of an heir. One can understand through the translation projects of the Asiatic Society how this law was at variance with the law of primogeniture within the English common law. Here, the property, according to the sutra, could be handed over to a large number of people. This completely went against the British notions of property inheritance.

The underlying idea of dharma in these sutras upholds not only the nature of morality but also the idea of how the law needs to be administered. Dharma is the social support, the main correlative that holds the law. This is the reason why the entire corpus of the law is built upon this very ephemeral and intangible idea. It is correlative with the idea of justice in today's times where the law can be administered. But unfortunately, due to the absence of moral–social support, it is constantly circumvented. This dichotomy is resolved in the Gautama Sutra. The sutra mentions that the legal assembly had to be comprised of an assembly of 10 individuals and, if this was not available, then one man who was proficient with the Vedas could comprise the assembly.[21]

The democratic nature of Hindu law is built upon the idea of consensus. It is not arbitrary in terms of a single person or a dominant group of people deciding and adjudicating over the matter of differences in the law. The sutra clearly states that, in terms of differences, there needed to be a committee of sorts which could arbitrate on the idea.

The law that emanates from the Dharmashastras might be redundant today in terms of a Hindu Personal Law, but what

---

[21] Gautama Sutra, 189; Olivelle, *The Law Codes of Āpastamba*, 189.
Also see Stenzler, Gautama Dharmasutra (with Haradatta's commentary by N. Talekar, 61; Poona, 1966; with Maskarin's commentary by L. Srinivasacharya. Government Oriental Library Series, Bibliotheca Sanskrita, 50. Mysore, 1917. Ed. with Maskarin's commentary by Veda Mitra (New Delhi: Veda Mitra and Sons, 1969. Tr. in Buhler 1879–1882).

appears within these old treatises is an amazing sense of fairness and mode of jurisdiction. Although much of the law is cultural in nature, pertaining to daily modes of behaviour within the four *varnas*, there is a surprising amount of material regarding the nature of the law, its administration and its geographical distribution. It gives a very clear indication of how early society worked and functioned within a clear codification of the texts. The texts in a larger symbolic sense signify more a way of life rather than a code that needed to be observed as the breaking of the law was more a break with dharma. It was unlike modern law and the Islamic law that preceded it.

The advent of Islam with the beginnings of the Delhi sultanate brought out a new kind of a public law that was state sanctioned. This did not preclude that the earlier laws of the Dharmasutras were negated; rather, they became more a part of the secular tradition, where the texts functioned in a more liturgical manner. There was a shift of these texts from the public sphere to a more private sphere. The Dharmashastras began functioning as liturgical texts that were more concerned with the notions of kinship such as marriage and rituals. These ceased to be objects of a public law that controlled inheritance, adjudicated disputes and decided the sanctity of *varna*. The public sphere with the advent of Islamic law became the repository of the Hanafi law.

Islamic and Hanafi Law

The period from the 12th century, with the beginning of the Delhi sultanate, actuates the application of Islamic law in India. The earlier period had the marked propensity of merging, following and the contestations of the Dharmashastras, depending on the religious patronage of the rule, be it Hindu, Buddhist or Jain.

Among the four religious Sunni Islamic schools of jurisprudence, the Hanafi school was predominant in India, with the other major schools of Sharia in Sunni Islam such as the Maliki, Shafi'i and the Hanbali. The earliest attempt of bringing in the

Hanafi school of jurisprudence begins with Sultan Mahmud Ghaznawi (988–1030). He is also reputed to be the author of a book, *Al-Tafrid*.[22] Ishaq Bhatti mentions[23] that there were 11 major fatwa collections in India, all belonging to the Hanafi *mazhab*. The *Fatawa Ghiyathiyya*, the *Fatawa Qarakhani*, the *Fatawa Tatarkhania* and the *Fatawa Baburi* are attributed to the following kings, respectively: Ghiyath-al-Din Balban, Jalal al-Din Khilji (1290–1294), Muhammad Tughluq (1325–1351) and Zahir al-Din Babur (1483–1530).

Fatawa al-Alamgiriyya and the Codification of the Hanafi Jurisprudence

In 1670, Aurangzeb ordered a compilation of extracts from authoritative works of the Hanafi school of jurisprudence. A syndicate of scholars was summoned to go through all the books on jurisprudence in the imperial library and the result was the *Fatawa al-Alamgiriyya*, which, according to Aurangzeb's admiring chronicler, rendered the world independent of all other works of jurisprudence.

The author of the Maasir-I-Alamgiri (completed in 1710)[24] attributes Aurangzeb's decision to make the Muslim act according to the legal decisions and precedents of the *ulema* of the Hanafi school. The compilation was translated from Arabic into Persian to make it more accessible, which became an authoritative source for guidance on interpreting Islamic law. At the same time, with the conquest of new territories, its application was actuated to new areas of the Mughal State under the jurisdiction of the *ulema*.[25] The *Fatawa al-Alamgiriyya* was made mandatory for

[22] Carl Brockelmann, *Geschichte der Arabische Litteratur* (Leiden: Brill, 1937), 36.

[23] Muhammad Ishaq Bhatti, *Barr-i-Saghir Pak wa Hind main 'ilm-i-fiqh. Idara-i-thaqafat-i Islamiyya* (Lahore: 1973), 30.

[24] Jadunath Sarkar, *Massir-I-Alamgir* (Calcutta: Asiatic Society, 1947).

[25] Lokhandwala M. F. Mirat-E-Ahmedi, *A Persian History of Gujarat* (Baroda: M. S. Uni, 1965), 248.

all citizens of the Mughal State to follow it, regardless of caste or creed. This rationalization had major problems for communities that did not follow Islamic codes, as their cultural practices did not come under a codified law which was very Arabic in character. This fatwa brought about a major change in the legal jurisprudence of the land, which till that time was governed by a variety of Dharmashastras and Dharmasutras in a flexible manner. This, and the imposition of the *Jazia* tax on Hindu subjects, has been a contested debate against the secular antecedents of Aurangzeb, though there is evidence of the same during the days of the Delhi sultanate. Aurangzeb intended to bring in all tenants of public governance within the larger ambit of the Hanafi codes. A particular emphasis was placed on non-Muslim subjects and according to the sharia, and all idol worshipers had to pay the *Jazia* tax.[26]

The imposition of this fatwa was a major intervention on Hindu's culture. One larger legacy of this fatwa was its evolution and acceptance within Anglo-Muhammadan law in British courts, where it was granted and deemed to be the law for all Muslim subjects of the colonial state.

Fatawa al-Alamgiriyya and the Problems

The coming of this fatwa changed the entire nature of penalties instituted by Akbar and the early Mughals. The Mughal penalties till the coming of Aurangzeb was more syncretic, keeping with the more tolerant policies instituted by Akbar. Till the time of Shah Jahan, even within the Muslim State, there was a larger tolerance towards local customs and beliefs keeping with the inter-community relations. This was especially compounded with the legal definitions and institutions of two legal entities, the office of the Kotwal and the *Muhtasib*. The period around the Delhi sultanate had the roots in the *ulema* and figured in a few constitutional figures such as the Kotwal and the Qazi, but it was

---

[26] Ibid., 296.

the advent of Aurangzeb's fatwa that two legal offices got massive emphasis. In the towns, it was to the kotwali *chabutra* that people brought their complaints of theft, assault and homicide. In Orme's description: 'one wants assistance to take, another has taken a thief: some offering themselves for bondsmen; others called upon for witnesses...'[27]

The Kotwal was responsible for the decision whether the case could be decided by him or could be referred to the Qazi for a trial. The Qazi was responsible for the cases linked to marriage, inheritance or property. The suits were not decided in the modern sense of civil or criminal offences; rather, it was seen whether the plaintiff had received his degree of satisfaction from the judgement.

According to the Mirat-E-Ahmedi, the Qazi was authorized to remove wine shops, stop gambling and enforce morals with the strict anti-drug and intoxication laws. The Qazi was also responsible for the standardization of all weights and measures used in the markets. This led, at times, to an overlapping of duties with the Kotwal.[28]

The beginning of the colonial rule brought about serious problems with the notion of the law of the fatwa. There was a wide difference in the nature of colonial law and the law that emanated within Aurangzeb's *ulema*. The differences and the clash of the two jurisprudence systems went on to become the problematic areas, particularly with the *Fatawa al-Alamgiriyya*. The Islamic law clashed with the English Civil Law, which was in the process of being instituted in the Supreme Court of Bengal and in the various Faujdari courts of the Muffasil areas of the British provinces. Just to put two issues that differed not only with the earlier Dharmashastra codes but also with the emerging

---

[27] James Forbes, *Oriental Memoires: A Narrative of Seventeen Years Residence in India*, vol. 2 (Berkeley, CA: University of California Libraries, 1834), 25.

[28] Mirat-E-Ahmedi, *A Persian History of Gujarat*, 222.

colonial laws were the treatises on theft and homicide. To explain briefly on *Theft*:

> With the role of theft penalty could only be imposed if the sum stolen was above a stipulated amount and if the amount stolen was deemed insignificant then flogging was imposed on the condition that the prisoner repented and this could also result in death if the offence was repeated often. With the issue of strangling the criminal was flogged and imprisoned. If the murder occurred out of drowning or in case the criminal had murdered the other by pushing him into a water body then the punishment was that he would have to give blood money as sanctioned by religion and the moral law.[29]

Fatwa al-Alamgiriyya on the issue of homicide presented a range of problems, especially with cases related to murder and the problems of judging it. One of the singular problems with the Hanafi school were the cases where a murder took place without a murder weapon. Within the law, a murder could take place only if blood was evident on the person and the scene of crime. Within this law, murder was visualized differently and not in modern-day understandings. For example, any death by drowning did not invite any penalty or any form of retaliation. The affected party was only liable for a similar penalty with the nature of crime.[30]

This was a major problem that colonial law had with the Hanafi codes. There was a major change in the colonial procedures, where the Hindu and the Muslim codes were to be declared to be personal laws. By the decree of the Privy Council, the Muslim Law was codified as a single personal law for all the sects under the Anglo-Muhammadan law,[31] and for civil matters there would be a standardization of the codes within the English Civil Law.

[29] Ibid., 248.
[30] Ibid., 248.
[31] Kashi Parsad Saksena, *Muslim Law* (Calcutta: Eastern Book Co., 1963), 13.

Conclusion

To conclude, India has seen a broad range of laws within the premodern society. The nature of the Dharmashastras and sutras bring out the essence of the law, which was largely based not only on *varna* but was also extremely liberal in terms of representing all social classes. One singular point of emphasis has been its emancipatory views of gender in terms of inheritance and succession. This nature of the law which was selectively followed broadly outlined the nature of the law before the advent of Islam and colonialism. One finds it pointing towards a multitude of laws and jurisprudence practised by people, and its subsequent decline as a law in the public sphere with the coming of the Hanafi codes. The larger resistance to the Hanafi codes emanates from the Abbasid sultanate as Hanafi code was at variance with the basic cultural codes that were part of the pluralistic customs of India. This encounter with the Hanafi school had a profound effect on the nature of the law during colonialism. What came out as change in the nature of the law was the institution of English colonial laws with an Indian touch, namely the Dharmasutras were translated and applied to Hindus and the Hanafi codes were applied to Muslims in colonial India. This was managed through the extensive translations that were initiated by the Asiatic Society. This advent of colonial law, which is not a subject of this chapter, saw a profusion of personal laws, especially with issues of inheritance. The legacy of the Dharmasutras goes on to institute a social code which is interpreted as caste today after colonial intervention. Moreover, it also laid the genesis for the future Hindu Personal Law after Independence. Earlier, the Hanafi law codes had formed the genesis of the Muslim Personal Law.

5

Kingship in Medieval South India

K. Srinivasulu

The study of ancient and medieval Indian political thought has largely been dominated by the Sanskritic dharma literature. The studies on scholarly and popular discourses in regional languages on the questions of state, sovereignty, kingship and legitimacy are very scanty. This is also because of the absence of a clearly discernible body of writing that could be called political. This becomes conspicuous when compared to the history of philosophical engagement with the political in the West. In contrast, in India, the political could be seen being articulated in the genre that largely gets identified with the literary. It thus makes it necessary to problematize the application of Western concepts/categories, intellectual discursive demarcations/disciplinary delineations to Indian intellectual formations. Instead, it would be instructive and fruitful to figure out the specificity of intellectual engagement with the social and political world of premodern India to make sense of the problem by identifying methodological differences and mapping thematic elaborations.

In this presentation, an attempt is made, against the above context, to examine ideas on kingship in medieval Telugu-speaking areas of South India, especially during the Kakatiya–Vijayanagara period and in the aftermath of the fall of Vijayanagara empire, which saw the rise of the *niti* school of political discourse centred around the idea and institution of king that was largely independent of and contrary to the prominent dharma school(s) in the dominant Sanskritic discursive formation.

The motivation for this exercise is to capture the regional variations in statecraft, governance and social policy in the medieval South India that get submerged in the pan-Indian generalizations. Such an attempt would make us appreciate the historical diversity in terms of regional political rhetoric, imagery and regime structures that continue to inform the context of increasing regionalization of Indian politics, especially in South India. The critical (re)appraisal of differential historical legacies and memories could open up the possibility of insights into the understanding of politics and governance styles by highlighting the continuities, differences and variations into the present tense.

What has held together the composite, pluralist, diverse and differential sociocultural formations that India has been constitutive of is the open, contestatory, dialogic and yet transactional character of the regions that comprise it. Any cultural formation to be resilient needs to open itself to internal questioning and strong enough to stand up to external challenges. The study of political thought in India seen in its regional diversity highlights and upholds this reality of the idea and imagination of India as this analysis seeks to demonstrate.

In this presentation, we first focus on methodological issues in the study of premodern Indian thought; second, we discuss the broader context of the discussion on dharma and *rajdharma* to highlight the importance of studying regional treatments of these issues; third, we examine the contestations between the dharma and *niti* schools that have flourished in Telugu language in the context of Kakatiya–Vijayanagara period and, fourth, we sum up the argument.

Some Methodological Issues

One of the most difficult aspects of studying premodern India and its social and political ideas is that they have been filtered through the prism of colonial modernity and its discursive, institutional and perspectival lenses.

Colonial modernity with its Orientalist problematic makes a radical distinction between the Orient and the Occident, the East and the West, and therein could be seen a paradox. While, on the one hand, it banks on denials, on the other hand, it seeks to look out for the attributes of the West to figure out the East. In other words, Orientalism, while 'othering' the East, could be seen to significantly fashion the East after the West.

This comes out strikingly enough in the field of social and political thought. From Socrates onwards, Western thought, drawing on the insight from Nietzsche, has evolved around the concept of doctrinal rational system.[1] Western political thought being system-centric has developed a whole complex of concepts such as state, society, class, sovereignty, law and rights, which have been paraded as universal categories of human concern.

System-centrism could also be deciphered in the positing of the evolution of the modern, secular state around the conflict between the Church and the State, ideas of separation of religion and politics, individual and collective, and freedom versus authority.

The question is whether these conflicts, controversies and concerns be seen and concepts be looked for in Indian history and collective experience with the same zest and rigour as in Western provenance. This in turn raises serious methodological questions, conceptual problems and substantive thematic issues for understanding India's past in its specificity.

---

[1] V. Tejera, *Nietzsche and Greek Thought* (Dordrecht: Martinus Nijhoff, 1987), see, especially Chapter 6.

The absence in India, for instance, of an organized and institutionalized religion like Christianity, with Church as a central institutional authority with a hierarchical structure to begin with, makes it to be different from the West. The social, cultural and religious practices in India defy institutionality and systematicity. The attempt at the discovery of system-likeness is a modernist response influenced and shaped by colonial and missionary intervention in India.

The social and cultural life in premodern India could be characterized as a fuzzy reality both in its spatiality and temporality, defying uniformity and patterned regularity in its social and cultural geography. The emergence of discrete categories of identity with clear markers is a result of the modern state's attempt at enumeration, which in the case of India was initiated by the colonial state, for instance, through the instrumentality of census operation.[2]

This is because the cultural life and belief system in India has been largely centred on rituals and practices that defied any clearly decipherable principles, ordering and regulation. To be precise, Indian experience has been ritual-oriented and practice-centric rather than system-centric.[3] This insight hopefully opens a new way of looking at India's past.

Further, it is unrealistic to talk about pan-Indian culture for cultural formations in India have been local, community-specific, practice-oriented and continuously evolving due to continuous shifts, regular disruptions, non-linearity of expansion and multiplicity of tensions. It is absurd to reduce the complexity of Indian

---

[2] For the distinction between fuzzy and enumerated community, see Sudipta Kaviraj, 'The Imaginary Institution of India', in *Subaltern Studies VII*, ed. P. Chatterjee and G. Pandey (New Delhi: OUP, 1992).

[3] Rani Siva Sankara Sarma, *The Last Brahmin* (Telugu; Hyderabad: Dasya Publication, 2016).

The discussion in this section draws on informal conversations with D. Venkat Rao on some of these issues over a period of time.

culture to religion as is often done. Although religious beliefs and practices are a significant aspect of Indian cultural formations, the latter cannot be reduced to religion. This is in sharp contrast to the predominant singularity of textual religions.

This methodological plurality and difference, when applied to the domain of politics, could hopefully open up fresh possibilities of enquiry. The questions that could thus be asked is as follows: can we look for 'state' in premodern India with the same clarity, connotation and implications?

This challenge, unavoidable, almost a *fait accompli*, needs to be critically engaged with in order to reach out to India's pre-modern past. In spite of the apparent disconnect with our own past, the traces or the fragments of the premodern could be found in communities, their oral cultures, folk memories, rituals and practices, largely because of their materiality in the life world of these diverse communities. In spite of the violence and disruption by modernity—colonial and post-colonial—there could be posited spaces, tropes and practices that leave memories, traces and markers of the Indian past on the present.

Conceptual Transference

The above methodological concern would throw a different light on the conceptual status of the category of dharma in general and of *rajdharma* in particular in Indian thought.

The category of *rajdharma* in dominant Indian thinking has to be viewed against the absence of a Western parallel of state, sovereignty as the source of law and of distinction and tension between the State and the Church. What is central to the consideration of *rajdharma* is *varna* dharma. Is *rajdharma* subordinate to *varna* dharma or independent of the latter? In other words, does the temporal authority of the Kshatriya (king) have to be submitted to the spiritual guidance, diktats of the Brahman who is the rightful interpreter of Dharmashastras?

On this, two viewpoints could be deciphered.[4] One is that, despite the exigencies of everyday governance, the raja is not the source of law for he does not make laws; rather, he is bestowed with the responsibility of implementing laws that conform to the Dharmashastras. In other words, the ruler has to follow the advice and instructions of the Brahman bestowed with the authority of interpreting the dharma, which is binding on the king. The second point of view is that though *rajdharma* has to be in harmony with the Varnashrama Dharma, this does not seem to imply subordination of the raja to the spiritual authority of the Brahman as often suggested. Both the Brahman and Kshatriya (the raja) have to adhere to their (*varna*) dharmas. This allows for certain freedom and authority to the king.

The nature of political authority of the raja, I would suggest, should be appreciated against the fact that, despite the theoretical grandeur of the *varna* and *ashram* vintage, in actuality, what governed life at the grassroots was a complex of informal rules and arrangements that were more decentralized, diffused, localized and community-centric. In other words, given the *varna–jati* nature of Indian social formation, there could not be a uniformly and singularly defined dharma as a moral code applicable to all sections of society.

[4] It may be instructive to note the characterization of dharma by P. V. Kane, an important figure in the textualization of Dharmashastras, which is a clear case of imitation of the Western tradition of text-based codification of law and acceptance of the superiority of text over practice, law over ritual. Thus, P. V. Kane emphasized dharma as codification:

> The conception of dharma was a far-reaching one embracing the whole life of man. The writers on dharmasastra meant by dharma not a creed or religion but a mode of life or *a code of conduct*, which regulated a man's work and activities as a member of society and as an individual and was intended to bring about the gradual development of a man and to enable him to reach what was deemed to be the goal of human existence.

P. V. Kane, *History of Dharmasastra*, Vol. II (Poona: Bhandarkar Institute, 1941), 2.

Further, due to the asymmetrical reach of premodern political authority to the high and low of social order and the centre and periphery of the Rajya, there was the possibility of decentred-ness, non-uniformity or plurality in the practice of dharma across social and physical space.

The conception of *varna–jati* social formation as a hierarchical one with a clearly defined ritual purity–pollution and differential endowments is a colonial modernist construction. This does not mean that there was no caste-based exclusion and discrimination. Given the caste–craft–occupation nexus, there was exploitation of labour. But to put it in a clearly definable and rigid ritual grid was a modernist innovation. With the spread of modernity, facilitated by the state intervention (for instance, policy of Census operation), political deepening and economic expansion, the fuzzy social ontology of caste–communities and their relations have assumed a more structural character both locally and over a larger spatial expanse.

But what could be noticed is the transference of the modernist picture onto pre-colonial/premodern India. As a result, it is assumed to be a prime task of the state to protect the *varna–jati* order in its hierarchical form.

It would be instructive to hypothesize that the premodern social arrangement, with certain delineation of occupations and tasks, was more of a heterarchical trope than a hierarchical structure. It may be noted that the European social theory, in its effort to define, understand or characterize a social formation, has deployed a methodological tool called contrastive definition, which is used to arrive at clarity about the formation to be defined by contrasting it with the already existing or known social form. This is found helpful and deployed by European thinkers like Hegel (Marx included) with finesse.[5] But, as a matter of fact, the statements on the formations that are compared with are not

---

[5] Sudipta Kaviraj, 'On the Status of Marx's Writings on India', *Social Scientist* 11, no. 9 (1983).

meant to be taken to be substantive, but only peripheral to the society that is being researched.

Seen in the light of this methodological insight, the Orientalist problematic, given its practical political exigencies, could be seen marked by a certain anxiety. Thus, the Orientalist anxiety to mark the difference between they (the East) and us (the West) has in a sense got overstretched and overplayed. This could be seen in the colonial, Orientalist representation of Indian society as homo hierarchicus as contrasted with Western homo aequalis (*a la* Louis Dumont) and the fixing of the ideas of dharma into the familiar grid of state–religion discourse.

Theoretical Shift

It is important to note that the Telugu region in South India saw two major kingdoms of the Kakatiya and Vijayanagara in sequence. During this period, political thought flourished in contrast to the well-known pan-India dharma tradition, a different tradition of *niti* got established and was also seen influential in the making of statecraft and guiding actual policymaking and governance.[6] This has not been paid sufficient attention by students of Indian political thought, though it was noted by literary

[6] Influential in the historical treatment of the question of sovereign power during the Vijayanagara period has been Burton Stein's concept of segmentary state. In his view, South India in contrast to North India has not seen a centralized state and bureaucratic fiscal administration as its corollary. The segmentary state is characterized as one which had a central authority concentrated in the emperor with actual control over a small core area, whereas the rulers of the peripheral areas (Samanta rajas) owing allegiance to emperor that was rather ritualistic. According to Stein, the segmentary state in the Vijayanagara empire was characterized by ritual sovereignty.

For a discussion on 'segmentary state' and 'ritual kingship', see Sanjay Subrahmanyam, 'Aspects of State Formation in South India and Southeast Asia, 1500–1650', *Indian Economic and Social History Review* 23, no. 4 (1986).

and social historians such as Velcheru Narayana Rao, Sanjay Subramanyam and David Shulman.

It is instructive to make a distinction between dharma and *niti* and, by extension, between *rajdharma* and *rajniti*. A substantial corpus of Telugu writing could be seen produced during this period, that is, from the 14th century to the 18th century within the dharma and *niti* traditions that reflected on questions pertaining to state, rule, the raja, government/administrations, rules of conduct for different sections of society, etc. Interestingly, though it reflects certain influence of the discourses in Sanskrit, it also shows a conscious distance from them with an attempt to capture the regional specificities of the context and issues examined. There is in contrast to the discursive formations in North India an absence of the influence of Islamic Persian ideas and concepts on this thought despite Persian presence and penetration in discursive formations, administrative culture and practices. This is one of the principal reasons for characterizing the Vijayanagara as a Hindu empire.

If Manu's Dharmashastra was the *locus classicus* of dharma tradition, then Kautilya's *Arthashastra*, with its elaboration of statecraft, is considered to be a canonical text of *niti* tradition. While the former is more identified with religion, the latter is noted for its non-theological character and for having drawn from practical experience and meant to have direct bearing on political practice. Since the scholars composing the vernacular texts during this period were equally proficient and even scholarly in Sanskrit as some of them having authored texts in Sanskrit, they undoubtedly had scholarly familiarity with the above classics. This is evident from the direct reference to the classical texts in their writings and also through the analysis of the intellectual atmosphere of the times. Yet what is equally important to note is that, given their specific regional, cultural, social and political location, their involvement in regional royal courts, and further given the fact that they were composing in Telugu for the particular audience that consisted of the royalty and scholars, the particular or specific has to be taken cognizance of and should not to be merged in the general or universal supposedly represented in the Sanskritic discourse. What would be instructive to note are the variations, contestations and thematic divergences across Sanskritic and Telugu language discourses on the one hand and different schools/perspectives within the *dharma* and *niti* traditions on the other.

In the next section, we try to capture the differences between the dharma and *niti* traditions that assumed prominence during the Kakatiya–Vijayanagara period. Ketana and Madiki Singana were two noted representatives of the dharma and *niti* traditions, respectively, in the medieval Telugu region.[7]

Dharma Tradition

Ketana is a major figure in the dharma school in the Telugu scholarly tradition. Apart from other works,[8] he is known for his *Vijnaneshvaramu*,[9] a Dharmashastra work based on the commentary of Vijnanesvara on the Yajnavalkyasmriti.[10]

Ketana, in the tradition of Dharmashastra, adheres to the *varna–ashram* dharma and accordingly highlights the importance of Brahman in the governance and recommends to the ruler to follow the advice and diktats of Brahmans knowledgeable in the intricacies of shastras. Ketana also invokes the Brahmanic

---

[7] The discussion in this section is inspired by and despite the difference in purpose draws largely on Velcheru Narayana Rao and S. Subrahmanyam, 'Notes on Political Thought in Medieval and Early Modern South India', *Modern Asian Studies* 43, no. 1 (2009), also reproduced in Velcheru Narayana Rao, *Text and Tradition in South India* (Ranikhet: Permanent Black, 2016).

[8] *Dashakumaracaritramu* and *Andhrabhashabhushanamu* (Telugu grammar) are other works of Ketana.

[9] Ketana, *Vijnaneshvaramu*, ed. C. V. Ramachandra Rao (Nellore, 1977); *Vijnaneshvaramu*, ed. C. Vasundhara (Nellore, 1989).

[10] Yajnavalkya, *A Treatise on Dharma*, Patrick Olivelle, ed. and trans. (Noida: Murty Classical Library of India; Cambridge, MA: Harvard University Press, 2019).

precepts of *paap–punya* in statecraft and recommends the ruler to follow them. It comes out clearly from the following passage, which defines the duty of the king centred around the concept of dharma defined by the learned Brahmans[11]:

> A king, without becoming greedy or angry,
> with dharma in his own heart,
> should decide issues of dharma,
> in the company of competent, well-known and scholarly Brahmins.
> In that group, he should have those
> learned in Veda, truthful,
> versed in the dharmashastras,
> and not given to love or hatred.
> Such Brahmins should be members of his council.

The inference that is clearly decipherable from the above passage is that *rajdharma* is not only an integral part of *varna* dharma but also secondary to and dependent on it, and the king and his legitimacy is drawn from his adherence to the sanctity of dharma as interpreted by the Brahmans, open to the latter's scrutiny and judgement.

This view is further emphasized by the invocation of *papam* or sin defined as a deviation from the thus stated dharma.

> And if the king does something unjust,
> and is supported by his council,
> they will be drowned in sin (*papambuna munuguduru*).[12]

Ketana emphasized the centrality of the king and his authority in safeguarding this dharma system and that, to keep this structure intact for him, it is necessary to hold the king (abiding by the

[11] These quotations are taken from translations into English by Rao and Subrahmanyam of Ramachandra Rao, eds., Ketana's *Vijnaneshvaramu*. The references to the Telugu text of Ketana as given in Velcheru and Subrahmanyam are retained. See their article 'Notes on Political Thought in Medieval and Early Modern South India', in Velcheru Narayana Rao, *Text and Tradition in South India*.

[12] Ketana, *Vijnaneshvaramu*, ed. Ramachandra Rao, 25, verses 1–3.

Brahman defined dharma) in high esteem for which he recommends severe punishments as a deterrence.

> If someone insults the king,
> Or reveals the royal secrets,
> His tongue should be cut out
> And he should be driven out of town.[13]

In Ketana's world view, *varna*/caste and the principle of hierarchy underlying it is decisive in the social system and the king's duty is to safeguard *varna* dharma and caste rules of behaviour. *Varna* is a central basis even in deciding of punishment. Depending on one's caste, the punishment would vary even though the crime is the same. In contrast to the *niti* tradition, as we shall see in the next section, following *Manuvadam*, it recommends adherence to *varna* hierarchy in the conduct of trials and the award of punishment not only disproportionate to but also, in fact, inversely related to the status of the guilty (higher status, lower punishment and *vice versa*) as the following excerpt shows.

> If a Brahmin commits a crime
> deserving capital punishment,
> this is what should be done:
> Shave his head,
> Mark his forehead with the sign of a dog's paw,
> Confiscate his money,
> sit him on a donkey,
> and drive him out of town.
> This is as good as killing him.
> But if a lower-caste person commits a crime
> that deserves capital punishment,
> taking his life
> is quite appropriate.[14]

The following extract further brings out the Brahmanical notion of crime and punishment tied up with the underlying concept of

[13] Ibid., 23, verse 134.
[14] Ibid., 27, verse 42.

paap and its caste-determined hierarchical order to be followed by the ruler in deciding the nature and quantum of punishment. The anxiety with possible violation of the sexual order is central to the purity and sanctity of the *varna* dharma structure. This comes out quite clearly with regard to the sexual relations intended prohibitions and prescribed hierarchy of punishments.

> If a person of a low caste
> forces himself on the wife
> of a man of higher caste
> he should be killed for it.
> that is the dharma of a king.
> If a man forces himself
> on a housewife of his own caste
> fine him a thousand panas.
> But if a man of high caste
> makes love to a woman of lower caste
> fine him five hundred panas.
> If a lower caste man
> makes love to a higher caste virgin
> he should be killed.
> But if he is a higher-caste man
> and the virgin loves him,
> the two should be married.[15]

Within the Brahmanical order despite the limited rather absence of gender autonomy, upper caste women are treated with certain leniency, as evident from the following:

> If a high caste woman
> Makes love to a shudra man,
> She may become pure again
> by ritual punishment (*prayascitta*).
> But if she becomes pregnant,
> her husband should leave her[16]

---

[15] Ibid., 21-22, verses 107, 108 and 110.
[16] Ibid., 10, verse 113.

The following brings out the sanctity of property in Ketana's view:

> If someone wishes to dig a well,
> or build a tank,
> on someone else's land,
> for the welfare of the people,
> he still must ask the owner's permission.
> and if the owner refuses,
> he is obliged to stop.[17]

On the basis of the above analysis and supported by the interpretation made by V. Narayana Rao and S. Subrahmanyam, the following observations can be made on Ketana's treatment of *rajdharma* based on Manu Dharma.

First, in Ketana's view, dharma ought to be the basis of social and political order because it has divine sanction. Without this, an orderly society and polity is unimaginable. This is sought to be impressed upon through the invocation of *daivam* and imparted justification by deploying a strong notion of *paap*.

Second, dharma in this view is the basis of and ordains the *varna* system. *Rajdharma* has to be part of dharma and defined and conceptualized accordingly. According to *rajdharma*, the prime duty of the king is to protect *varna* dharma and the social and political order based on it.

Third, the *varna* dharma-centric state not only governs politically but also regulates the social and moral life. Ketana defends the *varna* dharma-based caste relations, transactions, sexual economy, gender relations with clearly defined, hierarchically determined prohibitions, restrictions and transactions. Any transgression in social, sexual relations is seen as a violation of the *varna* order and thus as spelling disaster to social stability and harmony. Civil and criminal jurisprudence and the rewards and

---

[17] Ibid., 36, verse 149.

punishments are decided in tune with the hierarchical *varna*/caste gradation: the lower in the hierarchy, the greater the quantum and severity of punishment.

Fourth, in Ketana's discursive universe, we see a clear replication of the Manu Dharmashastra in medieval Telugu country.

The *niti* tradition of the same period could be seen radically departing from Dharmashastra jurisprudence and life vision, thus opening up a new notion of *rajniti* as part of a new social and political vision that even goes beyond the classical *niti* vision.

Niti Tradition

Madiki Singana is a major figure in the *niti* tradition in the medieval period. His compilation named *Sakala-niti-sammatamu* ('*Niti* acceptable to everyone')[18] is a major effort at bringing together important texts on *niti* in Telugu. It is a collection of 982 compositions from 17 *niti* texts authored by different people and also from oral sources. They deal with a wide variety of themes, pertaining to a code of conduct for rulers and instructions, relevant to different sections of people ranging from courtiers to scholars, artisans to common folk.

The non-inclusion in Singana's anthology of even a single verse from the 13th-century Dharmashastra works, including from Ketana's *Vijnaneshvaramu*, has to be seen as a demonstration of a clear perspectival and conceptual demarcation of *niti* from dharma.[19]

[18] Madiki Singana, *Sakala-niti-sammatamu*, Nidudavolu Venkataravu and P. S. R. Apparao, eds. (Hyderabad: Andhra Pradesh Sahitya Academy, 1970).

[19] The discussion in this section as in the section on dharma substantially draws on Rao and Subrahmanyam, 'Notes on Political Thought in Medieval and Early Modern South India', in Rao, *Text and Tradition in South India*.

Going by Singana, in the *niti* tradition, there is no place for any 'other worldly' authority. It does not shy away from emphasizing 'success' as an important criterion of assessment of one's actions as it is considered to be an acceptable basis of a good life, though all the ethical norms have to be adhered to in achieving success. In other words, social and political life is sought to be judged from a non-religious point of view but not amoral perspective.

Following Singana, it is clear that the *niti* texts deal with issues ranging from the protection of *durgas* (fortresses), system of spies, the logistics of waging a battle, invasion of enemy's territory, etc.

Singana's effort is to put together experience-based practical suggestions on the conduct of everyday administration and the problems one could face in the course of it. The following propositions highlight the importance of the raja, and what needs to be ensured in different fields such as law and order, crime, taxation and commerce to create and sustain an orderly society. The advice that flows from this amply demonstrates the central concerns of *niti* texts[20]:

1. The Niti school argues for the centrality of the king for an orderly society. The prime duty of a king is to rule. To rule is to command and to sustain it the king has to put in place a regime of punishments that does not distinguish the crime in terms of the near and dear. Thus the niti perspective focuses on the importance of danda in the statecraft.
2. It draws attention to the importance of fair practices in trade and commerce by ensuring uniformity in scales and measures, proper taxation, check over merchants who in pursuit of their profits could resort to greed and thereby ruin common people.
3. By punishing the wrongdoer the king would not only control crime but also win the trust of the praja—the people.

There are precepts concerning bad rulers which are informed by the experience with such kings. It not only identifies the harm that could visit one serving them but also renders practical advice as

[20] Ibid., 111–112.

to what is to be done in such instances. It is worth noting them in detail[21]:

* If anyone has caused you harm, go and complain to the king. But if the king himself harms you, who can you complain to?
* If serving a ruler causes incessant pain to the servant, the servant should leave such a master right away.
* He may be rich, born in a good caste, a strong warrior beyond comparison, but if a king is an ignoramus, his servants will no doubt leave him.
* If a king does not distinguish between the right hand and the left, a precious diamond and a piece of glass, it is humiliating to serve such a king-no matter how great a warrior you are.
* A bad king surrounded by good people turns out to be good. But even a good king is difficult to serve if his advisers are bad.
* A king who enjoys hearing stories of others' faults, who enjoys putting people through trouble, and steals other men's wives, brings calamity to his people.

Singana brings out the difference between the *niti* and dharma positions on the sovereign's status and powers. This is done by showing how Baddena differed from Ketana in the matters of king's place vis-à-vis the Brahmans. While Ketana, as we have seen above, emphasizes the importance of Brahmans and their knowledge of Dharmashastras to be the basis of statecraft, Singana argues for the king being in command and accessible to the people. Further, for Baddena, the king should treat his ministers as subordinates not as intellectual superiors and emphasizes the need for ruler exercising independent decisions as he says, 'A king should not direct his people and his servants to his minister for all their needs. The king should be his own minister and treat the minister as an assistant.'[22]

What is to be noted is that while the dharma position in Telugu discourse largely reflects and, in fact, loyally adheres to the Manu Dharma, the *niti* tradition could be seen making innovative moves

[21] Ibid., 112.
[22] Ibid., 113.

rather than repeating traditional *niti* precepts. Thus, in contrast to the dharma tradition, the *niti* perspective on the raja and statecraft could be seen being informed by political realism and sensitive to changing practical concerns of governance. It is a clear move from theological thrust in the vision of *rajdharma* wherein the king is to safeguard *varna* dharma to a *rajniti* view where the king is sought to be rendered independent of the interpreters of the dharma so that he can make laws and take decisions freely and be the master of his ministers and other state functionaries. What is further to be noted is a shift in the conception of the king from being protector of dharma to that of the *praja*. This could be seen as a reflection of changing times in which the king inclined to draw his powers moving away from other worldly sanctions to the earthly authority bestowed in himself and correspondingly had to make himself not only accessible but also acceptable to the *praja*.

Summing Up

In this analysis, we have tried to show how the treatment of the idea of kingship has varied both in time and space. The theory of kingship has both internal and external set of relationships. Most critical aspect in premodern India has been the relation between Brahman and Kshatriya, and the priest and the king.

The thinking on kinship in India has not been unitarian as sought to be viewed in the dominant perspective, which treats kinship from the dharma perspective and projects it as if it is universal and uncontested.

In the dominant dharma view, the Brahman is supposed to be teacher, adviser and guide to the king in the affairs of the state. The prime purpose and duty in this view for the king is to follow and enforce *varna* dharma so that the rules of *varna* are strictly adhered to. The association of *danda* with dharma is clear from the fact that any violation of the rules of *varna* conduct is punished. The dharma school prescribes a *varna*-based hierarchy of punishments for the same crime. This notion of a theocratic state in which the ruler is subordinate to the Brahman priest is not uncontested and not adhered to unchallenged.

The challenge to the dharma view of kinship has to be appreciated in the context of the emergence of powerful kings from non-Kshatriya or Shudra *varnas*. Such a challenge could be seen from the *niti* school which flourished in South India in the medieval period. This challenge is not merely in temporal–administrative practical terms but gains prominence for it provides a theoretical critique of the Brahmanical framework that posited the raja in the Brahman–Kshatriya matrix. The *niti* tradition provides an alternative view of kingship to address the challenges of statecraft based on the practical experience and political challenges. Thus, in the place of an idealist almost atemporal prescriptive dharma view, we find the flourish of a perspective that is grounded in practice and sensitive to the ground realities varying in terms of time, region, *varna/jati* regime and shifts in power structure.

6

Democratic Traditions in Lingayat Movement

Prakash Desai

Democracy as a well-established political system may be modern, but democratic ideals and experiences are quite old. Many societies, especially eastern societies like India, had ideals and experiences that could be recognized and theorized as democratic ideals and practices.

> It is commonly thought that most people in the world have no democratic experience, and that the democratic idea is fundamentally alien to most human cultures. This is what lies behind the catchphrase, 'the western concept of democracy'. On this basis, many scholars have concluded that efforts to establish democratic institutions outside of a few favored regions are doomed to failure.[1]

It was observed in the case of India too when it became a modern democratic republic.[2] According to the observation, India would not succeed as a democracy.

---

[1] Steven Muhlberger and Phil Paine, 'Democracy's Place in World History', *Journal of World History* 4, no. 1 (1993): 25. Available at https://www.jstor.org/stable/20078545 (accessed on 17 October 2018).

[2] See Selig S. Harrison, *India: The Most Dangerous Decades* (Princeton, NJ: Princeton University Press, 1960).

The research on democracy has supported the idea that 'Europeans have a special fitness for democracy (one more aspect of European uniqueness) by emphasizing every quasi-democratic institution or movement in European history while dismissing or ignoring identical experiences outside of Europe'.[3] Such ignorance or dismissal made others to explore the idea of democracy in different regions of the world. Consequently, many new ideas and perspectives have come to the arena of political theory on democracy. The effort to explore democratic ideas and institutions in India's past would help in clearing many generalizations[4] about eastern societies and such effort may enrich the discipline of comparative politics. The present chapter makes an effort to understand democratic experiences in India in its early history and how it was extended in Medieval India's socio-religious movements, especially the Lingayat Movement of the 12th-century South India. It tries to explore the change and continuity in the very debates and discussions on social, economic and political questions in the spiritual past of India.

Democratic Experiments in Pre-Medieval India

The experience of democracy, as it was in Greece, was also present in India.[5] The democratic thoughts produced by ancient Indian texts are witness to it. 'The Vedic polity consisted of three important components: the king, his royal priests and other kingmakers or *rajkartarahas*, the two tribal assemblies *Sabha* or *Samiti* (*Vidatha* also) and the *Jana* or people'.[6] These assemblies exhibited features that are close to certain democratic features.

---

[3] Muhlberger and Paine, 'Democracy's Place in World History', 25–26.
[4] Benoy Kumar Sarkar, 'Democratic Ideals and Republican Institutions in India', *The American Political Science Review* 12, no. 4 (1918): 606. Available at https://www.jstor.org/stable/1945832 (accessed on 17 October 2018).
[5] Muhlberger and Paine, 'Democracy's Place in World History', 34–35.
[6] Ashok S. Chousalkar, *Revisiting the Political Thought of Ancient India: Pre-Kautilyan Arthashastra Tradition* (New Delhi: Sage Publications, 2018), 15.

Although the early Aryans had the institution of monarchy and it had established itself on firm foundations, it was not absolute but limited in several ways. Certain democratic elements curtailed the absolute power of the king in many ways. These were: 1) the people's voice in choosing their king, 2) the oath that the king had to take at the coronation, and 3) the Assemblies of the people. It was the last institution that played a predominant part in curbing the power of the king.[7]

Regarding the role and responsibilities of the *Vidatha*, it is also observed that the *Vidatha* 'was largely responsible for the performance of religious ceremonies'.[8]

Apart from such political traditions, the social aspect of democracy and the way it is understood now also received some treatment. But in wider theoretical discussions on democracy, only the negative aspects of India's past appear to have been considered. The positive aspects which came in the form of protest movements, which stood for reason and rationality, are not sufficiently taken into consideration.

The impression of the western observers has been that Indian society historically has been unchanging, and even today it is strongly tradition-bound. Some critics have further alleged that on account of the lack of free thinking and of action-mindedness, the people of India were destined to remain a backward society.[9]

Such criticism may be true to an extent, but it cannot be outrightly stated that India did not have free thinking in its spiritual

[7] Janki Nath Bhat, 'Ancient Indian Democracies', *Civilisations* 4, no. 1 (1954): 51. Available at https://www.jstor.org/stable/41377595 (accessed on 17 October 2018).

[8] Jagdish Prasad Sharma and H. W. Bailey, 'The Question of the Vidátha in Vedic India', *The Journal of the Royal Asiatic Society of Great Britain and Ireland*, no. 1/2 (1965): 56. Available at https://www.jstor.org/stable/25202807 (accessed on 18 January 2020).

[9] G. S. Halappa, 'Sri Basavesvara and Free Thinking', in *Sri Basavesvara: Eighth Centenary Commemoration Volume*, ed. S. S. Wodeyar (Bangalore: Government of Mysore, 1967), 145.

and cultural past. It may be observed that the civilizational legacy of reason and rationality is responsible for India's survival as a democracy.

The ideas of democratic tradition such as reason, dissent and secularism were all part of ancient Indian society. Ambedkar has pointed out one of such ideas. He observed that India

> has seen the conflict between ecclesiastical law and secular law long before Europeans sought to challenge the authority of the Pope. Kautilya's *Arthashastra* lays down the foundation of secular law. In India unfortunately ecclesiastical law triumphed over secular law. In my opinion this was the one of the greatest disasters in the country.[10]

Buddhism as a socio-spiritual movement had contributed to the early experiences of democracy in India. The leadership for this movement came from the ruling classes of that time and was supported by merchants and craftsmen.

> When Brahminical orthodoxy was disputed in ancient India by members of other groups (including merchants and craftsmen), the fact that the protesters were often quite affluent should not distract attention from the fact that, in the context of Brahmin-dominated orthodoxy, they were indeed distinctively underprivileged.[11]

Their exclusion from spiritual sphere made them to question the orthodoxy. As India witnessed changes in sociopolitical and economic spheres, democratic tendencies began to wither. It is observed that the

[10] Quoted in Velcheru Narayana Rao and Sanjay Subrahmanyam, 'Notes on Political Thought in Medieval and Early Modern South India', *Modern Asian Studies* 43, no. 1 (2009): 176. Available at https://www.jstor.org/stable/20488076 (accessed on 26 July 2018).

[11] Amartya Sen, *The Argumentative Indian: Writings on Indian Culture, History and Identity* (New Delhi: Penguin Books, 2005), 10.

defeat of the democratic tendency in ancient Indian life was a complicated process, not simply the result of the greater military power available to a successful warlord. There was a revival of hierarchical thinking, and a willingness of the enfranchised members of *ganas* to accept it.[12]

The democratic practices which existed in early India could not be continued and Indian society had to come under the grip of non-democratic, non-secular empires. Certain practices, which can be considered as democratic, received major attention in the Bhakti Movement of Medieval India.

Democracy in the Lingayat Movement

One of the Bhakti Movements which gave wide scope to modern democratic practices was the social movement led by Basava in the 12th century. This is popularly known as the Lingayat Movement.

Buddhism influenced humanity for nearly a thousand years. Since Buddhism failed to develop its positive aspect, Indian society fell back and beat a retreat for a few centuries. The voice of people was curbed. The Manusmriti was revised with harsh injunctions so much so that Hindus were not allowed even to tour the foreign countries.[13]

The tradition of democracy again revived in the movement of Basava and his colleagues against the existing political system and hierarchical society. The monarchy which was upholding social order characterized by social hierarchy and discrimination was opposed and was dealt with intellectual and practical alternatives.

---

[12] Muhlberger and Paine, 'Democracy's Place in World History', 37.

[13] S. M. Hunashal, 'Basavesvara and Democracy', in *Sri Basavesvara: Eighth Centenary Commemoration Volume*, ed. S. S. Wodeyar (Bangalore: Government of Mysore, 1967), 485–486.

Democratic Narrative and Socially Marginalized

The significance of the Bhakti Movements lies in their efforts to democratize the social and spiritual spaces. The space that was dominated by force and manipulated by shrewdness was taken to task by intellectual and existential efforts. 'Movements against caste divisions that have figured repeatedly in Indian history, with varying degrees of success, have made good use of engaging arguments to question orthodox beliefs'.[14] Criticism of the dominant theology and internal criticism of their own ideas made Bhakti Movements to come up with fresh ideas in the realm of Indic thought.

> The Bhakti movement in India, by and large, was marked by the rejection of the existing ritual hierarchy and Brahmanical superiority; the use of the vernacular in preference to Sanskrit (the language of the elite); and the emergence of low-caste, non-literate persons as great spiritual leaders. There was large scale participation of peasantry, artisans, and other lower classes as well as ritually inferior but economically powerful groups such as skilled craftsmen in these devotional movements.[15]

As part of a kind of its political agenda, the literary tradition of the Lingayat Movement emphasized the common speech rather than the language of God.[16] The emphasis on Kannada language rather than the language of God enlarged its social base and, consequently, it became possible for everyone in society, from upper to lower strata, to express their social and philosophical views through their *vachanas*. The lyrical sayings of *Sharanas*

---

[14] Sen, *The Argumentative Indian*, 10.

[15] Vijaya Ramaswamy, 'Rebels—Conformists? Women Saints in Medieval South India', *Anthropos* 1, no. 3 (1992): 133. Available at http://www.jstor.org/stable/40462578 (accessed on 31 January 2018).

[16] T. R. Chandrashekhar, 'Vachana Samskruti: Ichina Oluvugalu' (Vachana Culture: Recent Leanings) in *Basavatatva: Samajika Badalavane* (Philosophy of Basava: Social Change), ed. Mahesh Tippashetti (Hampi, Karnataka: Prasaranga, Kannada Vishwavidyalaya, 2014), 105.

and *Sharanes*,[17] who participated in the movement are known as *vachanas*, and they are also referred to as *vacanas*.[18]

One of the efforts made by Basava and his colleagues 'in extending democratic space to articulation of contemporary issues was establishment of *Anubhava Mantapa*, the institution which became a democratic forum to deliberate on social, economic and spiritual ideas'.[19] In this forum, many issues were not only debated but conservative ideas were also rejected. Many *Sharanas* and *Sharanes* from socially marginalized communities participated in the debates on democratic ideals and principles. To name a few, Allama Prabhu, Madar Haralayya, Hadapada Appanna and Ambigara Choudayya set the agenda for discussion on social issues in *Anubhava Mantapa*. Allama Prabhu, the presiding *Sharana* of *Anubhava Manatapa*, came from the drum beaters community, which did not enjoy a good position in the social hierarchy. Many of colleagues or *Sharanas* of Basava were in the forefront in not only articulating spiritual matters but also issues related to human existence. Some of them, such as Haralayya and Maduvarasa, are remembered for making social life an inclusive one by taking an active part in encouraging

[17] *Sharana* means socio-religious reformer/revolutionary in the socio-religious Lingayat Movement in the 12th century. See S. H. Patil, *Community Dominance and Political Modernisation: The Lingayats* (New Delhi: Mittal Publications, 2002), 425. Men socio-religious reformers were referred to as *Sharanas* and women socio-religious reformers were referred to as *Sharanes*.

[18] *Vachanas* of the Lingayat Movement have their own place of importance in Kannada literature in the sense that they democratized the language itself. Language as an agency of communicating social truths beneficial to everyone in the society from the so-called upper to lower was not given much importance in earlier Kannada literary works. In fact, reflecting the conservative thinking had become a routine literary process and was respected and recognized in intellectual circles. *Vachana* literature with its simplicity in projecting the social vision and conveying the inclusive social message made huge impact on later stage wide streams of Kannada literary works.

[19] Prakash Desai, 'Exploring the Modern in Medieval: Political Ideas of Basava', in *Indian Political Thought: Themes and Thinkers*, eds. Himanshu Roy and Mahendra Prasad Singh (New Delhi: Pearson, 2017), 65.

inter-caste marriage. Thus, they made social life democratic and radical by annihilating barriers of caste restrictions imposed by the upper and priestly strata of the society.

Basava, as one of the leaders of the movement, cleared many prejudices which had been held as social truths. Basava 'in his zeal to bring home to those so called low castes who were suffering from extreme inferiority complex that the birth has nothing to do with greatness'[20] did not hesitate to criticize his own birth. He expresses in one of his *vachanas* that he is a son of the couple who were working as servants in the houses of two socially marginalized *Sharanas* belonging to the communities of cobbler and tanner.

> The son of the servant-maid in Cennayya's house,
> The daughter of the maid in Kakkayya's house
> Those two went out to gather dung
> And fell together: I the son
> Born of those two-so witness me
> Lord Kudala Sangama![21]

It seems that the *Sharanas* and *Sharanes* from socially marginalized communities further democratized the Lingayat Movement and its philosophy by critiquing the conservative ideas of some *Sharanas* belonging to the upper strata of the society. 'The cracks in actual experience, which theology tries to cover up, the vachanas open up'.[22] Religious literature does not try to expose actual social practices. Consequently, many social practices which are against humanism have retained their place in different societies. If there is an effort to criticize this tendency, there is a possibility

---

[20] Sri Shivakumara Shivacharya, 'Introduction', in *Vacanas of Basavanna: A Selection*, ed. H. Deveerappa (Sirigere, Karnataka: Annana Balaga, 1967), 22; Armando Menezes and S. M. Angadi, Vacanas of Basavanna: A Selection, ed. H. Deveerappa (Sirigere, Karnataka: Annana Balaga, 1967).

[21] Menezes and Angadi, *Vacanas of Basavanna*, 113.

[22] H. S. Shivaprakash, *I Keep Vigil of Rudra: The Vachanas* (New Delhi: Penguin Books, 2010), lxiii.

of such act being considered as heresy. Self-critique of the system is one of the exercises that *Sharanas* of the Lingayat Movement followed religiously. Basava, in fact, paved the way for such self-critique and later many of his colleagues went ahead to make it even more fierce in criticizing the actual practices of the society. In one of his *vachanas*, Basava observes:

> I bow down to the symbol
> When I see it.
> But, if there is no conduct
> To match the symbol,
> I sniff at it.[23]

Sharanas belonging to marginalized communities did not hesitate to pinpoint wrong ideas and beliefs.[24] When their food culture was objected to by the *Sharanas*, including Basava, they responded by questioning how the eater of the flesh of cow, a cobbler, became inferior when cow is an animal which provides nectar to Lord Shiva?[25] The difference is that one consumes milk and the other consumes flesh. The essence of their response must have been the rectification of the beliefs held by others on food culture. When the source for both milk and flesh is the same, how can the consumer of flesh become inferior and the other become superior?

The illogical and pompous life without practice and just with mere utterance of philosophical ideas has been severely condemned by Ambigara Choudayya, a *Sharana* belonging to socially marginalized communities.[26] The practices of priestly class in the Lingayat Movement came under severe criticism by Choudayya.

---

[23] Ibid.

[24] Shivarudra Kallollikar, 'Basavatatva: Talavargada Drushtiyalli' (The Philosophy of Basava: As Envisioned by the Marginalized) in *Basavatatva: Samajika Badalavane* (Philosophy of Basava: Social Change), ed. Mahesh Tippashetti (Hampi, Karnataka: Prasaranga, Kannada Vishwavidyalaya, 2014), 127.

[25] Ibid.

[26] Ibid, 124–125.

Providing religious initiation as a mere profession as practised by *Jangamas*[27] was not liked by him. For him, they and their profession of religious initiation looked like the practices of Vedic priestly class.[28] The claim of *Jangamas* that they would spiritually empower the marginalized angered Choudayya. The reason for his anger is the practice and belief of *Jangamas* that they are superior as well as their campaign towards preservation of their caste consciousness.[29] In one of his *vachanas*, he suggests punishment for such *Jangamas* who just preach without practice.[30]

The question of social hierarchy in the form of higher and lower caste was given sufficient rational treatment by *Sharanes* through their critique of the myths and prejudices associated with it. Kalavve, one of the *Sharanes*, exposes the myth of high and low status in society on the basis of the food one eats. She observed:

They say—
All those are high born
Who eat sheep, fowl and tiny fish,
They say——
All those are low born
Who eat the cow that rains on Shiva
Sacred milk sanctified five times.
What the Brahmins had eaten adorned the grass
And a dog licked it up and went away
What the cobblers had eaten adorned the grass—
Now Brahmins' ornament.
In other words
Bags are made of cow's hide
For ghee and for water
Senseless Brahmins who drink
Ghee and water from such leather bags
Thinking it sacred

---

[27] *Jangama* means the preacher, the one who initiates devotees into spirituality.
[28] Kallollikar, 'Basavatatva', 124–125.
[29] Ibid.
[30] Ibid.

They can't escape
Utmost perdition.
The master of Urilingapeddi
Doesn't approve of such men.[31]

Contemporary sociological works and social anthropologists have come up with critical remarks about Bhakti Movements. For some of them,

> they failed to make a dent on caste hierarchy, for at the village level, the system of production of food grains and other necessities was inextricably bound up with a caste-based division of labour. The moral is that ideological attacks on hierarchy and Brahmanical claims to supremacy failed to create an egalitarian social order since at the local level the production of basic needs was inextricably bound up with jati.[32]

Here, one needs to evaluate the impact of such movements on the effort of liberation from age-old slavery in the form of discrimination associated with caste. No doubt, they did not succeed in eliminating caste discrimination and continuation of the superiority complex, but they became the agencies of critiquing the very society which somehow managed to continue age-old practices in new incarnations. Apart from this, it needs to be noted that Bhakti Movements had become forums for internal criticism that came from marginalized communities. Their critique dwelt on the same age-old practices knowingly or unknowingly supported by some participants in the Bhakti Movements. Moreover, the labour which was considered as polluting practice received dignity and self-respect. 'Work itself is worship' (*Kayakave Kailasa*)[33] became the philosophy of Bhakti Movements like the Lingayat Movement.

[31] Shivaprakash, *I Keep Vigil of Rudra*, 81.

[32] M. N. Srinivas, 'An Obituary on Caste as a System', *Economic & Political Weekly* 38, no. 5 (2003): 458.

[33] Shivaprakash, *I Keep Vigil of Rudra*, lxv.

The Arguments of Women as Agencies of Democratization

The religious experiences of women in Vedic period were quite egalitarian.

> When examining religious experiences of Hindu women in the first, or Vedic, period, which lasts until the 6th century BC, one notices the distinct pattern of a number of women philosophers, such as Lopamudra, Gargi, Maitreyi, and others, living in an 'egalitarian' society, in which women enjoyed freedom and had access to all religious activities.[34]

But this did not last long. Whatever space was there for religious freedom and creative dialogue was lost. As time passed, women were forced to lead a marginalized life in society.[35]

> In a period roughly corresponding to that in which sati became prevalent, restrictions came into force on *Niyoga* (dead man's brother or next of kin marrying his widow) and on widow remarriage. From around AD 1000 total prohibition of widow remarriage seems to have become quite widespread. Decline in the rights and freedom of widows, fall in educational levels of women as well as greater prevalence of child marriage indicate a substantial reduction in women's status.[36]

Buddhism and Jainism have their own place in the efforts made to understand the space for women in social and religious order.

[34] Chandra Y. Mudaliar, 'Religious Experiences of Hindu Women: A Study of Akka Mahadevi', *Mystics Quarterly* 17, no. 3 (1991): 137. Available at http://www.jstor.org/stable/20717064 (accessed on 13 June 2015).

[35] Shamala Dasoga, Basavatatva: Mahile (The Philosophy of Basava: Women), in *Basavatatva: Samajika Badalavane* (Philosophy of Basava: Social Change), ed. Mahesh Tippashetti (Karnataka: Prasaranga, Kannada Vishwavidyalaya, 2014), 133.

[36] Sophie M. Tharakan and Michael Tharakan, 'Status of Women in India: A Historical Perspective', *Social Scientist* 4, no. 4/5, Special Number on Women (1975): 120. Available at https://www.jstor.org/stable/3516124 (accessed on 8 November 2018).

'Buddhism recognized the individuality and independence of women and their title to salvation in their own right whether married or single'.[37] Like Buddhism, Jainism created a religious space for women but its views on women in their social life came under certain criticism.

Jainism did admit women to the religious order of nuns. But there were some differences of opinion between Digambaras and Svetambaras, regarding their title to liberation. The former hold the view that they cannot become perfect without getting reborn as men while the latter maintain that they can, in their own right. The Jains maintain that in the monastic life, the nun is inferior to the monk![38]

The next stage of democratic experiences of women began to 'respond intellectually and spiritually to the state of decadence and oppression of the preceding era'.[39] The social order which considered women as inferior was questioned in the next stage. The idea of salvation for women as it was understood and practised by society was challenged. 'Generally, the brahmanical way of treating women's salvation was the surrender of the ego by becoming a self-sacrificing mother, a chaste wife and an obedient daughter. Obviously brahmanical society opposed their presence in the religious field as preachers'.[40] This opposition was challenged and proved as wrong by many women saints of the Bhakti Movement. India witnessed a number of saints and seers who played significant role in articulating feminist views in Bhakti Movements of the Medieval period. These Bhakti Movements have many outstanding women in them. They were considered on par with, and often superior to, men in their devotional and

---

[37] Sarojini Shintri, 'Basava and Womanhood', in *Sri Basavesvara: Eighth Centenary Commemoration Volume*, ed. S. S. Wodeyar (Bangalore: Government of Mysore, 1967), 152.

[38] Ibid., 153.

[39] Chandra Y. Mudaliar, 'Religious Experiences of Hindu Women', 137.

[40] Anjali Verma, *Women and Society in Early Medieval India: Re-Interpreting Epigraphs* (London: Routledge, 2019), 113.

intellectual pursuits.[41] Many of them questioned the intellect of the prevailing social order and also objected to its continuation among men who claimed to be progressive but remained the same on the question of women in spiritual and other matters. Thus, they paved the way for protests within protest movements if the basic objectives of very protests were not respected and fulfilled.

The period between the 11th century and the 12th century witnessed significant changes in the region of Kalyana ruled by the Chalukyas with respect to the status of women.[42] They not only occupied some important political and religious positions but also participated in philosophical discussions. However, problems such as the Sati system were prevalent, and marriage as a social union was strictly hierarchical.[43] Against such social practices and many others, the Lingayat Movement emerged as a protest movement in the 12th century to articulate views and practise the ideals. One of its objectives was to ensure equal space to women in the society.

The Lingayat Movement was a unique experiment as far as discussion on equal status to the women is concerned.[44] Nearly 60 saints of the Lingayat Movement were women.[45] 'These are not anonymous; they have legends and places associated with them, and many have left behind them bodies of poetry. The most famous of them is Mahadeviyakka'.[46] It was not just Akka Mahadevi who received equal respect for her intellectual and

---

[41] A. K. Ramanujan, 'Talking to God in the Mother Tongue', *India International Centre Quarterly* 19, no. 4 (1992): 55. Available at http://www.jstor.org/stable/23004008 (accessed on 19 July 2018).

[42] Indumati P. Patil, 'The Position of Women during 11th and 12th century A.D. (with Special Reference to Chalukyas of Kalyana)', *Proceedings of the Indian History Congress* 65 (2004), 126–130. Available at https://www.jstor.org/stable/44144726 (accessed 1 October 2019).

[43] Ibid.

[44] Vinaya Chaitanya, *Songs for Siva: Vacanas of Akka Mahadevi* (New Delhi: Harper Perennial, 2017), xxiv.

[45] Ramanujan, 'Talking to God in the Mother Tongue', 55.

[46] Ibid.

spiritual strength, there were many women writers of *vachanas* whose intellect was equally respected in the movement. 'Such equality applied not only in the matter of literary creation, which is a specialty, but in all aspects of daily life. Menstruating women, for instance, were not considered "unclean" and could attend worship like all others'.[47] The radicalism can be observed in the writings of both male and female saints of the Lingayat Movement. The significance of women saints of the Lingayat Movement lies in their approach to spiritual and social issues.

Like Akka Mahadevi, many of the female *vachanakaras* combined divinity and deviance, transcendentalism with powerful social protest and flouting of all conventions, whether social or religious. While the alternate voice of a 'counter culture' can be perceived in both male and female Virasaivites, the impact is much stronger in the case of the women because theirs is a dual defiance: a defiance of the Brahmanical system as well as of the patriarchal structure.[48]

In *vachana* literary tradition, woman is not just a biological component, she is also a social fact.[49] In this tradition, an effort has been made to understand gender relations socially. The concept of gender as philosophized by *Sharanas* and *Sharanes* is unique in the sense that they came with new observations which can be considered as a predecessor to modern arguments on gender. Jedara Dasimayya, one of the early *Vachanakara*,[50] questions the prevailing understanding with regards to a man and a woman. He said:

> If they see
> breasts and long hair coming
> they call it woman,

---

[47] Chaitanya, *Songs for Siva*, xxiv.

[48] Vijaya Ramaswamy, 'Rebels, Mystics or Housewives? Women in Virasaivism', *India International Centre Quarterly* 23, no. 3/4 (1996): 192. Available at http://www.jstor.org/stable/23004619 (accessed on 12 August 2013).

[49] Chandrashekhar, 'Vachana Samskruti', 98.

[50] *Vachanakara* means one who expresses his socio-spiritual ideas through his *vachanas*.

> if beard and whiskers
> they call it man:
> but, look, the self that hovers
> in between
> is neither man
> nor woman
> O Ramanatha.[51]

Siddharama, one of the *Sharanas* of the Lingayat Movement, says in his *vachana* that woman is not just a female sex and not a demoness even, but she is the very embodiment of God.[52] *Sharanas* not only tried to understand and make the status of women on par with men but also perceived them as divine beings.

By further extending their debates on the social and spiritual status, *Sharanes* gave radical and intellectual observations. Akka Mahadevi's place in the Lingayat Movement and philosophy is unique. Her views on divinity, marriage and freedom have much impact on the movement in the sense that the other *Sharanas* had to make much effort in questioning and responding to her on these ideas.

> Forced to a rash but courageous course of action, Akka mahadevi renounced her parents, her suitor, her home, and even her clothes and left her village clad only in her long tresses. Asserting that she could never wed any man, much less a Jaina, she revealed that she was already married to none other than the Lord Himself and that she would keep herself only unto Him.[53]

---

[51] A. K. Ramanujan, *Speaking of Siva* (New Delhi: Penguin Books, 1993), 92.

[52] For English translation of the Vachana, see Vijaya Ramaswamy (1996), *Divinity and Deviance: Women in Virasaivism* (New Delhi: Oxford University Press, 1996), x.

[53] R. Blake Michael, 'Women of the Śūnyasampādane: Housewives and Saints in Vīraśaivism', *Journal of the American Oriental Society* 103, no. 2 (1983): 363. Available at https://www.jstor.org/stable/601458 (accessed on 11 July 2019).

One of the *vachanas* of Akka Mahadevi is a critique of the marriage and the patriarchy associated with it. The *vachana* is as follows:

> To him with no death,
> No decay
> No form
> To the beautiful one
> I have given myself O Mother.
> To him with no place
> No end
> No space
> No signs
> To the beautiful one
> I have given myself O Mother.
> To him with no clan
> No country,
> To the peerless
> Handsome one
> I have given myself O Mother.
> For the reason
> Channamallikarjuna, the handsome one
> Is the man for me.
> These wasting, dying men—
> Take them away
> Throw them into the oven![54]

Seeking individual freedom and making the people of society to mind their own business was well expressed in one of the *vachanas* by her. The representation of the idea of individuality and, at the same time, thinking about community was narrated quite proficiently in the *vachanas* of Akka Mahadevi.

> Why do you make me talk?
> My hair is loose, my face is sad,
> My body is melting.
> O brothers, why do you make me talk?
> O fathers, I have been through much,

---

[54] Shivaprakash, *I Keep Vigil of Rudra*, 159.

Becoming has stopped for me,
Crooked ways are no more.
Becoming devoted, I have joined
Channamallikarjuna, jasmine-tender,
And am free of family.[55]

Arguments which do not favour egalitarian gender relationship are also traced in the *vachanas*. The concepts of woman, gold and land are used in discriminatory ways to state the arguments. Such arguments do not make differentiation between these concepts and almost treat women as a material thing that men try to gain and control in the same way they do with gold and land. For the understanding that woman, gold and land are enticements, Allama Prabhu observed in one of his *vachanas* that they are not, and that the real enticement is the insatiable appetite of the mind.[56] However, for him, the mind bothered more than the belief that equates women to a property to be owned.[57] Therefore, it is observed that *Sharanas* of the movement too had certain anxieties and complexities on the question of gender equality or equal space for women in all spheres of life.[58]

Even Basava, who is regarded as intellectual torchbearer of the movement, was not free from certain complexities and it cannot be said that he was completely liberal in this regard.

Committing adultery
Is an immoral act;
So, as she withdrew
To a broken wall
A scorpion stung her.
Hearing her shouts,

---

[55] Chaitanya, *Songs for Siva*, 128.
[56] For English translation of the Vachana, see Ramaswamy, *Divinity and Deviance*, ix.
[57] Mallika Ghanti, 'Basavatatva Mattu Mahile' (The Philosophy of Basava and Woman) in *Basavatatva: Samajika Badalavane* (Philosophy of Basava: Social Change), ed. Mahesh Tippashetti (Hampi, Karnataka: Prasaranga, Kannada Vishwavidyalaya, 2014), 145.
[58] Ibid., 144–145.

A guardsman robbed.
Her of her dress.
Going home in shame,
Her husband raised
Weals on her back:
Lord Kudala Sangama, the king,
Collected his fine![59]

Such *vachanas* appear sexist[60] because woman is perceived as responsible for deviation in moral order. Here, woman is looked upon as a criminal and the guardsman, the husband and the king are in the position of judges to judge the character of a woman. The way a woman is made responsible for an immoral act, the man is not made responsible and is free from punishment. One deserves punishment, and the other does not. Thus, it is brought to the notice that there is no uniformity in the vision and observations of *Sharanas* on the issues related to gender relation.[61] Often, patriarchal and biased arguments can be observed in their understanding.

The *Kayaka* philosophy of the Lingayat Movement has been religiously followed and philosophized by *Sharanes*. In this regard, several instances can be given. When her husband Marayya was merely chatting without doing his work, *Sharane* Lakkamma reminds and advises him about his work.[62] Thus, for her, work without devotion and devotion without work become meaningless. *Sharanes* such as Molige Mahadevi and Aydakki Lakkamma have made observations on worldly and otherworldly life.[63] They had to dwell on this effort because their husbands were inclined to think more upon the other-worldly life. They wanted to get rid of the worldly life and join *Kailasa* (heaven or abode of Shiva). For these illusions, they responded that there is no duality of death and *Kailasa*. According to them, the belief that

---

[59] Menezes and Angadi, *Vacanas of Basavanna*, 37.
[60] Chandrashekhar, 'Vachana Samskruti', 100.
[61] Ibid., 95.
[62] Ibid., 96.
[63] Ibid., 97.

one can go to *Kailasa* is an illusion. Mahadevi asserts that one should become Shiva himself than simply desiring that one can see Shiva in *Kailasa* and temples.[64] By considering her husband himself as Shiva, she rejects his desire of meeting Shiva and his abode.

Kayaka and *Dasoha* as Existential Episteme to Democratic Theory

Indian spiritual tradition has given importance to all spheres of life. It significantly deals with pertinent questions on material life. 'Indian materialism has a historical tradition dating much earlier than the rise of Carvaka or Lokayata school'.[65] It could not be developed as a school or system of philosophy, but its beginnings are found quite early in the history.[66]

> Indian religious thought does address this-worldly concerns. Philosophically, the Hindu tradition recognizes that ultimate reality (*Brahman*) is not only transcendent and impersonal, but is, also, immanent (intrinsic) and personal (an *Isvara*). The aim of life for the Hindu is not just *moksa*, or spiritual freedom, but equally *artha*, or material satisfaction. Thus, religion in the Indian tradition has not divorced itself from the secular affairs of society such as economic and political activity.[67]

To what extent these secular and materialistic traditions paved the way for democratic and egalitarian life is a big question

[64] Ibid.

[65] A. K. Sinha, 'Traces of Materialism in Early Vedic Thought: A Study', *Annals of the Bhandarkar Oriental Research Institute 75*, no. 1/4 (1994): 235–236. Available at https://www.jstor.org/stable/41694419 (accessed on 25 October 2019).

[66] Ibid., 236.

[67] Rajeev H. Dehejia and Vivek H. Dehejia, 'Religion and Economic Activity in India: An Historical Perspective', *The American Journal of Economics and Sociology 52*, no. 2 (1993): 145–146. Available at http://www.jstor.org/stable/3487047 (accessed on 20 July 2018).

that needs to be objectively analysed and explored. The answer for this question can be traced in Indic tradition of democratic experiments in Medieval India. What was philosophized was practised in the Indic Bhakti traditions of Medieval India. These traditions were not just mere seekers of liberation for the souls, they also celebrated their culture of work along with spirituality. Thus, they gave new meaning to human life that was to a major extent missing in the form of practice that was preached in our early history.

As a part of the main objective of creating egalitarian social life, Basava came up with two concepts, namely *Kayaka* and *Dasoha*. *Kayaka* means way of producing wealth and *Dasoha* means distribution of wealth.[68] 'Basava advocated toward building an egalitarian community based on the dignity of work, community service and sharing, diligence, thrift, and sobriety.'[69] These two concepts articulated by Basava and his colleagues became successful because they were religiously practised by the followers of the Lingayat Movement in democratizing the process of economic production. They can even be understood as egalitarian ideas and approaches for the genuine practice of democracy in the sense that they can clear the possible social and economic chaos in society which could ultimately affect democratic life.

There is an argument that political democracy would work better if it were accompanied by social and economic democracy.[70] Efforts have been made in this regard at both theoretical and practical

[68] S. S. Marulayya, *Basavannanavara Siddantagalu* (The Philosophical Ideas of Basava; Dharawad: Shree Basaveshwara Peetha, Karnataka University, 2003), 72.

[69] Danesh A. Chekki, *Religion and Social System of the Virasaiva Community* (Westport, CT: Greenwood Press, 1997), 59.

[70] Robin Blackburn, 'Economic Democracy: Meaningful, Desirable, Feasible?' *Daedalus* 136, no. 3 (2007): 36. Available at https://www.jstor.org/stable/20028127 (accessed on 26 October 2019).

levels. Ideas such as welfare state, social control over production and planned economy have been discussed and practised in different countries. However, the very aspiration of human beings to be equal even at a minimum level with everyone in their respective societies in social and economic spheres has not yet become a reality. The resultant inequality from social and economic chaos present in different societies is posing challenges to political democracy that is practised in its different forms such as elections, freedom and participation in decision-making. Spirituality and work that produce anything that is for the benefit of humanity can be a good combination of normative ideas to make democracy successful in its functioning. If the humanity becomes conscious about such ideas, they can be perfect guidelines or can act as alternatives to various ideas of making democracy both social and economic. 'If the theological formulations of the Sharana movement stand for the culture of the head, its devotional and mystical poetry represents the culture of the heart. The culture of the hand is represented by the philosophy of Kayaka'.[71] Thus, the concepts of *Kayaka* and *Dasoha* are indeed existential epistemes to democratic theory.

Conclusion

Democratic experiment of the Lingayat Movement cannot be considered as a complete success, but it laid the foundation for further experiments of a similar nature. It is because of certain firm civilizational democratic roots that democracy as an idea is being debated and discussed continuously in India. Any direct or indirect threat to this civilizational foundation cannot sustain but remain as mere, unwarranted phase in our history of the future. 'The "idea of India" is indeed an open, assimilative, and spacious one, sustaining a plurality of voices, orthodox and dissenting, of

---

[71] Shivaprakash, *I Keep Vigil of Rudra*, lxv.

many ages, regions, and affiliations.'[72] The Lingayat Movement was witness to debate and criticism among the *Sharanas* and *Sharanes* within the movement. When any arguments without much rationale and reason came to the fore, the same were put to harsh critique and debate in the movement by the *Sharanas* and *Sharanes*. Socially marginal voices succeeded in clearing the doubts of the leaders of the movement who wooed certain conservative lines on the questions of gender equality, social and spiritual space for women and the marginalized.

[72] Jonardon Ganeri, 'Intellectual India: Reason, Identity, Dissent', *New Literary History* 40, no. 2 (2009): 262. Available at https://www.jstor.org/stable/27760257 (accessed on 28 October 2018).

7

Interpreting Meerabai's Bhakti

Bijayalaxmi Nanda

Introduction

In the history of the Bhakti Movement in India, Meerabai is an important name—the saint, poet, lover, transgressor, deviant, revolutionary and devotee. To these adjectives, some have added the term feminist. In a quest to understand the roots of change in the Indic tradition, I strive here to interpret Meerabai's bhakti. But this is by no means the first interpretation. Many scholars in contemporary times have examined the life and times of Meerabai for a similar exercise.[1] According to Thaosen:

> tracing the roots of Indian Feminism led us to women in Bhakti, who challenged Brahminical patriarchy through their songs, poems

[1] Rashmi Bhatnagar, Renu Dube and Reena Dube, 'Meera's Medieval Lyric Poetry in Postcolonial India: The Rhetorics of Women's Writing in Dialect as a Secular Practice of Subaltern Coauthorship and Dissent', *Boundary* 2 31, no. 3, Fall (2004): 1–46.

Madhu Kishwar and Ruth Vanita, 'Poison to Nectar: The Life and Work of Mirabai', *Manushi* 19, no. 50–51–52 (January–June; 1989): 75–92.

Kumkum Sangari, 'Mirabai and the Spiritual Economy of Bhakti', *Economic & Political Weekly* 25, no. 28 (1990): 1464–1475.

and ways of life. At a time where most spaces were restricted to women, they embraced Bhakti to define their own truths to reform society, polity, relationships and religions. They broke all societal rules and stereotypes and lived their lives as they pleased.[2]

Apart from Meera Bai, other women saints who contributed to this upsurge of radical reconfiguring of the traditional position of women included Lal Ded, Akka Mahadevi, Ammaiyar and others.

This chapter (a) interprets the writings of Meerabai mediated through the interconnections of womanhood, culture and history, its influence on society in general and its implications on women in particular. It reflects upon (b) the historical account of her life in order to delve into the paradoxical tropes of devotion and social change and (c) it examines her struggle to move out of private domain and praxis. It finally interrogates the contemporary relevance of her ideas in order to engage with the possibilities of locating Indic roots of change.

Western feminism is popularly studied in waves and understood in terms of variants which include liberal, socialist, Marxist, ecofeminist and postmodern, among others. Feminism as an ideology and movement is committed to bringing about gender equality and countering various forms of oppression and subjugation of women. One of the core struggles of feminism is against the patriarchal order of society. Feminism in the West is traced to Olympe De Gouges, Mary Wollstonecraft and the suffragettes, among others. The narratives of Western feminism has been critiqued from within the feminist school in its different variants. Black feminism has emerged as a definable moment in feminist history to question White feminism for its exclusion of issues of Black women and women of colour. Post-colonial feminists have also provided a nuanced critique of Western feminist discourse for ignoring the perspectives emerging from other worlds than their own.

[2] Maduli Thaosen, 'The Bhakti Movement and Roots of Indian Feminism', *Feminism in India* (2017). Available at https://feminisminindia.com/2017/04/03/bhakti-movement-women/ (accessed on 14 January 2020).

The tracing of the roots of indigenous freedom, both individual and collective, for women in India requires recognition of the diversity of Indian society. There can be no one Indian freedom; one can only speak of multiple modes of Indian freedoms. By tracing the life and times of Meerabai, this chapter refrains from imposing this approach on the idea of Indic freedom. It is to map a journey which may throw up a few possibilities to understand a minute part of the diverse nature of feminisms or quests towards gender equality in India.

Bhakti and Gender

The meanings of bhakti have many interpretations. They remain intermeshed with culture, identity and personal political protests against power in multiple modes reflected in literature, poetry and religion. It is mostly associated with the alternative narrative of the oppressed providing voice to them. It also remains, at certain times, paradoxically linked to gender relations and reinforces class and caste power. How do we see gender and bhakti play out in the context of analysing society and the voices of women who played a significant role in the movement? How does it interact with the modern-day understanding of gender equality? Does bhakti have the ability to render itself to the kind of political sensibilities associated with gender equality?

Bhakti is not a monolith or a homogenizing force. There are as many variants of bhakti as there are bhakts. It is universally recognized that the Bhakti Movement emerged in the fifth and sixth centuries in South India and spread to other parts. The great Sanskritist, V. Raghavan, says that bhakti is 'a democratic doctrine which consolidates all people without distinction of caste, community, nationality or sex'.[3] Pauwels elucidates further on

---

[3] John Stratton Hawley, Christian Lee Novetzke and Swapna Sharma, eds., *Bhakti and Power: Debating India's Religion of the Heart* (Hyderabad: Orient Blackswan, 2019), 6.

this by distinguishing between *saguna* and *nirguna* bhakti, the former being worship of God with the attributes of Vishnu and the latter being the egalitarian worship of an abstract form.[4] However, she alerts that these pedantic distinctions cannot provide an explanation for what bhakti represents. The power of bhakti transcends religiosity and other forms of classifications referred to above. It emerges as a force which remains elusive to definition. Bhakti is a productive force interlaying memory with imagination. Both the political and emotive connections of the forces of love and power emerge within collectivized and enduring kindling of the same. Love and power remain interlinked and mediated in the movement. The interconnection and influence of bhakti on interrogating caste as a practice has been widely written about. But gender in the same context continues to be a neglected field. It is, therefore, important to carefully tread the path in recovering voices to underline the influence of bhakti on gender.

Bhakti requires a deeply introspective engagement with the narratives of the saints to extrapolate from there the nuances of history and its significance. Poems and narratives being mostly of the oral tradition escape the capturing of their true essence. It is only through secondary sources and through the lenses of writers and authors writing on bhakti that one can attempt to understand the same. The mediation of the academic and research writing fails us in delivering the uniqueness of the bhakti texts. The generic understanding of the Bhakti Movement can only be possible if one is aware of the intersecting and multi-layered approach required for the same. The interpretations over a period of time with different approaches provide us only certain fragments of truth. A mapping of the various sites of understanding and their interrelationship with a methodological

---

[4] Heidi R. M. Pauwels, 'Caste and Women in Early Modern India: Krishna Bhakti in Sixteenth-Century Vrindavan', in *Bhakti and Power: Debating India's Religion of the Heart*, eds. John Stratton Hawley, Christian Lee Novetzke and Swapna Sharma (Hyderabad: Orient Blackswan, 2019), 49.

rigour, however, helps unearth the essence of each bhakti voice.[5] According to Sangari[6]:

> Bhakti makes a language for aspiration and desire, through a notion of personal devotion and more direct communication with a compassionate god, which is embedded within an experiential base—particular sorts of hierarchical, patriarchal and feudal relations—a location which defines both the power and the vulnerability of such a language. Once assimilated into mainstream Hinduism, the critical edge of dissenting forms of bhakti is blunted, yet the language remains evocative, long after the movements have themselves waned, precisely because its experiential base has altered but not disappeared.

The enumeration of certain Bhakti saints, including Meerabai and others, provides traction to examine the influence of bhakti on gender. Their writings open a window to understand the Bhakti Movement, their own views, the status of women during that period and its contemporary relevance. The list of women saints of the Bhakti Movement includes Andal, Karaikkal Ammaiyar, Akka Mahadevi in the South, Lal Ded from Kashmir, Bahinabai and Soyarabai from Maharashtra.

However, in the telling and retelling of the stories and the capturing of the voices of resistance and protest to patriarchy, the context of time and space needs to be kept in mind. While the hymns, songs and poems of the women saints of the Bhakti Movement may have addressed the existential crisis of their lives as women located within a certain power structure, the value of their writings present themselves, for contemporary times, as a break or rupture from the past where they are located. Scholars have long debated how these expressions need to be examined, especially in the light of their inter-sectarian relationships. The poetry of the women saints proves to be both transformational and destabilizing. Their lives emerge as both real and imagined. It becomes a device to reflect on the world around her. The

---

[5] Ibid., 51.
[6] Sangari, 'Mirabai and the Spiritual Economy of Bhakti', 1464.

interpretations and the popular retellings also reflect the rebellious space it creates for those who are keen to use it for their own interrogation of caste, class and gender relations.

Thus, in the world of bhakti, home and protest intersected and overlapped for generations. Bhakti, according to Cherian, thus becomes a way of thinking through questions of the self, the family, the community and governance, and a framework in which experiments in self-governance were carried out. The power of bhakti then lies not in its ability to produce liberation or submission but in its ability to restructure relationships of liberty and submission[7] to expand the indigenous roots of struggle for the expansion of the periphery of freedom. The specific nature of her bhakti has to be understood in the context of its times—a rebellion against the medieval Rajputana traditions, the male domain of the prevailing religious texts and the unexpected popularity of the lone female devotional voice. Did the Bhakti Movement provide Meerabai the ability to persuade her family and utilize the momentum of the movement to propel her own spiritual quest through devotional poetry; or was she the radical transgressor who stood outside the circle of society to actively question the traditional norms; or was it an overlap or intersection of both these factors? It was a collective force of bhakti and the individual journey of a determined woman that reflect on the indigenous method to expand women's freedom in India.

Gender, Culture and Identity in Meerabai's Times

Simone de Beauvoir[8] famously said, 'One is not born but becomes a woman' in order to explain the social construction of biological identities, leading women to be reduced to inferior

[7] Divya Cherian, 'Fall from Grace?: Caste, Bhakti, and Politics in Late Eighteenth-Century Marwar', in *Bhakti and Power: Debating India's Religion of the Heart*, eds. John Stratton Hawley, Christian Lee Novetzke and Swapna Sharma (Hyderabad: Orient Blackswan, 2019).

[8] Simone de Beauvoir, *The Second Sex* (New York, NY: Vintage Books, 1973), 301.

position vis-à-vis men. The sex–gender distinction, as it came to be known later, became the mainstay of feminist critique, speaking of the essentializing of the biological differences of male and female into characteristics of masculinity and femininity, respectively. The sex–gender distinction debate has been subject to some revisions since then where even the idea of biology has been considered as constructed and the concept of gender fluidity in terms of an identity has emerged. This neat and universal delineation present in Western feminism is difficult to be adapted to the diversity of Indian society. A more nuanced Indic approach is necessary for it.

There are numerous historical accounts of Meerabai's birth and parentage. In biographies, the earliest are the Bhaktmal of Nabha Das (1667) and the Bhakt-maltika of Priyadas (1752), both based partly on her own compositions, her life, like the lives of all medieval saints and, more specifically, of women saints.[9] The most agreed upon date of her birth is 1498 AD. Her father Ratan Singh Rathore belonged to the Mertiya Rathore clan. She was thus a Rajput princess.[10]

The Rajputs controlled the erstwhile Rajputana states the from the 7th century onwards. They were extolled for their qualities of courage, chivalry and excellence in warfare. Their identity as a warrior race was honed because of their continuous warfare with the Turks, the Mughals and the Marathas. According to Jain and Sharma:

> In such a warrior culture, characterised by volatile and uncertain political conditions, not only men, but women were also obligated to inculcate the virtues of fortitude, bravery, discipline and sacrifice. In fact, women played an important role as wives and mothers of warriors in sustaining and preserving the chivalric ethos of the Rajput polity.[11]

[9] Sangari, 'Mirabai and the Spiritual Economy of Bhakti', 1464–1475.
[10] Kishwar and Vanita, 'Poison to Nectar', 75–92.
[11] Pratibha Jain and Sangeeta Sharma, 'Honour, Gender and the Legend of Meera Bai', *Economic & Political Weekly* 37, no. 46 (2002): 4646.

According to Sangari[12]:

> the fifteenth century sees the emergence of the word 'rajput' in its contemporary sense signifying not merely a caste but a ruling military aristocracy with its own ethos of marital valour, a claim to prestige and achieved status and its own patriarchal practices grounded in the clan system.

The conditions of insecurity and war led to a benevolent paternalistic position within the Rajputs as far as women were concerned, and the culture among the elite percolated downwards over the centuries. Male responsibility for safety and protection of women among the Rajput community was extolled, and women became repositories of community honour. The strict code of behaviour that emerged was a burden for both men and women. Both were shamed if they displayed any form of cowardice and stepped outside the boundaries of conventional norms. Marriage was the significant indicator in their lives. The elements of honour, purity, sexuality, courage and sacrifice became the defining elements of their lives. While their main roles were to support each other in times of need, they were also to be each other's inspiration and motivation to lay down their lives for the protection of the nation. Women were not passive victims, but their choices were mediated through the ideas of glorification of war, nation and sacrifice. Marriages among the elite were arranged for purely political reasons, where siblings were 'given away' for the greater good of the people. In this context, the social conditioning of women and girls was such that they considered it their duty and obligation to the nation and as a heroic act of sacrifice for their nation. It was mediated through the prism of the people and the nation. Marriage within such cultures took an intensely political avatar for the consolidation of rule, alliances, protection of boundaries and for power. It impacted the brides' and grooms' choices adversely, but it glorified their sacrifices for the greater good of the state and nation. So courage for women and men meant a certain degree of aligning themselves to the greater good of the state. The family,

---

[12] Sangari, 'Mirabai and the Spiritual Economy of Bhakti', 1466.

thus, no longer was part of the private sphere. It was, especially for the ruling clans, a desired part of the political.

Mewar ruled by the Sisodiya clan is believed to have the most pervasive cultural traditions regarding women. It was surrounded by kingdoms ruled by Muslims. The continuous warfare necessitated a protective stance by them through marriages and political alliances. According to Jain and Sharma, 'The concept of honour as it evolved in Rajputana states and particularly in Mewar, imparted a special character to the lives of women, their upbringing, marriage, education, day-to day life and social endeavours digressed from the normative pattern of women's lives'.[13]

The position of women also remained steeped in the role of wives and mothers, adorned with the symbols of marital status including jewellery, bangles and colourful sarees. The courage and bravery of women were harnessed for their commitment to the domestic and national realms, and for being the upholder of community's values and norms. While men did not view women as passive beings, strict restrictions on their mobility and on their sexuality were imposed by a social order borne both by women and men.

It is in this cultural setting that Meerabai was born and brought up, imbibing the values of the community around her. However, she transcended all boundaries and norms set by both her natal and marital family, and she remains one of the most significant transgressors of her times. Her celebration as a saint and devotee in the same community which she defied continues to evoke surprise and inspiration.

Expanding Freedom through Devotion

How did Meerabai get away with her so-called 'deviant ways' in medieval times is a question that warrants intense enquiry. The various historical accounts of her life have acquired folklore status.

---

[13] Jain and Sharma, 'Honour', 4647.

One of the most commonly accepted versions is that one day, a 4-year-old Meerabai was watching a marriage procession pass by from her window, and her interest piqued by the bridegroom and she asked her mother the question 'Where is my bridegroom?' Meerabai's mother guided her to the puja altar and, pointing to a small statue of Lord Krishna, jocularly announced 'this is your bridegroom.' The Rathores belonged to the Vaishnavite traditions and the worship of Krishna was common to all households. The young Meerabai accepted this with all earnestness and worshipped Krishna as her consort with a passion and dedication that is characteristic only of prodigal saints.

When her wedding was arranged with Bhoj Raj Bhoj of the Sisodiya clan, Meera refused to accept him as her husband. She refused to consummate the marriage; neither did she accept the family deity of the Sisodiyas. She announced her status as the wife of Krishna and continued with her devotion for him. Her husband Bhoj Raj Bhoj did not force Meera to conform to the traditions and norms of his clan. One of the various accounts mentions that Bhoj Raj Bhoj died early. Meerabai refused to be sacrificed as a Sati on her husband's funeral pyre; nor did she agree to lead the life of a widow. Her widespread popularity on the basis of her devotion, ecstatic poetry and melodious singing gave her a unique status and distinction. Her poetic refrain *mere to giridhara gopala dusro na koi* was her claim as the status of Krishna's consort and a rejection of her role as Bhoj Raj's wife.

However, while the Sisodiya clan protested against it, they found it difficult to punish her for her transgressions in the face of popular sentiments which had already anointed her a saint. There were attempts on her life. But it made Meerabai resolute. She decided to cross the boundary of the home, shunned all signs of family life, dressed in the garb of mendicants and joined male mendicants on a pilgrimage to places associated with Krishna. Her singing and dancing devoted to Krishna in her pilgrimage enticed many devotees. Her fame spread far and wide. It is believed that Akbar and Tansen (both in disguise) visited her when she was in Chittor to hear her bhajans. Meerabai also became the disciple of Ravidas, who was from a marginalized caste. While her marital family remained resentful, her status as a saint and singer made her popular among all classes and castes.

Her bhakti became an effective strategy to break away from the structures, roles and institutions associated with marriage and motherhood. The Ranas also tried to persuade her to return to her marital home by sending priests to Dwarka where she had been residing in the Krishna temple. Meerabai asked them to wait for the night while she remained in the temple. In the morning, they found she had disappeared, her mendicant cloth wrapped around Lord Krishna's statue. Her devotion to the Lord had become enshrined in the collective memory of the people.

This folklore has enough detractors. S. M. Pandey, however, provides Ram Chandra Shukla's account. According to Shukla, Meerabai's husband died shortly after her marriage and so did her father in a battle with Babar. Meerabai was thus left alone in her marital home sans her husband and father. The family norms of the Sisodiyas tightened on Meerabai because she did not conform to the norms of widowhood. She refused to be sacrificed at her husband's funeral pyre and 'commit Sati', as was the order of the day, and she roamed free with male saints while celebrating her devotion to Krishna. Meerabai's constant reference to her tormentor in her poems was about a Rana about whom most biographers believe was her husband's younger brother. He took over the reins of the kingdom after her husband's death. While much is also made of Meerabai's acceptance of Ravidas as her mentor bringing in a gender and caste intersection. According to Pandey, there is no evidence to substantiate the assertion that Ravidas mentioned in Meerabai's poems is the famous Ravidas. He cites Parshuram Chaturvedi, who says that though Ravidas of the saint tradition may not have been the direct guru of Meerabai, there is a possibility that Ravidas' influence was exerted through his writings, and that when she says 'Guru milia Raidas', she probably is making an allegorical reference and not literal. Pandey also cites Chandrabali Pandey, who believes that the Ravidas cited in the poems of Meerabai is another Ravidas, belonging to the same tradition. Also, Meerabai's meeting with Akbar and Tansen, his court singer, is questioned for its historical accuracy.[14] Pandey then goes on to discuss Meerabai's last days. According to him, Mirabai left Mewar and lived for a long time in Vrindavan and then moved to Dwarka, where she spent her last days and passed away probably in 1546.

Historical accuracy notwithstanding, the legend of Meerabai gained strength from its telling and retelling. While the authenticity of her biography continues to be questioned, the influence of Meerabai on the Bhakti Movement and her status as the most famous female saint of the 15th century remains unquestioned. Unravelling the subversive elements of her writings, especially in relation to patriarchy, has been an engagement for many. The quest to examine the roots of an indigenous questioning of gender discrimination thus becomes important here.

Roots of Indian Feminism: Meerabai's Contribution

Questioning inequalities or discriminatory practices had strong roots in the Bhakti tradition. Irrespective of the critique or its appropriation for such academic purposes, it is clear that the Bhakti Movement provided space for questioning rigid social norms and protested against it. The movement in that sense became an enabler. The literary and poetic traditions lend credence to the voices of women in their many quests to reject rigid medieval controls of the domestic sphere, which speak of a higher idealized devotion emphasizing a choice-based intense mystical experience. The transgression of the boundaries of their role is exemplified in the life, writings and practices of the women saints of the Bhakti Movement, beginning from the 6th-century Tamil poet Ammaiyar to the later saints which included Lal Ded and Meerabai. Their devotional poems found their way from homes to temples to offices to fields and forests. It spoke the language

[14] S. M. Pandey and Norman Zide, 'Mirabai and Her Contribution to the Bhakti Movement', *History of Religions* 5, no. 1 (Summer; 1965): 58.

of the common people and found its acceptance in their everyday lives. Lal Ded wrote in the vernacular Kashmiri, and Meerabai wrote in the Braj Bhasha, a local dialect of Rajasthan.[15]

The mystical nature of her poems was intertwined with the rebellious ideas against cultural norms and roles for women. She fearlessly spoke of love and desire when she said *bhakti bhav se mast doli...giridhar pe balijaye* (Behari quoted in Wasia).[16] She rejected her marriage and motherhood striking at the very root of the glorification of women in the Rajput traditions. As she says in a poem:

> *Jeevado mai vaar dalungi haan*
> *Tere haan jog dharan lok laaj kuldhar.*

(Yes I will give up my Life for Him. Because of you. Worldly modesty and family restriction)[17]

When questioned about her free interaction with male saints, she said:

Rana, to me this slander is sweet
Some praise me, some blame me, I go the other way.
On the narrow path, I found God's people
For what should I turn back?
I am learning wisdom among the wise, the wicked look at me with malice.
Mira's lord is Giridhar Nagar: let the wicked burn in a furnace.[18]

---

[15] Wasia, 'Poetry of Defiance: A Comparative Study of Lalleshwari (Lal Ded) and Meerabai' (Dissertation submitted as a fulfilment of the requirement for Integrated MPhil/PhD Programme in English; Srinagar: Department of English Central University of Kashmir, 2014). Available at https://shodhganga.inflibnet.ac.in/bitstream/10603/205505/9/09_chapter04.pdf (accessed on 7 January 2020).

[16] Ibid., 133.

[17] V. K. Subramanium, *Mystic Songs of Meera* (New Delhi: Abhinav Publications, 2005), quoted in Wasia, 'Poetry of Defiance'.

[18] Kishwar and Vanita, 'Poison to Nectar', 82.

Meerabai's revolutionary and transgressive poems can be said to contain the germs of ideas that may be recognized as feminist in the present context. First, it was her rejection of the roles of wife and mother. Her domestic role in her marital home was shunned by her, irrespective of the stranglehold of the norms to be performed by wife and mother. In fact, she vehemently opposed it. She called her marriage an illusion and a lie. Her transgression achieved legendary status because of this revolutionary stance where she denied both the sexual and reproductive roles of the wife. It was not without its own set of risks. She was coerced in different ways and stigmatized also for the same. However, her nonchalance in the face of it, because of her spiritual quest, provided her the ability to break free from the regulations of her sexuality and mobility. The disentangling from the illusory nature of human bonding of marriage is well stated by her.

Tum hi jhuthe ham bhi jhuthe jhutha hai sab sansaara
Stri purush ke sambandh jhuthe, to phuthya hai ya tumhara
Tum hi kaho ardhangha hamaari, hamku lagaayo kaara
Koti brahmand me vyapy arahiyo hai to nij var hamaara.

(You are a lie, and I am a lie. Everything is useless and illusionary. Tell me O' husband of mine, I have been stigmatized. The whole world knows that you are my bridegroom).[19]

She also rejected the practice of Sati and absolved herself of her marital status by escaping the stigma of widowhood. Her emphasis on her status as the wife of Krishna gave her the freedom to escape that stigma. Her ability to exercise her choice of worship, to continue with the Vaishnavite traditions of her natal home as opposed to the Kuldevi worship in her marital home, was courageous. This questioning of the identity of the woman as a daughter and the entrenched image of the wife as the only role embedded in the marital home was one of Meerabai's first transgressions. She shunned not only the role of the dutiful wife but also the rituals and customs of the marital home. Another

---

[19] Sangari, 'Mirabai and the Spiritual Economy of Bhakti', 1467.

important aspect of this is captured in Meerabai's critique of the practice of *Bidaai* or the traditional sending off of a daughter from the natal home to the marital home, making the daughter an outsider to her parents, to be recognized to belong to only marital home. Meerabai transcended this ideological content and channelized it towards her public identity, outside the domestic sphere, which was mediated through spiritual quest. Interestingly, whenever Meerabai made references to *Bidaai* in her poems, these were addressed to her childhood female friends and spoke about breaking of natal ties to move towards a self-chosen path.[20] So, in a way, Meerabai encompassed the understanding of sisterhood and female friendship reflective of most feminist principles that emerged centuries later in France, in the 19th and 20th centuries, and in contemporary times. It is also the foremost feminist ideal that one can retrieve from her life and practices.

Come my friends! Let's play and not go to other houses.[21]

The third is Meerabai's chosen life devoted to spiritual quest and poetry by shunning her domestic role. She refused her wifely duties and stood outside the heteronormative sociocultural construct of a married life. She crossed the threshold of her home to the public arena. It was, in that sense, an empowered and informed choice. Her poetry was not just musings, the quality was of a higher order. But it was also accessible and within the reach of the masses. Her ability to sing and perform amass a wider audience is also part of legendary folklore. So, in that sense, her dedication, passion and talent in her chosen field are reflective of a public role that she excelled in. Meerabai, thus, crossed the domestic sphere and was able to enjoy the status of a saint

---

[20] Wasia, 'Lal Ded and Meerabai: A Feminist Perspective' (*National Conference cum Workshop on Recent Trends in Technical Language & Communication: Emerging Requirements*, 21–22 April 2017). Available at http://data.conferenceworld.in/NCCW/P01–13.pdf (accessed on 10 January 2020), 10.

[21] Subramanium, *Mystic Songs of Meera*, cited in Wasia, 'Lal Ded and Meerabai', 10.

through spiritual awakening. Her travels, her intermingling with male mendicants, people of other castes and communities and her ecstatic singing, dancing and writing poetry, all encompassed an absolute transcendence of all the cultural norms embedded in the medieval Rajput elite practices. By her commitment to her works, Meerabai exemplified a woman who lived on her own terms, a rarity in her times. Her donning of the mendicant garments and her shunning of the feminine ornaments and adornments, including jewellery, was the final nail in the coffin of the feminine ideal. Her passionate love for Krishna expressed in her poems is about desire and pining for the beloved. In this sense, her poems engage unambiguously with the sacred and the erotic. Speaking of desire for Lord Krishna in her poems, Meerabai transgresses every role set for the married woman in society; yet, by her spiritual practice and devotion, she balances the crossing over in a way that that both shocks and inspires.

> I don't like your strange world Rana
>
> A world where there are no holy men and the people are trash.
>
> I have given up ornaments and given up braiding my hair and I have given up putting on kajal.
>
> Mira's lord is Giridhar Nagar, I have found a perfect husband.[22]

And another where she says:

> O Friends of all my lives! I cannot forget you day or night for
>
> When I do not see you I am restless and my heart burns. I mount the high places to watch for your coming and from sobbing my eyes become red
>
> The ocean of life is false and false are the bonds of the world and family.
>
> Beholding your beauty every moment, I become intoxicated. Mira's lord is Girdhar Nagar and a love for him has welled up in her heart.[23]

---

[22] Cited in Pandey and Zide, 'Mirabai and Her Contribution to the Bhakti Movement', 57.

[23] Ibid., 71.

According to Kumkum Sangari, 'Meerabai aimed at making the world understand that that choosing a lifetime ideal was an effective way to counter medieval Rajput patriarchal ideology'.[24] Her voice was a radical one, breaking all stereotypes associated with medieval Rajput elite practices. Her method was to transcend worldly pursuits and break all the gender binaries which many male bhakti poets and saints had associated themselves with. She remained on her own, mingling with everyone and belonging to none. Meerabai's refusal to be 'part of a sect—she wants to belong to the world and to leave her work to the world rather than to her Rajput lineage—opens up the possibility of co-authorship by diverse sections of subaltern classes'.[25] Meerabai's poetry offers radical criticisms of the caste systems and the exclusion of women from full participation in religious customs.[26] Her poetry, life and practices provide us with a powerful narrative to engage with the roots of Indian womanhood. However, it is fraught with contradictions and paradoxes. The first critique is one of reductionism and appropriation. Meerabai was one of the foremost Bhakti poets in the lines of saints such as Kabir, Surdas and others.

Her abstinence from the medieval heteronormative order was common to all of them. Associating her with feminism may seem far-fetched in that sense. However, one cannot disagree that her life and praxis have provided an understanding of her basic questioning of gendered norms. By breaking medieval norms and practices and popularizing it through her poetry, she provided a sense of freedom to women. Her voice lends credence to the aspirations of work ideals for women beyond their constructed domestic roles. It is true that her spiritual quest provided her the public legitimacy and so did the context of the Bhakti Movement. It is also important

[24] Sangari, 'Mirabai and the Spiritual Economy of Bhakti', 1464–1475.
[25] Bhatnagar, Dube and Dube, 'Meera's Medieval Lyric Poetry in Postcolonial India', 10.
[26] Amy Carr-Richardson, 'Feminist and Non-Western Perspectives in the Music Theory Classroom: A Study of John Harbison's "Mirabai Songs"', *College Music Symposium* 42 (2002): 20–36.

to recognize that while she faced innumerable obstacles in her path imposed by the princely lineage to which she belonged, it is also important to note that it was the support of the larger society around her that allowed her to have the conviction and strength to move forward with her life goals. Her ability to refuse her marital role, her refusal to be Sati and her widespread travel also require a nuanced enquiry into the prevalence of gender freedom in her times. Was it her spiritual quest which restrained coercive acts to be applied to her or was it her popularity as a poet–saint which provided her that freedom? While the traditions of the medieval times in Rajput lineage are one which seem to obstruct her, it is also important to engage with a more nuanced understanding of the popular support she received.

Indian feminists today treat Meerabai as the foremother of Indian feminism. She inspired many women to break boundaries, transcend and seek liberation from rigid social norms. Her works, praxis and poetry may be the forebearer of Indian feminist thought.

Conclusion

Meerabai's praxis for personal freedom of women continues to be relevant. Reflected in the form of poetry and sainthood, she is celebrated till date. She is the part of folklore. But her transgression from wifely duties remains a sore point among some of the subsects of the Rajput community. The name Meera is used to refer, contemptuously, to a transgressor or to an ascetic and asexual woman who is spiritually inclined. While the colonial and post-colonial eras have brought in numerous changes in women's position in India, there remains several issues that continue to act as obstacles in the path of women's freedom. The institution of marriage continues to be steeped in traditional conventions. Choice marriages outside caste and community are still frowned upon.

The status of women who are single continues to remain problematic. Women's identity is still linked to marriage and motherhood. While many stereotypes abound women and are reinforced, Meerabai's legacy has provided us with many answers to the existing issues. No wonder, Gandhi considered her the paramount *satyagrahi*. Contemporary feminists are influenced by Meerabai and draw on her for inspiration. Kamla Bhasin believes that Meera is a role model for the rebel in every woman to break the shackles of patriarchy through a rejection of all that has been imposed on her. It was a choice of a life of freedom coming from her spirit of renunciation. While it may appeal to a certain variant of Indian feminism, it is not without its critique emerging from Dalit feminism.

To conclude, Meerabai, through her life and writings, questioned gender relations and chose a life dedicated to her works, providing inspiration and motivation for freedom in both mystical and social sense. Her critical role in resisting patriarchal forces and changing them in the face of severe opposition provides contemporary feminist struggles in India with various possibilities of resistance. Whether one wants to recognize it as overtly feminist or not, Meerabai's life provides us the lens to understand the indigenous roots of cultural resistance to multiple gendered relations. It also requires us to question the monolithic understanding of it in her times. While Meerabai resisted the ideological forces of the medieval society, her resistance was by no means a single voice. She was joined in unison by many others who supported her and continued to speak of her in order to support her freedom to choose. The intersectional issues present in the interrogation of gender, culture and identity in Meerabai's times are nuanced and defy a single narrative or explanation. Her struggle moulded and reshaped gender relations of her time and expanded the periphery of individual and social freedom.

8

Indic Islam

Himanshu Roy

Introduction

This chapter explores the journey of political–Arabic Islam in India, analyses its impact on different facets of Indic society, the encounter it generated and the role of social process that transformed it into Indic Islam. Indic, it may be explained here, has been changing its meaning from territorial to cultural to religious. It was used by the Greeks for the residents settled in the regions of the Sindhu river. Herodotus called them Indons, a term which primarily denoted territoriality. In course of time, its usage was enlarged to include contemporary Afghanistan, Pakistan, India and Bangladesh; and it also acquired cultural and religious forms. Megasthenes' *Indica* and other works reflected the society and polity of the Indons. It may also be explained here that by political–Arabic Islam, it is meant that a new emerging segment of Muslim elite began to dominate the monarchy and ruling structure since the 8th century AD, beginning from Sindh, which had alien, non-Indic religious and cultural beliefs and followed a different administrative and judicial apparatus inherited from Arabic–Persian history and polity. This elite, in course of history, expanded its religion, culture, population and political dominance in India for the

next 1,000 years, beginning from 712 lasting until 1774, when
Warren Hastings had refused to recognize the Mughal state as
the sovereign power of *Hindustan*, and its symbol, the monarchy, was formally abolished in 1858.

Political Islam

Politically and religiously, the Muslim monarchs in India were
sovereign and were not dictated by the Arabic–Persian monarchs, clerics or local mullahs. The Muslim elite composed
of local nobility (max up to 30%) and nobility of the foreign
origin (Turks, Persians, Arabs and Uzbeks more than 70%).
Their strength was approximately 5 per cent of the total Muslim
population. The elite of the foreign origin had contemptuous
attitude towards Indic Muslim, for both elite and the Arjal and
Ajlaz. It was more contemptuous towards Hindus and Kafirs,
particularly the non-elite population. Al-Biruni[1] had observed
in 1030 AD that 'they (Hindus) differ from us in everything' and
there is an 'increasing ideological and emotional hostility between
the Hindus and the Muslims'. He had noted that Muhammad
(of Ghazni) had 'utterly ruined the prosperity of the country,
and performed there wonderful exploits, by which the Hindus
became like atoms of dust scattered in all directions'. He had
added that Muhammad bin Qasim had entered Sindh penetrat-
ing even as far as Kannauj…'sometimes fighting sword in hand'.
Biruni had also written that Hindu science had retreated far away
to those parts of the country which were not yet conquered by
the Muslims, or that inter-caste marriages were common among
the *Antyaja*. Al-Biruni was a Persian who had stayed in Ghazni
and had travelled to India for six years. His description of the
Muhammad's rule is an eyewitness account. Ghazni, the capital
city, built so arduously by Muhammad with the loot of India (e.g.,
136 metric tons of silver were looted from Kangra fort alone) was
subsequently plundered for seven days by another Muslim, and

[1] Al-Biruni, *India* (New Delhi: National Book Trust, 1983), v, xx, 9, 10.

then set ablaze (a Ghurid chieftain[2] in 1150 AD). Their internal conflict notwithstanding, the far West region of India by that time had begun to witness mass conversions,[3] which had a substantive presence of Buddhists, who, in turn, were largely Dalits. The invasion of India by the Muslim kings, here it may be stated, had begun during the rule of Caliph Umar, when the prohibition against expeditions to India was removed and plans to invade it began. The first invasion took place as early as 644 which was repulsed.[4] A better plan began in 710 AD.[5] During the Prophet's time, or as far as 636 AD, during the Caliph's time, invasion to India was disapproved as it was the land of perfect freedom.[6]

Majority of the Indian Muslims (approximately 95%) were Dalits and Other Backward Castes who had converted to Islam but continued with their hereditary caste roles. The percentage of Muslim population to Hindus was approximately 6–7 per cent. It was this demographic asymmetry and the fear of possible local revolts or the loss of political power that restrained the Arabic–Persian elite in its forced conversion of Hindus. Here, two points may be noted: first, the Indic residents had enjoyed large degree of freedom contextualized in its history despite graded hierarchical duties and rights which checked the conversion of the local residents to Islam. Second, Islam in India was 'casteized' which checked the acceptance of Indic Muslims by non-Indic elites. It substantively reduced their chances of vertical–horizontal social, economic mobility and kept them rooted to their castes. In other words, despite their conversion to Islam, their social status remained rooted to their castes resulting into

[2] Ravi K. Mishra, 'Islam in India and the Rise of Wahabism', *IIC Quarterly* 46, no. 2 (2019).

[3] Aniruddha Ray, *The Sultanate of Delhi (1206–1526)* (New Delhi: Manohar, 2011), 22.

[4] A. M. Zaidi, *Evolution of Muslim Political Thought in India* (New Delhi: Michiko & Panjathan, 1975), 25.

[5] Richard M. Eaton, *India in the Persianate Age* (New Delhi: Allen Lane, 2019), 32, 34.

[6] Ibid., 161.

their castes' imprinting Islam, and substantively Indianizing it. Simultaneously, the Arabic–Persian Islamic culture also arrived with the foreigners, percolated downwards over the centuries, and crept into the culture of the local Muslim converts who imitated the Arabic culture. The non-Indic Muslim elite, who had felt superior, prided itself of being non-Indic, and looked at the Indic residents contemptuously, was substantively responsible for partitioning India in later years when, demographically, Western and Eastern India became Muslim majority regions.

The political Islam entered into India in the 8th century AD as stated earlier; and it expanded to Punjab, Delhi and in other parts of India in subsequent years. Since then, until 1858, when the monarchy was abolished, Muslim monarchs through their rule for 1,000 years enacted two major changes that Muslim traders in India were not able to do in the pre-Sultanate years. They created, maintained and expanded their separate Islamic religious identity. Unlike pre-Islamic invaders, they did not adopt and merged themselves with Indic religions; and, second, they impacted Indic culture, language, literature and administration or Persianized it substantively. They also brought in new technologies, food, animals and plants that enriched India with diversity. In course of its expansion to new territories, it gradually, however, became Indic not only because of its political compromises it made or due to the social–cultural modifications it underwent over the centuries that facilitated its transition, but because it was subsumed by the liberality of the Indic civilization, which has been accommodative, flexible, tolerant and open to new ideas; or, at worst, as critics have argued, it had been indifferent, insular to the new development, which enabled the new immigrants to subsist and grow. In both cases, however, the Indic was not swamped over by Arabic Islam, which had originated and expanded with the idea of revealed knowledge primarily applied and accepted through propagation and conversion in the form of one book, one God, one religion, and of its world views treating others as Jahil, lacking wisdom, knowledge and consciousness; in other words, those who were not imbued with it were ignorant and needed to be brought out of Jahiliyyah[7]; also, it subtly sent a message of pre-eminence of Islam and Prophet as the awakened consciousness in relation to Kafirs, infidels and pagans.

In Indic Islam, there was no dual sovereignty like medieval Europe. The monarch was absolute sovereign who never shared his political supremacy or tolerated any encroachment to his power from any. The spiritual–judicial authorities had their autonomous domains, but they were always under the monarchs. With the consolidation of the political power in North India, particularly from the 12th century AD, the Muslim monarchs became more autonomous of the Arabic–Persian political culture. In other domains, however, non-political culture impacted deeply about which we will discuss later.

The Shariat was applicable only to Muslims who had accepted it. The demand to apply it on all was rejected by the monarchs.[8] The fear of popular revolts in the absence of homogenized Muslim community who were numerically miniscule, their sectarian conflicts among themselves and their lack of popular support to the elite restrained the monarchs in their Islamic acts.[9] The Muslim elite, in order to rule, expand and stabilize their regimes began to co-opt local elites in their structure as subordinate partners, which facilitated their public acceptance. The arrival and expansion of Sufi culture in the Indic region, which had emerged in Persia from below, further helped them. The expansion of it (Sufi) was with the tacit understanding of the ruling elite to deflect possible popular rebellion, if any, against the elite. The culture of the Muslim elite, in the meanwhile, had also begun to percolate downwards, substantively facilitated by the Sufi.

[7] Muzaffar Alam, *The Languages of Political Islam in India* (New Delhi: Permanent Black, 2004), 19.

[8] See Himanshu Roy and Muzaffar Alam, 'Zia Barani: Good Sultan and Ideal Polity' in *Indian Political Thought*, eds. Himanshu Roy and M. P. Singh (New Delhi: Pearson, 2017), 81.

[9] Alam, *The Languages of Political Islam in India*, p. 83.

The first major change in the polity was the formulation of a 'ranked and salaried bureaucracy' for the collection of land revenue and the functioning of the military's rank and file. It was the system of *iqta* and *iqtadar* inherited from Arabic–Persian world— a unit of land and its revenue collector—who was 'required to recruit, train, equip and command, a stipulated number of troops who would be available to the Sultan on demand'.[10] For, the very nature of their warfare and military organization was different from the Indians. The Turks were faster and their horse-mounted archers were better trained. The second major change was the system of jurisprudence, in which alien book and practices— the Quran, Sunnat, Hadith—written in an alien language had become the major source of delivering justice; and the third major change was the trappings of the *durbar*—the office of the Sultan—the kingship which drew its symbols and praxis premised on the legacies and inheritance from the Arabic–Persian world. In the initial few centuries of its rule in India, the rulers were the vassals of Persian monarchs. Only from the late 13th century, it began to acquire independent status. As their rule expanded to the new territories, which was purely due to the power of the sword, the three major changes, outlined earlier, were also extended to it with modifications and adaptations in the contextualized history of the time. In many territories, and on many occasions, the changes percolated downwards at their own, as these were associated with the ruling class; and at many places, they broke the temples and the Gods to subjugate, to instil fear and to convert the local residents to Islam to expand their political base; for, their political legitimacy in the initial centuries of their rule was from Muslims. Muslims from all over the world were welcomed and were suitably rewarded and placed in the administration, military, judiciary or durbar.

There were changes in the dynasties of the Muslim rules over the centuries; but the fundamental of the polity, as explained above, remained almost similar with minor modifications. Few

---

[10] Eaton, *India in the Persianate Age*, 35.

nomenclatures did change such, for example, as the *iqta* of the Sultanate period was Jagir of the Mughal times, which was more rationalized and nuanced; or Arabic–Persian became the official language of the state, administration and the court. The co-optation of defeated rulers as subordinate partners of the new ruling elite was now more pronounced, widespread and visible at this time. Or the rulers adopted different Indic cultural symbols in their royal insignia, but their feeling of insecurity in an alien land haunted them. 'The Hindus here are in such number that the Muslims in their midst are like salt.... As the Muslims and their army grow in strength, I shall then give the Hindus the choice of Islam or death.'[11] The Muslim elites kept on coming to India as invaders and immigrants till the 18th century; and the feeling of being a ruler kept on recurring till the end of the 19th century, as best reflected in the writings of Sir Syed Ahmad Khan[12] and in the presidential address of Rahimtulla M. Sayani of the Congress in 1896. Sir Syed Ahmad Khan had explicitly posited 'that Mahommedans can never accept Hindus as their rulers'. However, notwithstanding this, the popular praxis among the Ajlaf and Arjal, who were local converts, was largely Indic.

The political Islam was also manifest in the application of religious taxes and in jurisprudence which were reflected in the forms of *jazia* and Sharia; while *jazia*, the tax was imposed on Hindus, Sharia, the Islamic law, was not officially imposed; but many Hindus received judgements within its legal framework. In fact, in the administration of justice, which was headed by a *Qazi* who was familiar with the Sharia and other Islamic laws, it was easier for him to deliver justice accordingly. The Hindu subjects accepted their judgements on issues which were part of non-religious, secular–economic domain linked with trade conflicts, land disputes, etc. In case of conflicts between Hindus and Muslims, or in cases of rebellion against the state, the punishment for

[11] Iltutmish cited in Alam, *The Languages of Political Islam in India*, 83.

[12] For details, see Himanshu Roy, ed., 'Religion, Minorities and the Indian State in Narendra Kumar', in *Politics and Religion in India* (London: Routledge, 2020).

Muslims was minimal, while the Hindus were punished severely. For a lighter punishment, they had the option to convert to Islam. The *Qazi* and the jurisprudence were largely guided by the Hanafi Sunni Islam, at least Aurangzeb tried to apply it in his kingdom.

The political Islam actuated two contradictory trends. It created a unified political kingdom from Gandhara to Dhaka but, simultaneously, also created two religious communities. Instead of merging with the Indic, as all the preceding invaders had done, it rather converted the Indic subjects to Islam. It did not remain, like a salad bowl, static with an Islamic identity. It was dynamic and competed with Hinduism. Maybe, therefore, Hindus looked down upon Islam with hatred, as M. N. Roy had stated. Dinkar substantiated it by stating that Muslims' brutality (*atyachar*) in India was incomparable. What the Hindus had received from Islam that is the image they have about Islam,[13] which remained distinct despite passage of time.

Cultural Islam

The new ruling Muslim elite brought in its wake a new script and a language of administration, which gradually became the state language and, subsequently, also the ideological state apparatus. This was a non-Indic, alien language and script that was imposed on the Indic subjects from the top, which had the backing of the sword. It was the part of political Islam. In course of time, dictionaries were created to translate Indic words to Persian or vice versa for a better understanding of subjects and their history; or Indic, Persian interchangeably texts were translated for pedagogy. A partial organic growth of language, Urdu–Rekhta could emerge only in the 18th century, the script remained Arabic and the language became Hindavi–Hindustani. But it too remained confined to urban centres and within the precincts of the non-subaltern sections; the vast majority of rural subjects remained confined to

[13] Hazari Prasad Dwivedi and M. N. Roy, cited in Ramdhari Singh Dinkar, *Sanskriti Ke Char Adhyaya* (Patna: Udyachal, 1990), 263, 272.

their regional dialects and scripts, which had received a boost in their growth after the arrival of political Islam.

Political Islam had imposed its culture as the culture of the new ruling elite. The new Arabic–Persian culture was first adopted by the defeated Indic rulers who were co-opted as subordinate partners in the elite structure, which remained confined to urban centres. What was considered as a composite culture was essentially a result of conversion, converts adopted the Islamic culture while also carrying the Indic culture; this was partly midwifed by the Sufis. In the process, Islam was partially Hinduized with *mazar*, music and pomp. Equally important in the Hinduization process was the prosperity and climate of India that had impacted the immigrants in their everyday routine which was visible in their food, clothing and housing; their own cultural background, in return, impacted the architectural design, cuisine and culinary habits of Indic residents. Its adoption by Indic converts, and later on, by Hindus was more in urban centres. Those who intended to join the administration were persuaded to adopt Persian culture. Rural India, which constituted 90 per cent of the population, remained largely Indic. Villages, particularly in North India, where Muslim immigrants were granted lands for their settlements, adopted elements of Arabic–Persian culture.

As this elite structure weakened, particularly in the 18th century, and in subsequent years, the composite culture grew faster. But it was not a homogenized culture that transcended religious identity. The religious identities remained, but the non-religious elements became similar adopted by the Indic subjects which was more urban, segmentary and sectional; it was not universal or pan-Indic. Imposition, imitation and conversion had played an important role in the spread of this Persian culture. Here, a pertinent point emerges which needs to be explained: why Islamic precepts were not acceptable to the majority of Indic subjects despite its rule and message of equality preached for approximately 1,000 years in a graded society of pre-democratic, medieval India. To answer it, it may be stated here that the Indic civilization has been wide open to new ideas, had a wide degree of individual and social freedom in comparison to other premodern civilizations and provided wide opportunities of livelihood and freedom of development to everyone, which was even endorsed by Prophet Mohammad and the first two Caliphs. It was only during the period of the third Caliph (Usman) that the permission to attack India was granted. This freedom and opportunities for which invaders and immigrants came to India was the impediment in the expansion of Islam here, which, despite centuries of rule, could not conquer India in terms of religion. Hardly 7–8 per cent of the population, mostly subaltern, converted to Islam, which was substantively midwifed by the Sufis. Unlike Hinduism and the other Indic religions, Islam lacked religious pluralism and tolerance; instead, it perpetuated one book, one flag and one Prophet. It did not permit religious freedom out of this perimeter. Even within Islam, it did not tolerate Shia, Ahmadiyya, Khoja and Memon. It was a Sunni-dominated sectarian religion. Furthermore, its arrival in India was graded and hierarchical. So its messages of equality were more of a hoax in praxis. It did not appeal to Indic subjects who were habitual to wide freedom. They saw through this façade their dichotomies and the inner functioning of this religious community. It was this rejection, even by the Arjal and Ajlaf who were part of the graded Indic social structure, that restricted the expansion of conversion to Islam.

But, unfortunately, a section of new converts acted as instrument in the expansion of Islam, many times being at the fore front. Thinking of themselves as fellow religionists of the new ruling elite, they acted in the mission mode in propagation and conversion. The feeling of liberation and equality gave them new energy to act with the missionary zeal; they began to flaunt and looked towards Mecca–Medina or Arab–Persia as their own. It was their cultural uprooting. The tragic part was that the Arabs did not consider them as their own and looked at them contemptuously. This pincer-like cultural dichotomy pushed them into an alienated, insecure social position where they were neither religious nor cultural. Both religions and culture impacted each other to an extent, but they never fused into one. They remained two parallel separates entities. The Arabs always respected and trusted their fellow Arabs, not the Indian Muslims. Even Hindu converts who were part of the Muslim elite structure were not trusted upon; they were rather suspects, at least in the eyes of the mullah and the Arabs.

Some of the cultural elements that emerged out of the interactions between the two religions and cultures over the centuries are interesting to note here. *Taziya*, for example, was one such case which was not in practice in the Arab world. Another was Shab e-Barat; the third was the Khairat; the fourth was public bathing and many such elements were imitated from Hindus, particularly from the marriage and death rituals. Hindus learnt or enforced the purdah on their women in the public domain,[14] particularly the elite. It was less enforced on the subaltern women; it was not possible to be in purdah while working in the fields. *Jauhar* was another Hindu phenomenon that was adopted and enacted for the women of the harem of the ruling elite to protect their honour when it lost the battle against the Muslim invaders. Then, food, clothing, etc., were adopted from the Arabs. Many of the new technologies came with Arabs: rahat (Persian wheel) driven by animals to draw water from the well or paper to write were their new contributions.

They were also meticulous history writers, unlike the historians of the pre-Islamic India who lacked the art of comprehensive history writing. The problem was of accuracy, details, dates, years, context, writing style, etc. While the history of the Islamic period was written in prose and was filled up with details, the same cannot be said about the pre-Islamic historians. It should be clarified here that more than 90 per cent of the manuscripts of the pre-Islamic period are yet to be translated. But based on what is available till now, the observation may not be out of place. Many of the translated manuscripts are commentaries on particular important texts such as, for example, Manusmriti,

---

[14] Ibid., 472–473.

Shukraniti, Arthashastra, etc. The training schools focused on the art of memorizing and style of debating in the Hindu tradition rather than on the art of history writing as it was practised during the Muslim rule.

The focus of education and the method of imparting skills to students in Hindu and Muslim schools varied. While the language of education was mother tongue or Sanskrit or Indic in Hindu institutions, in Muslim *maktabs* and madrasa, it was Arabic–Persian, and the Quran was an important component of the syllabus. The subjects also varied. But it was not a compartmentalized kind of manual. There were interchangeable and interlinked learnings.[15] As the time passed by, many of the Muslim scholars produced literary works on local themes, while Hindus wrote in Persian, particularly after the imposition of Persian as the state language by Akbar. It also marked a shift that forced many Hindus to learn Persian for livelihood and upward social mobility. It also led Hindu students to study in Muslim schools. Persian acquired importance, and its acquaintance was tagged as suave and urbane. In both religions, caste was not an impediment; students from all castes were present in schools run by Muslims or Hindus.

Women seclusion was more stringent in upper-class Muslim women. Hindu converts, particularly the Arjal and Ajlaf, imitated them. Yet it was not so fastidious due to their works in the fields, *karkhanas* or homes.[16] Widow remarriage and divorce were prevalent among them, which was also applicable to subaltern Hindu women, who enjoyed more individual and social freedom as they were earning members of the family. Among the upper castes, it was restricted. Hindu girls had the freedom to go to schools, while Muslim girls were educated at home, particularly about the teachings of the Quran.

The Islamic culture was more widespread in the urban centres in the north-west India, northern India, Bengal and its adjoining

[15] Alam, *The Languages of Political Islam in India,* 178–179.
[16] Neena Kumari, *Madhya Kaleen Bhartiya Samaj and Sanskriti* (Hindi) (New Delhi: Research India Press, 2019), 161–165.

parts of Assam. Rural India and South India had lesser impact because they were not so intensely deep into it. But they were not insulated either or remained pure. Its arrival and expansion into the newer segments of subjects created tension and social distancing, alienation, brutality and energetic outbursts.

Social Structure of Islam

Islam became Indic substantively only when it was taken over by castes. Families that converted to Islam continued to perform their caste professions. There was no structural rupture; rather, Muslims were co-opted and adopted. Invaders and fellow immigrants–co-religionists—who came to India from all the regions of Arab, Persia, Turkmenistan, Uzbekistan, etc.—became the ruling elite. They were called as the Ashrafs, Sajjads, Turks, Pathans, Sheikhs, etc. There was an internal hierarchy and there was internal jostling for being higher on the social ladder. Brahmans and Rajputs who converted to Islam were co-opted as Ashrafs. Slaves who came to India with their masters, if they were in prominent political administrative positions, were part of the upper crust of Indic Islam; the others worked in *karkhanas* as skilled craftsmen or as support auxiliary staff of their masters.

Muslim invaders kept on coming to India until the 18th century and their co-religionist immigrants until the first half of the 19th century. It was this elite which imposed its administration, language and mosques by sword when it conquered the territories. Their continued existence as the rulers forced the Indic subjects to adopt the minimum of it required to survive. Centuries later, the conversion of Sufis and the compulsion of rule generated a composite culture that was more urban and segmentary, and had emerged only in the 17th century and early decades of the 18th century. Marriages which were the best reflection of this social composition were arranged according to the internal hierarchy of cultural backgrounds of the elite. Pathans married Pathans, Turks married Turks, Iranians married Iranians and so on. There was no transcending of this internal hierarchy.

The girls of Hindu elite families were gifted to Muslim elite families to enhance their political–administrative status. But the reverse, from the Muslim to the Hindu, was rare. Apart from it, from the 1870s, political and social tensions emerged when the bottom erupted in support of Indic languages. The Muslim elite had become desperate to hold on to their privileges and political power, which was not forthcoming after the 1857 revolt, as reflected in their insistence on perpetuating Arabic–Persian scripts and languages; or in seeking political parity with Hindus in legislative bodies. The façade of composite culture in the absence of political power had blown off. Their Islamic, in fact Arab, identity, its fangs and fightback had become visible by the end of the 19th century. This was more manifested in the Ashrafs, who were once the ruling elite. But being a tiny segment among Muslims, they needed the support of the Ajlaf and Arjal to realize their objective, which could come forth on the premise of Islam. The slogan 'social justice for Muslims' linked all the three caste blocks among Muslims and provided the Ashraf unprecedented support in their quest for power.

The Ajlaf, the middle castes of Indic Muslims with their largest number, are the traditional village craftsmen now known as the Other Backward Castes who were the last among the Hindus to be converted to Islam. The Arjal, the untouchables, were the first among the Hindus to be converted to Islam as they were at the bottom of the social rung who had nothing to lose. The political elite among the upper castes Hindu, who were to lose their power if they did not become Muslims, converted to Islam early to retain their power as co-opted, subordinate partners of the Muslim invaders. All three caste blocks were multi-layered and plural with all their caste features. The only similarity among them was their Quran, Prophet and flag. Many of the families still carry their Hindu gotras, family and village lineages, deities and rituals.

Among the crafts that Ajlaf practised were of *lohar* (ironsmith), nai (barber), weaver (*Julaha*) and carpenters or of any mid-level crafts that varied by location. They owned land, cultivated their family landholdings, received their wages in grains or cash in lieu of their services and products provided to the villagers or local businesses. Within them, there is hierarchy; in fact, there is untouchability,[17] particularly among the Arjal; marriages are held within their castes and professions. But the commonality among them, apart from their religion, is that they all have access to the households of upper caste families, who were their *jajmans* or primary customers. This was akin to the functioning of Hindu castes,[18] which were specialized skills constantly required for production as India was the trading centre of the world in pre-colonial times. The conversion to Islam, therefore, did not make a dent to the caste structure. The requirements of the specialized products and services in society kept the Ajlaf engaged with their Hindu *jajmans* despite their conversion. It was equally applicable in reverse order where the *jajmans* were Muslims and the services were provided by the Hindus. There were wide regional and sub-regional variations among Muslims, just as there were among Hindus. The perpetual shortage of labour with the expanding villages and the constant requirement of skilled labour for export kept the castes interdependent despite their religions.

The last among the Muslim castes were the Arjal, who were the untouchables and practised untouchability among their fraternal castes, akin to Dalits among the Hindus and performed their hereditary professional works. Their works varied in different regions, but, despite conversion, their professional works continued. Positional shifts in their works, particularly due to social mobility and trade requirements, were occasional, episodic occurrences, not recurring, constant process. The change was a group occurrence. Their conversion to Islam, in early years, was

---

[17] Imtiaz Ahmad, ed., *Caste and Social stratification among the Muslims* (New Delhi: Manohar, 1973), 24. In his introduction, Ahmad writes that the members of groups within the higher categories do not eat or drink with the Lal Begis, a caste of Muslim scavengers. The Dafalis, who work as priests for the Lal Begis, or the Qalandars who sometimes live in their neighbourhood, refuse to accept food or water from Lal Begis.

[18] Ibid., 23. Imtiaz Ahmad writes, 'this pattern does not constitute a basic departure from the Hindu Caste Pattern.'

also a group occurrence. The conversion was aimed to upgrade their social position; but, despite the objective, they continued with their past, practised untouchability within the Arjal castes and rationalized it in religious terms.[19] In fact, it was equally applicable to Ashraf and Ajlaf as well. It was argued in academic discourse that 'caste was consciously adopted by the Muslims in India as a compromise which they had to make in a predominantly Hindu environment'[20] which may not be accurate as later research have shown otherwise. Imtiaz Ahmad has argued that 'Islamization serves to reinforce rather than weaken or eliminate caste distinctions.'[21] Invaders and immigrants, the new Muslim ruling elite, who had acquired power by sword, were treated locally as equivalent to the upper castes. They comprised 2–3.5 per cent of the elite, with the upper caste Hindu converts accounting for the remining 2.5–3 per cent of the elite. Together, they constituted 5–6 per cent of the Muslim elite, the Ashraf. Except for these immigrants, the Muslim converts broadly reflected the caste composition of the Hindu social order, with 75–80 per cent of the Other Backward Castes, the Ajlaf, and 15–20 per cent of the Scheduled Castes, the Arjal. They performed similar works, by and large, what their counterparts among the Hindus did; or, in other words, they continued with their profession despite their conversion to Islam. This continuation of castes among the Muslims kept them Indic. Their cultural continuation remained substantively rooted in the castes—the skilled labour—and the localities—the local cultural ethos—despite imitating an alien history and rituals of Islam after their conversion, which had created an abrupt social hiatus in the localities and in pan-Indic society.

The conversion, however, had partially made them global through their cultural imitation of the Muslim elite, who were Arabic–Persian and perpetuated their religious cultural identity without merging with the Indic as the earlier invaders had done. The Arabic–Persian elite was highly contemptuous of the local

[19] Ibid., 28.
[20] Ibid., 29.
[21] Ibid., 30.

converts—the Ajlaf and the Arjal—but needed them for the stability of their rule, which was midwifed by their religious identity of Islam.

Conclusion

Islam in India could not convert the whole of Hindus to its ideology in its ruling years as it did in the whole of Arabic–Persian world. It did, however, succeed in creating an identity of its own and a social hiatus that still persists. It partitioned the land and people based on Islamic identity that bonded the Ajlaf and Arjal with Ashraf. It simultaneously broke up with the Hindus; whenever they were in psychological crisis, they looked towards the Arabic world for their succour. In fact, they felt pride in it and insisted on maintaining their Arab identity. Sir Syed Ahmad Khan had argued that Muslims were a separate *kaum*, that Mahommedans can never accept Hindus as their rulers and that

> they are ready to sacrifice themselves for that glory which they still inherit from their fore fathers who were erstwhile rulers of India.... We are those who have ruled India for six or seven hundred years.... Our nation is of the blood of those who made not only the Arabia, but Asia and Europe, to tremble. It is our *kaum* which conquered the whole of India by sword, although its people were all of one religion.[22]

The tragic part of it was that 3 per cent of the Muslim invaders and immigrants succeeded in perpetuating their culture in the 97 per cent of Muslims who were Indic, the local converts. In their everyday praxis, they remained rooted to their localities, and they equally felt diversified in non-religious culture with their co-religionists who were from other regions. They continued with their diffused landholdings, customary rights and enjoyed a wide degree of social–individual freedom. The Caliph was, at best, of notional, symbolic value with no effective command; there was

---

[22] Zaidi, *Evolution of Muslim Political Thought in India*, 25.

no extension of his episcopal order. Their professional skilled labour, of different castes, continued; their marriages and social relations remained endogamous within castes and the *jajmani* system continued.

In a nutshell, Muslims in India had dichotomous existence. The conversions to Islam created the dichotomy. The Muslim invaders and immigrants considered themselves Arab; the percolation of this identity among local converts, and their acceptance of it, was the root cause of this social disconnect. More the Arabic and Wahabism of Islam for religious purification, more was the social disconnect of the Muslims with the Indic. Had they rejected this identity, the social disconnect with the Indic world would not have happened. The rejection of one's own history and the acceptance of other's history as their own becomes problematic in history.

9

Idea of Justice in Tribes of Manipur

Vijaylakshmi Brara

Background

Justice, like truth, does not vary from place to place or from time to time. Yet the manner in which it is sought may differ. The broad sense of justice is divided into distributive justice and corrective justice by Aristotle. Distributive justice works to ensure a fair division of social benefits and burdens among the members of the community. It serves to ensure equilibrium among the members of the society. When this equilibrium gets disturbed by an act of an individual or a group by way of violence, robbery and any other such crime, the balance is restored by forcing the wrong doer to compensate by means of serving a punishment or any other restitution. This is called corrective justice. In a modern society, punishments are such that they act as deterrent and are preventive as well as reformatory in nature. The tribes in Manipur as elsewhere may not have equivalent terms for distributive and corrective justice, but they do have a strong sense of what is right and wrong.

Somewhere down the line, the state and the policy initiators put the traditions of a sense of justice into a bracket of customary laws confining them to their geography while adopting a foreign model in their pursuit of becoming 'modern'. Hence, laws were framed and not evolved; jails were constructed, and the whole system was geared towards 'punishing the guilty'.

This chapter has tried to understand the sense of justice among some of the tribes in Manipur through their indigenous outlook of bringing equilibrium rather than secluding the guilty. Of course, it is not left without a critique. I conclude this chapter by bringing in the issue of the codification of customary laws and the impact on women. This chapter also dwells on the background, drawing comparisons from other Northeast states. More specifically, the Tanzania case study is the focus of attention as it strikes a parallel with the understanding of the philosophy behind the customary laws. Part I deals with the concepts and the customary laws of various tribes. Part II deals with the more specific question of customary laws and their impact on women, along with the issue of their codification. This chapter is the outcome of a study of both written and oral repository of the customary laws. The oral information was sought from the tribe's elders through long interviews.

Part I

The indigenous communities have had their laws of life sustenance. But with modern institutional frameworks, they also have to incorporate modern jurisprudence simultaneously. In India, one is the Indian legal system, based on the written Indian Constitution, and the other is based on the tribal customary laws. The Indian legal system has codified laws which are written down along with the detailed guidelines and the procedures which need to be followed. It is based on the philosophy of retribution. The underlying theme of retributive philosophy is that the suffering of the culprit should be coterminous with the suffering of the victim. Therefore, punishing the guilty is the main premise. The punishment aims to satisfy the victim and/or his/her family and friends. Society wants the offender to pay a certain debt to society so that some kind of normalcy can be restored. The Indian penal code only focuses on a particular crime. The court room procedure is there to see whether the person is guilty or innocent with the interplay of evidence, witnesses and arguments. The opposing groups do not interact much and remain hostile to each other.

The philosophy of customary laws, on the other hand, is thoroughly enmeshed in the mores of society. The natural world, the human world, agricultural practices and the rite of passage are placed in a harmonious manner, the balance of which is the prime aim of the indigenous world view. According to **Ada Pecos Melton,** these laws

> Are guided by the unwritten customs, traditions and practices that are learned primarily by example and through the oral teachings of tribal elders. The holistic philosophy is a circle of justice that connects everyone involved with the problem or conflict on a continuum. The crux of the matter is to deal with the underlying issues that need to be resolved to attain peace and harmony for the individuals and the community.[1]

There is a certain continuity that starts with the disclosure of the crime, followed by discussions and resolutions with the ultimate aim of making amends and restoring relationships. The main aim is to heal society, to bring back harmony with all beings and the surrounding nature.

Imbibing the Values of the Right and the Wrong

The lessons through stories and anecdotes are a starting point of transmitting indigenous knowledge into the young minds of the children in their respective tribes. The kitchen, with its burning hearth, is the centre around which these tales are told and retold. The tales range from the idea of goodness, truthfulness, sense

---

[1] Ada Pecos Melton, 'Indigenous Justice System and Tribal Society,' *Judicature* 79, no. 3 (November–December 1995): 126–133, available at https://www.ojp.gov/ncjrs/virtual-library/abstracts/indigenous-justice-systems-and-tribal-society (accessed on 28 June 2021).

of justice, respecting elders, understanding land use, knowledge of different herbs, agricultural cycle, to the art of weaving and the art and ethics of war. There are no formal classrooms, but knowledge is transmitted by the elders of the family through *phunga wari* (stories around the kitchen hearth). Such a transfer of indigenous knowledge gets imbibed into the very psyche of the children of each tribe. The knowledge imparted within the household gets its institutional bases in the youth dormitories, separate for boys and girls, in each village. They are generally called the *morungs* among the Nagas and *som inn* among the Kuki-Chin-Mizo tribes. These *morungs* are fully residential and have a strict regimen. The boys and girls are responsible for all the collective festivals, *jhum* (slash and burn) and other activities of the village. A boy or girl coming out imbibing the traditional knowledge systems assimilates the values of right and wrong very strongly. But on my recent visit to some of the villages, I was told that these traditional institutions are losing their base because the new religion does not favour the continuation of the preaching of the ancient faith. In fact, it was very difficult to gather information on the indigenous knowledge systems in this part of the region.

Punishment is seen very differently in tribal societies. But today, many indigenous communities have started to desire a confinement kind of punishment for heinous crimes. The customary practices of punishments still revolve around ridiculing, shaming, whipping in public, expelling from the village, taking away the right to a member of the community, fines in cash and/ or kind and committing to social service.

Among the Paite community (one of the tribes in Manipur), the variety of penalties is limited to compensation. Even in the extreme case of murder, although the compensation becomes very high (10 mithuns or equivalent cash and a shawl), there does not seem to have laws of imprisonment or a death sentence.

Recent studies have shown that customary laws and institutions are the most influential in land and water allocation and settling land and water use disputes. Moreover, customary laws and institutions are viewed to be more successful in managing rural water resources than imposing formal laws. This is because most State centred policies for managing natural resources have failed due to faulty designs for resource management programmes, inefficient implementations, and corruption.[2]

Although this quote is from a case study of Tanzania, it can be tailor fit to describe the situation in India vis-à-vis customary laws, especially in Manipur state.

The reason why I am citing this study is because African political systems, just like the political systems of Manipur, are characterized by each tribe's customary laws. Although this study primarily focuses on customary laws in the management of drinking water in Tanzania, the reason why I am taking this up is to understand that there is a need to compliment the statutory laws for them to be implementable. At the same time, statutory laws need to learn from customary practices the essentials of preserving and protecting the biodiversity and indigenous knowledge systems.

Nkonya's study of Tanzania indicates that most rural people in this country have formulated their own laws to effectively manage their water resources and are not very aware of statutory laws relating to water. Since they themselves formulated and regulated the laws, the simple fact of their participation made these laws effective and implementable.

This is true of customary laws across the globe. The participatory nature, the fact that they have been imbibed since birth and is therefore very well understood and sanctified by society, gives impetus to their practicability when it comes to their implementation vis-à-vis land and other natural assets as well as intratribal equilibrium. Yet one cannot ignore the group/elite/gender bias

---

[2] Leticia K. Nkonya, 'Customary Laws for Access to and Management of Drinking Water in Tanzania,' *Law Environment and Development Journal* (2006): 50, available at *http://www.lead-journal.org/content/06050.pdf* (accessed on 28 June 2021).

present in these laws, which renders them restrictive and regressive and becomes exclusive in nature, debarring a certain category of people to enjoy their societal rights as well as natural resources.

There are at present 33 Scheduled Tribes recognized by the Government of Manipur. These tribes can be broadly classified into the Naga and Kuki-Chin groups. Amongst the Naga tribes, the traditional village administration is looked after by the village chief with the help of the village elders, who may be elected or hereditary, who normally decide the disputes on the basis of a collective decision. On the other hand, amongst the Kuki-Chin groups, the administration is concentrated in the hands of the village chief, who owns the land and will enjoy absolute power over the villagers. Even now, both in remote Naga and Kuki-Chin areas, people do resort to resolution of disputes at the village level through customary laws.

According to Cobo, 'among the most distinctive features of the tribes are their unique cultural patterns, social institutions and legal systems.'[3] How these practices and features get assimilated into the systems of government of their respective regions varies according to their varied ideologies, ranging from highly centralized to federal political institutions. It's a matter of great satisfaction that, even though the tribes live within the broader state systems with written and formalized laws, many of their customs and traditions, what we refer to as customary law, continue to be upheld. But at the same time, it is been seen that, increasingly, there are moves whereby these laws are getting eroded or assimilated. With growing ideologies as well as the move towards centralization, the customary laws, each peculiar to their respective tribes, are suffering from neglect in the policy initiatives of various countries. This move towards marginalization, particularly in the Asian region, has been initiated since the

[3] José Martínez Cobo, 1986, *Study of the Problem of Discrimination against Indigenous Populations*, United Nations NE/CN.4/Sub.2, available at https://www.un.org/development/desa/indigenouspeoples/publications/martinez-cobo-study.html (accessed on 28 June 2021).

times of conquests and colonization. Nevertheless, we can see from countries such as Philippines, China and India that many tribes have been able to retain a lesser level of political, but a fairly substantive level of legal, autonomy. In the Manipur context, in addition, conversion to Christianity has also weakened the base of customary laws, as now most of the decisions are undertaken by the respective churches or by the village council based on the rules laid down by the Bible.

Administration of Justice among Some of the Tribes of Manipur

The Marings

The Marings are mostly inhabited in the Chandel district of Manipur, bordering Myanmar. The term Marings is derived from the word Meiring, which means 'the people who keep the fire unquenched'.[4] They are believed to come out of the cave with the help of a black mithun with white spots. That is why mithun has a special place in all of their rituals.

So far as land is concerned, all land in the Maring villages belongs to the village community and not to any chief. But an individual family can acquire permanent rights over homestead land, terraced, wet rice land and *jhum* land for which the individual households are not required to pay anything to the village council, authority or the chief. The land is divided into two categories for revenue purposes.

As regards the administration of justice is concerned, in the past, they had institutions of chief priest, *khulpu*, and the administrative chief, the *khullakpas*, who were the highest authority. These offices were hereditary. But in the present context, the elected village authority, headed by the chairman, carries out the village administration. In addition, there is also a council that is

---

[4] Jeuti Baruah, *Customary Laws of Maring Nagas of Manipur* (Assam: Law Research Institute, Guwahati High Court, Sponsored by NEC, 2007), 2.

elected from within the village. The present system of administration of justice has three levels. The first is the village council,
which is headed by the traditional head, the *khullakpa*. Its functions are executive, administrative and judicial. The members of
the council formulate policies in conflict as well as in peaceful
times. They make and amend unwritten laws which are religiously
followed. The second is the area council or *chingshanglak*, which
has members from the surrounding villages. These members are
elected from the representations of the surrounding village councils. The third level is the Maring Council or Maring Uparup,
which is the apex body representing the whole tribe. This is not,
by any means, a government institution. It is a body to look after
the welfare of the whole Maring tribe. Crimes, such as infighting,
theft and cheating, are usually resolved by letting the offender pay
a fine for some hens, pigs, rice beer or some cash. But crimes or
disputes related to land bring in some magical elements. In cases
where no evidence can be found, the judgement is usually done
by dipping into the water. Out of the two contesters, whoever
comes out first is declared guilty. Alternatively, the village council
takes a handful of soil from the concerned land and mixes it with
the water and makes both the parties drink it. The person who is
not the real owner of the land hesitates to drink it as it is believed
to have a strong curse. The judgement is hence declared, and a
fine is imposed on the guilty. Another area of emphasis is on the
crimes involving adultery/immorality. The customs lay down
detailed procedure for a variety of ways in which adultery or an
immoral act can happen. A person leading an immoral life, 'liber-
tine' or playing 'harlotry', can even be excommunicated after the
warning given to him is not heeded. Among the Marings, gongs
are the most expensive and prized procession. This is included
in the fine along with a long list of rice beer, one mithun, three
hogs, five hens and a fine of some cash. This is the fine imposed
on a man who refuses to take back his wife or betrothal after she
is forcefully or even intentionally made to marry another man.
The man who married another man's wife or has a betrothal is
charged comparatively lesser fine of one mithun, two pigs, three
hens and two pots of rice beer. Similarly, the customary laws of

the Maring perceive immoral conducts in dormitories very seriously, as these are the places where a good Maring way of life is actually taught. Defiling such places is taken as an insult to their basic world view.

The Rongmeis

According to Vidyarthi and Binay Kumar, 'Every Rongmei village is ruled by its own chief called *Nampou*. The chief is given a prominent position at all social and religions gatherings and festivals of the village. The words of the chief are obeyed diligently.'[5] Parry describes the Rongmei chief as a leader in war, the owner of the village land and protector of the village.[6] And Rao has focused on his entitlements to portions of the meat of all animals killed in the village hunt during the festivals. The youths of the village help him in cultivating his fields and in the construction of his house. He is always offered the best rice beer (zou-ngao) during the festivals.[7]

Even though the Rongmei chief enjoys enormous powers, in the sense that he is considered as the supreme authority in almost all affairs of the village, in the administration of his village and for the welfare of his subjects, the village council, composed of the village elders, keeps a strict watch over his duties and functions. The elders maintain a balance by checking any misconduct by him. The jurisprudence of customary laws, looking after the development of the village and performing rituals have to be looked after by the chief. On the whole, the whole gamut of village life revolves around him.

Yet the highest decision-making body remains the village council or *thoubei*, also called *peikai*. *Peipouk* is its head, who

---

[5] L. P. Vidyarthi and Binay Kumar Rai, *The Tribal Culture of India* (New Delhi: Concept Publishing Company, 1985), 31.

[6] N. E. Parry, *The Lakhers* (reprint, Kolkata: Firma KLM Pvt. Ltd, 1998), 248.

[7] V. Venkata Rao, *A Century of Tribal Politics in India* (1876–1974), S. Chand and Company, Delhi, 118.

heads the pei or the village court. The other elderly men in the village are its members. There is customarily no seat or position for women of any age.

Just like the Tanzanian traditional laws relating to water, the customary laws of the Rongmeis are implemented effectively as they are ingrained in the psyche and minds of the people of this tribe. There is no death penalty. The resolution is through the imposition of hefty fines as well as the ouster from the village if the crime is of the most heinous kind. There is no book of laws. It's all oral handed down from generations.

As stated earlier, the village court consists of the village elders (only men) who are also members of the village council. The chief heads this court and decides on civil as well as criminal cases. In small cases, only a few members of the village court settle it. But in cases such as murder or adultery or rape, the members of the extended lineage from both sides are required to attend the proceedings. Any dispute within the same clan is resolved by their own clan's male elders.

The belief that the guilty will be punished by divine intervention where there is no other option left brings in the concept of taking an oath. An oath is kind of confession to the God. It is believed that if a person is guilty and also when he/she is not telling the truth, he/she will be inflicted by God's wrath. This belief is so strong that the village council, the elders and the chief are convinced that the accused will not dare tell lies. They are convinced that the God will surely punish the guilty if he/she does not confess the true facts. The oath is a submission of bare facts, and therefore, whatever is submitted is nothing but the truth. It is symbolically portrayed through fire. The guilty person holds the fire taken out of the furnace and swears in the name of the God. He/she then dips the fire into the water with a proclamation that he/she may also extinguish the fire if he/she is telling a lie. There are other symbols, like consuming powder made out of iron or earth collected from the site of landslides and even the symbolic forms of thunderbolts. By holding objects which are truly through the act of God, the wrong doer will be punished with the same power.

Other forms of ordeals as evidence of proving oneself innocent are as follows:

- Biting the teeth of a tiger (*kamang neih kaimei*): Here, the accused as well as the aggrieved party bite the tiger's tooth before the *peikai gandai* (village authorities). And it is believed that the one who is guilty will be eaten by the tiger.
- Immersion in the river (*dui khou-lupmei*): This is the most common form of ordeal undertaken to prove one's innocence. Both the complaining parties immerse themselves in the water simultaneously. The longer time one stays inside the water than the other comes out innocent.

The ultimate aim of these forms of trials is to end hostilities among warring groups and restoration of peace: in other words, as stated earlier, to maintain harmony and normalcy. The punishments are usually compensatory in nature. They involve payment of fines and/or kind. The amount increases with the severity of the crime.

The Maos

The Maos inhabit the Senapati district of Manipur. The topography is fully laden with megaliths of various sizes as well as memorial stones. These monoliths/megaliths are erected to commemorate the giver of the feast at the stone pulling ceremony called *zhoso,* which is the most prominent feature of the Mao way of life. Out of all the villages, Makhan is one of the oldest and the largest, consisting of five sub-villages.

The Maos are very strict regarding the customary rules of clan exogamy, though the strictness of the rules does not correspond with the level of punishment. All it needs is a blessing from the elders after performing certain sanctified rituals and offering a cow or a pig and some drinks to the village elders.

Land is considered the gift of God, and therefore, any attempt to collect revenue or impose taxes is strongly protested against. Maos have a homestead land which is inheritable. The woodland commonly known as *Shiikhu* is divided into segments, each of which is owned by a family, clan (khel) and the village community as a whole. The land next to *Shiikhu* is agricultural land, public land and terraced land which is owned by individual families and also by clan members and the community and is controlled by the village chairman. These lands are leased out to individuals who do not have land of their own.

The administration of justice in Mao society was carried out by the village authorities called *kotsiimeii*. Each village had its own village court called *makrii kasiina*. And its decision was final and binding. In earlier days, this was the only justice system and was confined to the village limits. In a dispute where there is a lack of evidence, an oath and ordeal play an important role. In disputes about land, an oath on the earth is taken, and in the case of timber, an oath on an axe is taken. If there is a dispute between two villages, then an oath to a cat is taken. The Mao justice system has four tiers: the clan elders, the village council, the area council and the Mao council. The Mao council is the apex body of all Maos. Lately, it has been called the Mao Naga Social Welfare Board. All these tiers pronounce judgements based on customary practices.

In cases dealing with murder where there is a lack of evidence, oath taking becomes an important act to prove that one is not guilty. In fact, oath taking is one of the prominent methods of redemption and is taken very seriously by the Maos. In the Mao customs, both the accuser and the accused are put on trial by taking an oath in order to find out who is right and who is wrong. The oath taker accepts the curse of God to fall upon him/her or on them by cutting short their lives if they are guilty. There are four kinds of oaths among the Maos. The first is for the least serious cases, *ochii ojii kahaino ai ekhulo*, which means 'if I am guilty, let the curse of heaven and earth fall upon me by cutting short my life.' The second is a little more serious case. It is done by holding a ginger stem in the hand of the oath taker and stating that if he/she is guilty, let the curse of God fall upon him/her by losing his/her offspring, like the disease that is infected by the ginger stem. The third kind of oath is usually between two villages where the eldest member of the clan holds his testicles in his hand and pronounces that if they are guilty, then let them and their offspring vanish from the earth. The fourth one is for the most heinous crimes in which the two parties hold a living cat and cut the cat into two pieces by saying that if the group involved is guilty, then let God kill them immediately. Naturally, the oath is taken with utmost sincerity and total belief in the curse of the almighty. Although serious research is needed to see how much this institution of oath taking has been eroded or metamorphosed into a new form by Christianity and Christian values.

The Tangkhuls

The Tangkhul society village headman is called an *awunga*. *Awunga* is regarded as the founder of the whole village. He is also the permanent leader of the whole village, whose position is hereditary. The chief of every clan is called *pipa*. A *pipa* of a clan can exercise veto power in taking any decision in the village council. The village council is called *hanga*. It consists of *pipas* of the clan and other nominated members who are known as *haugba*. *Awunga* is the head of the council and also the chief judge of the village court. The village court is in the residence of the *awunga*. The functions of *hanga* are general administration of the village, administration of justice, religious affairs, developmental activities, maintenance of culture, customs and traditions and defence of the village. The *hanga* has further different organs. The *Yaron Long* is the house of the unmarried male in the village. All the important works, such as games, sports, songs and dances, protection of any unusual happenings and even village defence, is assigned to them. *Ngala Long* is a dormitory for unmarried girls. But these institutions are today being replaced by schools, youth clubs and other organizations. Village assemblies are the highest decisions-making body, meetings of which are held twice in a year.

The whole system of Tangkhuls is built upon the clan system. The clan or *shangnao* is an association of people linked by uni-lineal descent.

As far as the land use is concerned, like the Maos, the Tangkhul land is also divided into the homestead (kha), the woodland, which can be owned by individuals as well as by the village, and adjacent to the woodland is the agricultural land. There is also public land which is used for planting useful trees which can be used by people by paying tax to the village council. The last is the terraced land, the ownership of which is with the individual families.

The administration of justice has three tiers among the Tangkhuls. The village court, the regional courts (*luiyan*) and the apex body are called the Tangkhul Naga Long Court. The mode of trial is the usual hearing, collection of evidence, swearing as well as the unusual ones which are immersing in river, drinking mud of the disputed land, throwing spears at each other, by waging war between two villages for seven years and fighting with a stick. Here again, oath taking is taken extremely seriously, and it is done when there is no evidence or witness to the said crime.

The Paite

The Paites belong to the northern Chin subgroup of the Kuki-Chin group, along with the Thadou, Vaiphei, Gangte, Hmar and others. It is believed that their ancestors migrated from Southwest China. They also call themselves Zoumi, literally meaning 'people of hills'. The Paites want to assert their own identity, and till now, only Thadao have accepted the term Kuki for themselves in Manipur. They mainly live in the Churachandpur district of Manipur. Unlike the Marings, Maos and Tangkhuls, the chief among the Paite occupies a very high position among the villagers. The chief is known as *hausa*. His office is hereditary. He is assisted by the village elders (upa), but his decision is final. But the Manipur (Village Authority in Hill Areas) Act, 1956, has given legal recognition to the term *khullakpa*. The chief, who is the *khullakpa*, automatically becomes the chairman of the statutory village authority. There is no classification of the land as the whole land belongs to the chief. The chief allots the land for different uses. He can expel a villager and can also bring new persons to cultivate the land. He even charges a premium while settling on fresh land. Every male adult pays the chief a basket of paddy called *taangseu* annually as a rent for farming on his land. If the chief is very oppressive, the villagers simply move to another village.

The traditional Paite court had the power to try cases from theft to homicide. But, unlike the other villages mentioned above, people in this community are moving to statutory institutions, such as the police and the magistrates' courts, especially for serious cognizable offences. Thus, the number of serious cases tried by the traditional village court is decreasing. Matrimonial cases, including elopement, adultery and rape, are still decided by the traditional village council. Other cases, such as violations of customary law, theft, abuse of all sorts and land disputes, also come up for trial in the chief's court. The punishment varies from arranging to give mithuns, pigs, jars of wine and, nowadays, even a sum of money. In extreme cases, the offender is excommunicated.

Although most of the time, the villagers are satisfied by the village court's verdict, those dissatisfied seek redressal in the government courts of the subdivisional magistrate's courts. The church nowadays plays a crucial role in dissolving cases through mutual reconciliation. The customary practices of the Paites are enforceable only within the boundaries of the village. For any intervillage dispute, the settlement is sought in the other government courts under the Indian Penal Code.

The Hmars

Besides the Paites, the Hmars also occupy the Churachandpur district of Manipur. There are two versions regarding the origin and meaning of the term Hmar. In one version, it means 'north', implying living north of Mizos. But that would mean that the term came into existence only after their settlement in Mizoram. This is untenable for many. Therefore, they seek another meaning. They say that Hmar is derived from '*Hmarh*', which means 'tying of hair at the nape'. Earlier writers, both British and Indian, were confused about the identity of the Hmars and put them under the Lushai or Kuki tribes. All this confusion was set aside when the Government of India put Hmars as one of the 31 Scheduled Tribes of Manipur.

Like the Paites or any other Kuki tribe, the village land belongs to the chief. This has drawn lot of silent resentment among the villagers. They used the villagers as personal servants without any wage, except giving food, shelter and clothing. Even in selecting the councillors he chose his own kinsmen and friends. Therefore, in deciding to distribute the *jhum* land, the councillors were given the most fertile land. With the introduction of Manipur Hill Village Authority Act of 1956, the chief became the ex-officio chairman of the village council, and the council members were directed to be directly elected through adult franchise. But since traditions are very deep set, the system more or less remained the same.

The land among Hmars is divided into two: the hill area where *jhum* takes place and the plain land for wet paddy cultivation. The hill is further divided into agricultural, forest, homestead and village common land.

The administration of justice is the prime function of the chief and his councillors. It tries all cases from theft to homicide. The most common conflict according to a survey[8] was defamation on the lines of sexual relations between boys and girls and also rape cases. According to this report, this was understandable with the absence of social restraint on the mixing together between

---

[8] Jeuti Baruah, *Customary Laws among Hmars with Special Reference to Their Land Holding* (Assam: Law Research Institute, Guwahati High Court, Sponsored by NEC, 2007), 55.

boys and girls.' There is a detailed and minutely laid down laws related to the defaming the women in Hmar society. It has been particularly emphasized in various documents related to Hmar customary laws. Earlier, there was a peculiar custom by which the murderers or other criminals took refuge in the chief's house to escape from the consequences. They surrendered before him and became his slaves (*chemson bawi*). But his safety was only guaranteed within the premises of chief's house. The system of ordeals and oath is not so much prevalent in the Hmar justice system, but a person's oath by placing a tiger's tooth in his mouth and saying that he may be devoured by a tiger if he is lying or diving in the water or swearing in the name of God did sometimes help the man to claim innocence. Fines have been the best way of retribution.

The Thadou Kuki

The chieftainship among Thadou Kuki has seven-tiered structure with the *hausapu* (chief) as the head. It has *semangpa* (prime minister), *pachong* (secretary), *thiempu* (physician and a priest), *thihiu* (blacksmith), *chonloi* (treasurer) and *lom-upa* (leader of the youth) and *kho-sam* (caller and announcer of the sermons and judgements). Here also, just like the Hmars, all crimes, including the most heinous ones, are punished through fines. Among the Thadous, the oath is taken by placing a bear or tiger's skull on the ground along with betel leaf, paddy husk and a sword. The person comes forward and pointing to the skull says, 'If I break faith, may a bear or tiger devour me and may the seed I sow be as fruitless as the husk and may I be hit by the sword. Heaven and earth now witness this oath.' Then, there is the dipping in the water and whoever brings any stone or mud from the surface faster is declared not guilty. Even in the case of murder, there are fines stipulated to represent certain parts of the body. *Dahpl* (gong) represents the head of the victim, *khichoung* (beads) represent the eyes, *khivui* (garland) represents the umbilical cord in addition to *puondum* (black cloth) to cover the dead body and *kosa*, a meal served to all the guests coming for the bereavement. *Hem kham* is stopping the sharp edge of the knife by the chief which symbolizes the restoration of peace is also very popular.

Compensation versus Vendetta

With the above description of the prevalence of customary laws, it is clear that the tribal community has a very strong sense of right and wrong. One of the most intriguing points is that every dispute gets resolved through compensation, even the most heinous ones. Revenge gives rise to further revenge and that, in turn, to further revenge. This thought must have worried the elderly, who then thought of restoring the equilibrium disturbed by any wrongs through compensation. A thief has to return to the owner the article stolen in addition to a little more payment. An adulterer has to pay compensation to the husband, an amount equal to that which would be required to marry a new bride. The wife who divorced her husband would have to return the marriage price. In this manner, the scales of compensation for all crimes have been evolved. Even in the extreme case of homicide, heavy compensation paid to the relatives of the disease assuaged the bitter feelings of the family, at least to the extent that it refrained from retaliation. Once the compensation was paid, society's equilibrium got restored.

P. P. Trivedi, the member of the Planning Commission, way back in 1983, said,

> The tribal system of administration of justice in the north eastern hilly areas has some inherent features which make for its strength and relevance, namely proximity, accessibility, speed and credibility. The venue of offences as well as well as the location of parties and witness is close to the place where justice is administered. The decisions are delivered in an open meeting in presence of the villagers where everybody knows everybody else. The proceedings are simple and do not involve much expense. It is relatively easy to seek and get redress. Due to proximity and accessibility the system

is most expeditious. The proximity, accessibility and speed make for the credibility of the system.[9]

The participatory nature of the customary laws as stated above, the fact that they have been imbibed since birth and therefore very well understood and sanctified by society, gives impetus to their practicability when it comes to their implementation. Yet one cannot ignore the group/elite/gender bias present in these laws, which renders them restrictive and regressive and becomes exclusive in nature, debarring a certain category of people to enjoy them in an egalitarian manner.

Part II

Women and Customary Laws

I move this section with the agreement that customary laws have given us the assured environmental safety net as well as a trust in human values, such as speaking the truth, confessing to a crime and a collective wish to fulfil the promises made by the ancestors to maintain peace harmony and equilibrium in the society. Yet it will be half-truth if we also do not accept the fact that these laws have shown certain regressive tendencies too. Earlier, they were based on egalitarian principles, but now, we see a tendency towards elitism and stark class divisions. Although the Kuki chief perpetuated it earlier too, political leaders in other tribes are also taking on. Hence, given that they are the primary beneficiaries, they are comfortable in their positions. These comfort zones are a bit uncomfortable as they narrow down the customs to suit the elite as well as men. In other words, it is perpetuating the regressive elements in these laws. In this customarily accepted system, decision-makers and the people in authority are all men. And this is a major lacuna

[9] Quoted in J. N. Das, *A Study of Administration of Justice among the Tribes and Races of North Eastern Region, Excluding Nagaland and Meghalaya* (Assam: Law Research Institute, Guwahati High Court, 1987), 682.

hindering any progression in the customary laws. Even when there were institutions where women were the heads, they were slowly filtered out in the selection–deletion process of writing history and culture. In the matrilineal societies of Meghalaya, the Khasis have a traditional institution called the *Dorbar*. Here also, women are not allowed to be members. So even though the lineage head is a woman, the authority rests on her brothers. Hence, in the famous enquiry of the students of sociology where they seek to answer whether matrilineal societies are the mirror opposite to patrilineal societies, the example of Khasi society is given to disprove this claim. The answer lies in not confusing lineage system with the notions of power. Patriarchy can exist in varied degrees in both patrilineal and matrilineal societies. The women in this part of the region, therefore, don't want to codify their customary laws as yet. While accepting the importance of preserving these laws as an integral part of their identity, they want to amend and make them gender inclusive and then to go ahead with the codification.

In Manipur, in the valley, inheritance is in the lines of the Hindu Succession Act since the majority of the community has been Hindu since the 17th century, when Hinduism became a state religion. How and why the tribes surrounding the valley did not convert to Hinduism has certain geohistorical as well as sociocultural reasoning. But that's a matter for another discussion on some other platform. Hence, in the valley comprising Imphal—east and west—Thoubal and Bishupur, sons and daughters have an equal right to inheritance. Yet in the necessity to fix the patriarchal image, many women with their benevolent daughter/sisterhood role forfeit their claim to inheritance. Cultural moors override the legal statutory provisions, again indicating that customs and traditions are more intrinsic to the society's collective consciousness.

Among the hill tribes of Manipur, the situation is quite grim when it comes to the inheritance rights of women. Here, customary laws are more stringent and in practice. The women, therefore, do not have many avenues for redressal. If you are a woman and a widow, you cannot demand any share in the property of your husband, which goes to the nearest male relative. This is an example of the Kuki tribe, but the same goes for the Tangkhuls, the Kabuis, the Marams and the Maos. Ironically, there is a historical legacy of women occupying a seat of power among the Nagas, according to Dr Jeuti Baruah. According to her,

> In times of war a woman named Maram Harkhosita was the supreme commander, village Kangpot and Thowai had a woman chief and Tolloi village council members were also women. Women were given the responsibility of the village granary. In granary festival (*Chumpha*) women were given the position of priest hood to perform rituals over grain store *Pukhrelas* were the daughters of the village who were given the responsibility of ushering in peace between two warring villages. *Meithalung* means oven and it broadly means kitchen government. Three stones are erected one for eldest son, the father and the mother. In the event of mother's death no body except the eldest daughter in law can take that seat and that too only if she is officially been ordained by the mother in law.[10]

When did women forfeit their political leadership roles among the tribes of Manipur as well as the other Northeast states? It is a matter of serious future research. Until now, I have not been able to find an answer to this exclusionary, hegemonic epistemology. There seems to have penetration of hegemonic patriarchal notions seeping in over a period of time among these communities. In the present scenario, barring the ritual importance given to women over the protection and decision over the granary, they have not been recognized as possible owners of agricultural lands or chieftainship.

---

[10] Jeuti Baruah, *Customary Laws of the Paite of Manipur* (Assam: Law Research Institute, Guwahati High Court, Sponsored by NEC, 2007), 45; Jeuti Baruah, *Customary laws of the Maos of Manipur* (Assam: Law Research Institute, Guwahati High Court, Sponsored by NEC, 2007); Jeuti Baruah, *Customary laws of the Tangkhul Nagas of Manipur* (Assam: Law Research Institute, Guwahati High Court, Sponsored by NEC, 2007).

Codification of Customary Laws

Customary laws are appealing and understood and, therefore, easy to implement. Since they are in accordance with culture and traditions of the society, they are imbibed and followed with an aim to receive justice and societal equilibrium. It is also an important marker of the respective tribal identity.

Over a period of time, with the establishment of a modern state with a centralized Constitution, there is also a growing fear that small communities, such as the tribes in Manipur, may get subsumed into the wider notion of the nation. Hence, there is perseverance in asserting the indicators of their identity through geography, beliefs, dress, food as well as the laws entailing their customs. Going back to their traditions is a way of asserting their identity. Thus, the tradition–modernity interface is a crucial component both in their identity reassertion and conflicts. It has implications both from a gender and a class perspective.[11]

Some tribes are trying to undo a few historical wrongs against women. For instance, the Paite tradition did not allow parental property to be passed to the daughter even in the absence of a son.

> The Paite Tribal Council in a 2004 amendment to this law introduced provisions in favour of daughters, widows, illegitimate or adopted and other disinherited sons. They allow the father to appoint one of his daughters to inherit property if he does not have a son. Her in-laws cannot force a widow to go back to her parents if she wants to stay unmarried in her late husband's house to look after her young children. A debate is also taking place among them on whether women should enter their decision-making bodies.[12]

---

[11] National Commission for Women, 'Land Rights of Women in Tripura', a monograph based on a research study undertaken by Tripura Commission for Women, available at http://ncw.nic.in/sites/default/files/LandRightsWomeninTripura.pdf (accessed on 28 June 2021).

[12] H. Kamkhenthang, *The Paite: A Transborder Tribe of India and Burma* (New Delhi: Mittal Publications, 2005), available at https://www.google.co.in/books/edition/The_Paite_a_Transborder_Tribe_of_India_a/n7CdTs3Iq78C?hl=en&gbpv=1&pg=PR3&printsec=frontcover (accessed on 28 June 2021).

They have a long way to go to attain equality but this is the first step.

According to Lucy Zeol, 'The community on its part needs no recognition to live according to its tradition. Its members follow the law out of respect or fear of the divine or because the community leaders use them as a social control mechanism.'[13] That creates the first contradiction between the formal and informal systems. Society or any social group is not a static organism. It is constantly evolving and is, by nature, dynamic. Since there is progression, the customs change or acquire new meanings. Customary laws, therefore, also need to undergo changes in their content, interpretation and enforcement in response to the situations that society faces in the present times. If a society refuses to change with the changing times, it gives its law a rigid interpretation, especially if the customs continue when its social base has disappeared. It then justifies its continuance or avoidance by attributing it to its ancestors or to its identity. For example, in some tribes, in which women have made progress in education and other spheres, men resist their access to equality by citing tradition and even quotations from the Bible to prove their applicability in modern times.

Malleability is essential for the customary laws to evolve from within. First and foremost, the issue of gender disparity needs to be addressed. The Paite community has shown the way. Despite the rise of the tribal women in education, visibility and breaking glass ceilings in various fields, customary laws keep women subordinate and deny them the right to participate in decision-making bodies and inheritance. The customary laws, therefore, have to encompass and recognize such societal changes. The plausible solution is for each tribe to document its laws and for women's leaders to initiate a debate on gender and class issues and introduce clauses that take them towards equality.

[13] Lucy Zehol, *Ethnicity in Manipur: Experiences Issues and Perspectives* (New Delhi: Regency Publications, Astral International, 1998).

References

R. Brown, *Statistical Account of the Native State of Manipur, and the Hill Territory under Its Rule* (Calcutta: Office of the Superintendent of Government Printing, 1872).

T. N. Subba, Joseph Puthenpurackal, and Shaji Joseph Puykunnel, eds, *Christianity and Change in Northeast India* (New Delhi: Concept Publishing Company, 2008).

Aboriginal System Implementation Commission, *The Justice System and Aboriginal People* (Manitoba: Government of Manitoba, 2015), available at www.ajic.mb.ca/volumel/chapter2.html (accessed on 28 June 2021).

10

Colonial Roots of Aryan Invasion Theory

Kundan Singh

Introduction

William Jones famously, by identifying close linkages between Sanskrit and European languages, gave birth to the idea of common ancestry between Indians and Europeans. In the earlier years of contention on the matter, he considered India as the cradle of civilization and Sanskrit as the mother of all Indo-European languages. With the rise in the imperial power of Europe over India, the cradle of civilization, however, began to shift outside India and ultimately landed in Europe. Simultaneously, the idea of the invasion of India by the 'Aryan race' or the Aryan invasion theory (AIT) was promoted. Since then, however, one archaeological finding over the other has consistently refuted the AIT, proving it false. As flawed as it remains, this theory has nonetheless persisted and morphed into its current form as the Aryan migration theory (AMT) and continues to find mention and favour in contemporary academic discourse. In mainstream academia today, whether in grade-school texts or in texts meant for undergraduate and graduate study, whenever India and Hinduism are mentioned, the coming of the Aryans from outside of India and establishing Hinduism and civilization in India are discussed as veritable facts.

By placing the discussion in anticolonial and postcolonial contexts, we show that, despite considerable archaeological evidence refuting either the invasion or the migration of Aryans into India, it is because of the theory's embeddedness in the notion of the racial superiority of Europeans or people with European ancestry that the theory does not fade into oblivion.

Genesis of the AIT

William Jones[1] outlined the connection between Sanskrit and European languages, contending for a common ancestry between Indians and Europeans. He was a student of languages, and in his view, Sanskrit is profoundly copious and far more refined than Greek and Latin are, and that these languages bear similarities in grammatical forms and verbs, which could not have been produced by chance. He also held that Sanskrit has similarities with the Gothic and Celtic languages and Persian, and thus, they belong to one single family.

The common ancestry theory, however, was not born with Jones, as Bryant[2] demonstrates. Such conjectures were prevalent even before him. Scholars such as Pere Coeurdoux, as early as 1768, have contended that Sanskrit, as the language of the Brahmins, came to India from Caucasia. There were others such as Nathaniel Halhed and James Parsons, a physician by profession and a fellow of the Royal Society and the Society of the Antiquities, who in the year 1776 had already drawn a connection between Indian and European languages. It was the reputation and stature of William Jones, who was a judge at the Supreme Court in Bengal, which engraved this idea in stone.[3]

---

[1] William Jones, 'On the Origin and Family of Nations,' *Asiatic Researches* 3. Reprinted in *The Collected Works of William Jones* (New York, NY: New York University Press, 1792/1993), 185–204.

[2] Edwin Bryant, *The Quest for the Origins of Vedic Culture: The Indo-Aryan Migration Debate* (New York, NY: Oxford University Press, 2001).

[3] This section of the book chapter is largely inspired by the research work of Bryant, *The Quest for the Origins of Vedic Culture*. Adequate attention has been paid to give credit to his ideas.

In the initial years of common Indo-European ancestry, India was the cradle of civilization. Thinkers of the Modern Era, such as Voltaire, Sonnerat, Schelling and Schlegel, argued that the epicentre of civilization was India, and that Europe owed its cultural and philosophical origins to India. Monboddo,[4] Halhed, Schlegel and Kennedy[5] believed that Greek and Latin were derived from Sanskrit. The mother tongue of all the Indo-European languages was Sanskrit. This theory, however, did not remain static. With the political ascendency of Europe over India, the mother-tongue theory began to fade into oblivion. One of the first people to challenge it was Franz Bopp, who felt that there was instead an 'original' tongue out of which Sanskrit as well as European languages were derived, though Sanskrit was able to preserve its originality better than others. The original tongue was termed the Proto-Indo-European language, of which Sanskrit became one of the daughters, albeit the eldest of them all. For the people thus represented by these ideas, the terms Indo-German, Indo-European and Aryan came into use beginning in the nineteenth century.[6]

With the decline in the status of Sanskrit as the original mother tongue of all European languages, India as the mother region of all Indo-Europeans also began to recede. Friedrich Schlegel's brother, A. W. von Schlegel, in 1842, asserted that, instead of migration happening from India to Europe, there existed some central region from which people went in different directions to Europe and India. Benfey, consequently, contended that since Southern India consisted of a 'tribal' population (and hence, by implication, inferior given the prominent discourse of the times), they had to be subjugated by the invading 'superior' Aryans from the North. Muir,[7] torturing the Sanskrit texts, claimed the gradual advance of the Aryans from the Northwest of India to

---

[4] J. B. Monboddo, *Of the Origins and Progress of Language* (Edinburgh: Balfour, 1774).

[5] V. Kennedy, *Researches into the Origin and Affinity of the Principal Languages of India* (London: Longman, 1828).

[6] Bryant, *The Quest for the Origins of Vedic Culture*.

[7] J. Muir, *Original Sanskrit Texts* (London: Trüber, 1860).

the East as well as to the South. The AIT was thus born. Post the First War of Indian independence against the British in 1857, as the British established their political suzerainty over most parts of India, neither India, as the home of the Aryans, nor Sanskrit, as the mother tongue of the European languages, remained. Chakrabarti writes, 'With the Raj firmly established, it was time to begin to visualize the history and cultural process of India as a series of invasions and foreign rules.'[8]

Given that colonizers and missionaries more often than not have been in cahoots with one another for the purpose of the global subjugation of peoples and cultures, both the parties seized the opportunity and began driving the AIT hard. A common ancestry of the Hindus and Europeans was an idea that had made most of the missionaries and colonizers uncomfortable. Missionaries, such as Alexander Duff and William Hastie, and colonizers, such as James Mill, opposed the idea tooth and nail and were more inclined to emphasize the differences between Indians and Europeans than their similarities. Disparaging Indians—their culture, civilization, traditions and religion—was the master note of their utterances instead of focusing on convergences or similarities. With the 'revelation' by the Madras School of Orientalism that Sanskrit and southern Indian languages did not come from a common root,[9] the aforementioned notion of 'Aryans' invading the 'Indians' began to gain further currency. The Vedas were further tortured to depict white and fair 'Aryans,' coming through the northwest, in conflict with the dark-skinned and flat-nosed 'Dravidians,' described as the original natives of the Indian subcontinent. The corollary to all this, as Trautmann[10] shows, was that the European Aryans brought civilization and Sanskrit to India. The conclusion fitted extremely well with the 'civilizing mission' notion of the Europeans: just as the Aryans of

---

[8] D. K. Chakrabarti, 'India and the Druids,' *Antiquity* 50, no. 197 (1976): 66–67.

[9] Bryant, *The Quest for the Origins of Vedic Culture*.

[10] T. R. Trautmann, 'Elephants and the Mauryas,' in *India: History and Thought*, ed. S. Muckerjee (Calcutta: Subernarekha, 1982), 245–281.

the past brought civilization, language and culture to the Indians of yore, the colonizers and missionaries were bringing a second wave of civilization to the intermixed and corrupted (hence, by default, inferior) Indians. The AIT served many different political ends for missionaries, colonialists, and 'native' Indians.[11]

The movement of the Aryan homeland from India to 'somewhere in Asia' to Europe also happened in successive stages. It was assisted by German philology. As an emerging nation, Germany had found itself lagging, in becoming a colonial power, behind some other European nations, such as England, France, Spain, Holland and Portugal, and it was desperately looking for sources that could bolster its national identity and ego. Sanskrit and India came in extremely handy for such an objective. If the Germans could show that they were the original Indo-Europeans, who were the cause of various European nations and India in history, their national pride would be stamped beyond question. This was the basis of their quest for a pure Indo-German race. The Indo-Germans could consequently not have a homeland in Asia. Therefore, the homeland of the Indo Germans/Indo Europeans/Aryans had to be changed first and had to be moved to Europe.

And indeed, the process began. Robert G. Latham, in 1862, proposed a European homeland for the Indo-Europeans. In 1878, the German philologist, L. Geiger, contended that Indo-Europeans were blond and blue-eyed people, and that these characteristics had become diluted and darkened where there had been an intermixing of genes.[12] Since the contention served the European sense of superiority, in no time, it began to gather steam and get regurgitated. Finding evidence of unadulterated blond, fair and blue-eyed Indo-Europeans in the areas of Germany, Austria, Switzerland and Belgium was easy. And thus, this area became the original homeland of the Indo-Europeans. The rise of Nazism was exclusively related to this appropriation, though

---

[11] Bryant, *The Quest for the Origins of Vedic Culture.*
[12] Ibid.

one must say that in the quest for the original homeland of the Indo-Europeans, scholars have virtually pointed to almost every part of Europe.[13]

In this melee, there emerged the German Indologist, Max Müller, who had been hired by the East India Company for the translation of the Sanskrit texts in its possession. He arbitrarily attributed the date of the Rigveda to around 1200 BCE. The arbitrariness of the dating was criticized by his contemporaries, to which he responded in 1890 that the dates were hypothetical, that it was difficult to tell when the Vedas were composed, and that he doubted if it would ever be determined whether the hymns came into existence in 1000 BCE or 2000 BCE or 3000 BCE.[14]

Consequently, the coming of the Aryans to India in 1500 BCE was determined—a date which gets regurgitated in all mainstream academic literature on India and Hinduism.[15] Before we address the contemporary archaeological evidence regarding the AIT, the following are three points that emerge from the above:

1. The issue of the Aryans and India has not been static. Over a period of time, the spectrum has evolved from India being the cradle of the Aryan civilization to being invaded by fair, blond and blue-eyed Aryans who had their homeland in Europe.

2. It has changed with the changing fortunes of India. That the 'Aryans' invaded India from the north-western frontier was a theory developed during the times when suzerainty of the British over India was almost complete.

3. The AIT is not divorced from—on the contrary, contiguous with—the imperialistic designs of the colonialists and the

---

[13] Ibid.

[14] B. B. Lal, 'Aryan Invasion of India: Perpetuation of a Myth,' in *The Indo-Aryan Controversy: Evidence and Inference in Indian History*, ed. Edwin F. Bryant and Laurie L. Patton (New York, NY: Routledge, 2005), 50–74. He cites Max Müller's own words in this regard.

[15] For instance, Gavin Flood, *An Introduction to Hinduism* (Cambridge: Cambridge University Press, 1996).

evangelical zeal of the missionaries. Depending upon the political and missionary expediencies, the AIT was used by various parties involved.

Indus Civilization and Contemporary Discourse on Archaeology

The truth has its own way of springing surprises. The established and dominant narrative at the beginning of the 20th century was that India knew no civilization before the coming of the Aryans. This was to change when, in 1924, Sir John Marshall (through the excavations initiated by R. D. Banerji and Daya Ram Sahni, respectively) announced the discovery of two ancient Bronze Age civilization cities—Mohenjo-Daro and Harappa—of what he called the Indus civilization (also known as Harappan civilization in the current discourse), as both the cities were situated in the river valley of the Indus. John Marshall was then the Director General of the Archaeological Survey of India. The subsequent decade-long excavations (excavations continued even later) revealed that the cities of the Indus civilization were massive and extremely well planned. They were marvels of urban engineering at the time they were built. They had roads intersecting at right angles with carefully laid out drainage and covered sewage systems. Mohenjo-Daro made use of baked bricks, which were quite unheard of in other Bronze Age civilizations. The houses of the inhabitants were well planned, with many of them having at least two storeys. They also had brick-lined wells, bathing facilities, privies and drainage connected to the city's main sewage system, suggesting that town planning and cleanliness were of utmost importance to the Harappans.[16]

Their economy was quite complex, with various craftspeople, metalworkers, seal cutters, architects and engineers living in the city. The Harappans were wealthy people who traded as far away

[16] G. L. Possehl, *The Indus Civilization: A Contemporary Perspective* (Boulder, CO: AltaMira Press, 2002).

as Mesopotamia, Sumer and Egypt. The technological sophistication of the Harappan people can also be seen in the making of metal alloys such as bronze, square seals, high-quality faience, high-quality ceramics, especially stoneware and jewellery—in the cutting, polishing, etching and drilling of long carnelian beads. The metalworkers worked with copper, tin, arsenic, lead, silver, gold and electrum. They also built small ships which could sail as far away as 4,000 miles to distant lands. The Harappan way of life was not possible without an in-depth knowledge of urban engineering, chemistry and navigation.[17]

The discovery of Mohenjo-Daro and Harappa struck at the very root of the then prevalent discourse that the Aryans came to India in 1500 BCE and consequently established civilization. One would think that, with the massive amount of evidence against it, the AIT would suffer a fatal jolt. However, the ideas of European superiority and supremacy prevailed, and throwing all academic integrity to the wind the new evidence was reinterpreted. The Aryans still came as invaders. This time, instead of defeating the civilization-less original inhabitants of India—the 'Dravidians'—they defeated the civilized Dravidians and pushed them to the southernmost corners of the Indian subcontinent. The Vedic and Puranic texts were twisted and tortured for the desired outcomes.

In 1944, when the Second World War was coming to a close, the Brigadier General of the British Army serving on the North African front, Robert Eric Mortimer Wheeler, became the Director General of the Archaeological Survey of India. Shortly after, he made a trip to Harappa, which was under excavation at that point in time, and within a couple of hours of being at the site, he concluded that the mound at Harappa was a citadel—constructed to fend off the invading Aryans. Wheeler's view was that because Punjab was at the frontier of invasions since antiquity, the cities built walls and forts for protection. He connoted the mention of 'pur' in the Rigveda with forts and ramparts and

---

[17] Ibid.

contended that since Indra, an 'Aryan War God,' is also known as 'purandara' meaning destroyer of 'purs' or forts and ramparts, it was the invading Aryans who had destroyed the cities—with their forts and ramparts—of the indigenous people, thus making the oft-quoted statement: 'On circumstantial evidence, Indra stands accused.'[18]

Wheeler's contentions have not held the test of time. Excavations reveal a different picture at Harappa and Mohenjo-Daro and the rest of the 1,050 sites of the Indus civilization (to date, approximately 1,052 sites of the civilization have been either identified or excavated),[19] which many scholars would rather prefer to call as Indus-Saraswati Civilization. This is because of the finding of over 500 sites on the currently dried-up riverbed of a mighty ancient river, Saraswati, which is called Ghaggar in India and Hakra in Pakistan. It flowed from the Himalayas to the Arabian Sea.[20] Tectonic movements around the beginning of the second millennium BCE made a part of the river go into the paleochannel and another meet the river Yamuna, which was not as big then as it is today.[21] Satellite images have proved the existence of this river in the past, and even today, all over India, there are Brahmin communities which call their *jati* by the name of the river Saraswati—they call themselves Saaraswat Brahmins or Brahmins who lived by the banks of Saraswati at one point in time. Gregory Possehl,[22] who was engaged in archaeological research on the Indus civilization in both India and Pakistan for close to four decades, holds that the Indus civilization began around 7000 BCE and entered its mature phase, called the Mature Harappan phase, between 2500 BCE–1900 BCE, in which its

[18] R. E. M. Wheeler, 'Harappa 1946: The Defences and Cemetery R-37,' *Ancient India* 3 (1947): 58–130, 82.

[19] Possehl, *The Indus Civilization.*

[20] Ibid.

[21] D. P. Agarwal and R. K. Sood, 'Ecological Factors and Harappan Civilization,' in *Harappan Civilization: A Contemporary Perspective*, ed. Gregory L. Possehl (New Delhi: Oxford and IBH Publishing Company, 1982), 223–231.

[22] Possehl, *The Indus Civilization.*

numerous cities flourished. These cities had declined long before the mythical invasion of the mythical Aryans. Mohenjo-Daro, along with many other cities in Sindh, Balochistan and Cholistan, came to an abrupt end around 1900 BCE, and as far as the other cities are concerned, there was either a progressive decline or a relocation of the civilization eastwards towards the Indo-Gangetic plain in the late Harappan period (depending upon the region, the time span of this phase is either 1900 BCE–1300 BCE or 1900 BCE–1000 BCE).

Possehl[23] writes that, in the western and north-western regions of civilization, there was either an abandonment or a severe thinning of the population. These settlements include Balakot, Kot Diji, Chanhu-Daro, Kulli, Allahdino, Nindowari, Mehi, Nausharo, Ropar, Kalibangan, Surkotada, Dholavira, Lothal and Desalpur. The economy in the region was disrupted, and the 'production of a wide range of special materials, many of which seem to be luxury items, was curtailed'.[24] Correspondingly, settlements in Haryana, Punjab, Western Uttar Pradesh and Northern Rajasthan saw an increase in number, though the Gujrat region of civilization did not see any decrease or increase—it fundamentally remained stable.

Jonathan Kenoyer,[25] who has conducted excavations and research at both Mohenjo-Daro and Harappa, having worked in western and central India, also holds a similar position: that the urban centres of the Harappan civilization moved towards the Gangetic plains and the Malwa Plateau. There is a migration of political, social and economic activities eastwards.

Jim Shaffer, another archaeologist who has conducted extensive fieldwork on Neolithic and Bronze Age Civilization sites in both India and Pakistan—holding the drying of the river

[23] Ibid.

[24] Possehl, *The Indus Civilization*, 237.

[25] J. M. Kenoyer, 'Culture Change during the Late Harappan Period at Harappa: New Insights on Vedic Aryan Issues,' in *The Indo-Aryan Controversy: Evidence and Inference in Indian History*, ed. Edwin F. Bryant and Laurie L. Patton (New York, NY: Routledge, 2005), 21–49.

Saraswati as the cause—along with Diane Lichtenstein, supports the findings:

> While the quality of the survey data is regionally variable, it is sufficient to show a gradual and significant population shift from the Indus Valley eastward into the eastern Punjab and Gujarat, beginning in the late third millennium BC and continuing throughout the second millennium BC.[26]

As mentioned earlier, whereas the city of Mohenjo-Daro was abandoned around 1900 BCE, Harappa did not suffer a similar fate. Harappa continued to exist in what is called the Late Harappan period and saw a decline in constructional quality, which has been assessed by the quality of the bricks used. Town planning plummeted, and there is evidence of encroachment and over-crowding: '*There is no concrete evidence for the appearance of a new biological population* (Hemphill et al. 1991; Kennedy 1992, 1995). This suggests that the changes and discontinuities reflect a transformation of the local population rather than the appearance of new people and the eradication of the Harappan inhabitants.'[27]

We have commented earlier that the faience industry and bead making—an aspect of the lapidary industry—were quite developed in the Mature Phase of the Harappan civilization. Kenoyer[28] notes that the making of stone beads became less common in the Late Harappan period and was substituted with glass beads. The production of glass beads in Punjab continues all the way up to the Painted Grey Ware period (1400–1000 BCE) and later till the Northern Black Polished Ware period, showing continuity between the Late Harappan period and the Early History. In effect, if we take the evidence of the bead and faience

---

[26] Jim G. Shaffer and Diane A. Lichtenstein, 'South Asian Archeology and the Myth of Indo-Aryan Invasions,' in *The Indo-Aryan Controversy: Evidence and Inference in Indian History*, ed. Edwin F. Bryant and Laurie L. Patton (New York, NY: Routledge, 2005), 75–104, 86.

[27] Kenoyer, 'Culture Change during the Late Harappan Period at Harappa,' 23, italics mine.

[28] Ibid.

industry into account, there is a continuity coming to the current times. The state of Gujarat, which is the southernmost area of the Harappan civilization, still has the city of Surat as one of the leading centres in the world, even today, in terms of the lapidary industry. The city is the biggest centre in the world for the cutting and polishing of diamonds and gems.

What about the citadel theory of Wheeler, standing on which he gave archaeological evidence to the AIT? Possehl[29] contends that the elevated mound was not a citadel—on the contrary, it was an elevated area, fortified with retaining walls to hold the mud used for its construction, on which buildings of significance such as the Great Bath (taking the example of Mohenjo-Daro), warehouses and other large buildings could be built; it was some sort of an ancient Indian acropolis. If it were meant for defensive purposes, then the western side of the Mohenjo-Daro mound would not have been open to the Indus plains.

In the excavations at Mohenjo-Daro, there were some human remains that were found—a total of 42 skeletons, interned in a rather hasty manner in different places within the city; no cemetery as yet has been found there. At one site, which is called the 'HR Area Tragedy' site—located in the HR-B Area, Block 2, House V, Room 74—a total of 14 skeletons (13 adult males and females and one child) were found. Wheeler immediately connected this to the invasion of the Aryans:

> That final blow has often enough been described. It is represented by groups of skeletons—men, women and children, some bearing axes or sword-cuts—which have been found lying on the topmost level in the sprawled or contorted positions in which they fell. They had been left there by raiders who had no further use for the city which they had stormed. In that moment Mohenjo-daro was dead.[30]

[29] Possehl, *The Indus Civilization*.
[30] M. Wheeler, *Early India and Pakistan: To Ashoka* (New York, NY: Frederick A. Praeger, 1959), 113–114.

Dales[31] and Kennedy[32] have refuted these contentions. Kennedy, who investigated the skeletons, holds that though there was trauma on skeleton 10, the death did not seem to have occurred from the trauma because 'the cut is not fresh and its margins are characterized by considerable bone absorption.'[33] Or even if the death had been caused by the wound, the wound must have been caused anywhere between 30 and 70 days earlier. Therefore, despite that there were skeletons found in one room, all but one did not have mortal wounds. Though the skeletons suggest a hasty internment, there is no conclusive evidence to suggest that the people were put to death by any invading army. There are other three 'massacre' sites where clusters of skeletons have been found. However, all of them belong to a period (the Late Harappan period) when civilization at Mohenjo-Daro had already come to an end. Possehl concludes:

> Some experts on ancient Indian history have faith in the preposition that these deaths were cause (sic) by invading Aryans. There are, however, many problems with this theory, not the least of which is chronological: While there may have been speakers of one or more Indo-European languages in the Greater Indus region earlier, there is a gap of centuries between the abandonment of Mohenjo-daro at about 1900 B.C. and the documentation found in the Rgveda, which probably dates to circa 1000 B.C. Also note that the Rgveda is a not a text documenting the invasion and

[31] G. F. Dales, 'The Mythical Massacre at Mohenjo-daro,' *Expedition* 6, no. 3 (1964): 36–43.

[32] K. A. R. Kennedy, 'Skulls, Aryans and Flowing Drains: The Interface of Archeology and Skeletal Biology in the Study of the Harappan Civilization,' in *Harappan Civilization: A Contemporary Perspective*, ed. Gregory L. Possehl (New Delhi: Oxford and IBH Publishing Company, 1982), 289–295; 'Trauma and Disease in Ancient Harappans,' in *Frontiers of the Indus Civilization*, ed. B. B. Lal and S. P. Gupta (New Delhi: Books and Books, 1984), 425–436; 'Identification of Sacrificial and Massacre Victims in Archeological Sites: The Skeletal Evidence,' in *Man and Environment* 19, no. 1–2 (1994): 247–251.

[33] K. A. R. Kennedy, 'Trauma and Disease in Ancient Harappans,' in *Frontiers of the Indus Civilization*, ed. B. B. Lal and S. P. Gupta (New Delhi: Books and Books, 1984), 425–436, 429.

conquest of the Subcontinent, but speaks of the feuding among the Aryans as well as with the indigenous peoples. Sindh is a peripheral area in the Vedic literature: The center of this world was the Punjab. It is therefore noteworthy that there is no evidence for massacre at Harappa or any of the other Indus settlements in the geographical area described most prominently in the Vedas.[34]

Kenoyer seconds: 'One of the most important results of the current work at Harappa is that there continues to be no support for the earlier interpretations of Vedic-Aryan invasions and the destruction of Harappan settlements.'[35] The AIT, thus, stands refuted. *But just like the earlier situation where the emergence of the ruins of the massive cities of Harappa and Mohenjo-Daro did not refute the AIT but rather was appropriated to continue the narrative, the profound refutation of the AIT has morphed into a new theory: the AMT.* The AMT now contends that the European Aryans may not have come as invading armies, but they still came as wandering pastoralists. The idea of European Aryans was racist and imperialistic right from the very beginning, and it remains racist and imperialistic today in whatever guise we may experience it—within its scholarly facade, it continues to deny India its history and the cultural, philosophical, spiritual, artistic, architectural, scientific and technological accomplishments of its ancestors. What is most surprising is that the same archaeologists, who refute the AIT, promote the AMT on either weak or no evidence, even when they have to contradict themselves. For instance, Kenoyer writes, 'At the opposite end of the spectrum is the misconception that the Indus people as a whole represent the communities referred to in the Vedic literature.'[36] This is despite his own contentions as quoted above: 'During the Late Harappan period there is evidence of overcrowding and encroachment rather than abandonment and decline.... *There is no concrete evidence for the appearance of a new biological*

[34] Possehl, *The Indus Civilization*, 164–165.
[35] Kenoyer, 'Culture Change during the Late Harappan Period at Harappa,' 44.
[36] Ibid., 45.

population.[37] The non-appearance of a new biological population in Late Harappa should have been sufficient to contest the AMT theory. Kenoyer, however, takes a contrary route:

> According to many scholars, the chronological framework for the final phases of the Harappan and the Late Harappan occupation at Harappa does correspond broadly with the time frame for the Ṛg Vedic period. Therefore, it is not improbable that some communities referred to in the Vedas were passing through or living in the regions controlled by Harappa during both the Harappan (Period 3C 2250–1900 BC) and the Late Harappan times (1900–1700 or 1300 BC).[38]

This is also despite reporting the similarities in burial practices mentioned in the Vedas and found in the late Harappan period:

> The Ṛg Veda refers to several types of burial, including earth burials and cremation. It is clear from the careful reading the excavation reports of Vats that there is no evidence for cremation at Harappa, but there are earth burials in Stratum II of Cemetery H. In later texts dating to c.800 BC, there are detailed instructions on how to collect bones that have been either buried or exposed for a specified length of time and place them in a pot with a lid that is then buried in a pit.... Pot burials from the later Stratum I in Cemetery H could reflect an earlier example of this type of secondary or fractional burial. However, the limited nature of the data makes it impossible to make any conclusive statements about the presence or absence of Vedic communities at Harappa.[39]

With the above data, Kenoyer could have taken the position that perhaps both the dating of the Vedas as well as the coming of the Aryans into India are profound myths created to bolster and enhance European supremacy over the native Indians of the Indian subcontinent. He, however, did not and consequently perpetuated the AMT. This is despite his familiarity with the fact that the date of the creation of the Vedas in 1200 BCE, on

---

[37] Ibid., 23–26, italics mine.
[38] Ibid., 46.
[39] Ibid., 45.

which the coming of the Aryans in 1500 BCE was predicated, is arbitrary—his colleague and fellow archaeologist, B. B. Lal, as we saw earlier, has been quite vocal about it.

What has happened now is that the time of the coming of the Aryans has been moved backwards by a few centuries. The possibility that the Harappan civilization was an indigenous creation of the Indian Aryans is yet to be acceded to by most Western archaeologists. Gregory Possehl,[40] who, as we have seen earlier, has comprehensively refuted the AIT. However, he also does not find the idea fantastical that wandering pastoralists could create a massive civilization which made India the jewel in the crown of the British empire—after having achieved a golden age in the early centuries of the first millennium CE—but not indigenous people who were already massive city builders with a highly advanced civilization for their times, who would disappear without a trace or leave a little trace (particularly when they were not invaded and consequently decimated). Mere wandering herdsmen, because they simply were European, could become harbingers of a profound ancient Indian civilization, the full scope of the achievements of which in current times is yet to be fully traced and unfolded:

> I believe from linguistic evidence that the homeland of the Indo-European peoples was somewhere in the temperate forest regions of Eurasia, so they came to the subcontinent from somewhere else. When the speakers of an Indo-European language(s) first came to the Subcontinent is not known. They first appear in the Near East just after 2000 B.C., but this is from linguistic evidence and they could have been there much before this, as would be the case for the Subcontinent.... No one knows for sure when the Indo-Europeans who spoke Vedic Sanskrit came to the Subcontinent, or how they got there. Speakers of other Indo-European languages were in the Near East early in the second millennium, and this may approximate the date of the Aryans into the Subcontinent. *But there is no evidence for an invasion, and most contemporary scholars who deal with this issue think more in terms of the movement that characterizes cattle pastoralists because of their need for*

---

[40] Possehl, *The Indus Civilization*

pastureland, than military conquest. Moreover, the Aryans may have come to the Punjab over a long period of time (a matter of centuries), not in a great rush, as an invasion would suggest.[41]

And they came so comprehensively that, in no part of the world, they left any trace of their language, culture, philosophy, etc., other than the Indian subcontinent. Forget about evidence to refute the AMT, this theory militates against common sense. Given that Possehl earlier attested to the movement of the Indus civilization eastward after 1900 BCE, how does he explain the migration and the eclipsing of its fabulous urban centres? Comical as it may sound, Possehl holds that the Indus Civilization was so good that it failed. Its failure was not because of 'flood, avulsion, drought, trade, disease, locusts, invasion, or any other of a myriad of "natural" or "outside" forces' but because of 'sociocultural flaw'.[42] It was a social system that achieved great heights because of 'social harmony in human relationships and with the environment.'[43] He stated that it was too good for its own good. Citing Heesterman,[44] he feels that if a society does not have inner conflict, it cannot last for long because it is the inner conflict which allows the inhabitants to be in a 'constant state of negotiating, resolving, dealing with maladaptation or lack of harmony in their lives,'[45] and because the Indus civilization built a system based on social harmony among and with one another, which included the environment, it collapsed under its own weight—it was too good for its own survival. The above position of Possehl is completely conjectural—as conjectural as the AMT. It is true that there seems to be an absence of big temples and palaces within the Mature Harappan civilization, quite unlike Mesopotamia and Egypt, but creating a comprehensive idea of an entire social system based on the lack of these artefacts is nothing but a conjectural projection. Possehl created the radical 'other'

[41] Ibid., 249, italics mine.
[42] Ibid., 244.
[43] Ibid.
[44] J. C. Heesterman, *The Inner Conflict of Tradition* (Chicago, IL: University of Chicago Press, 1985).
[45] Possehl, *The Indus Civilization*, 244.

of the Egyptian and Mesopotamian civilizations in the Harappan civilization and based his theory on it. He writes:

> One of the more interesting observations about the Indus Civilization is that no temples have been found. Nor is there much to be said of monumental architecture with a religious function or monumental architecture of any kind. The temples and pyramids of Dynastic Egypt and the ziggurats of Mesopotamia have no parallel in the Indus Valley.[46]

He contends further that it is not that religion was not there in the civilization; it certainly was, as is evident from structures such as the Great Bath in Mohenjo-Daro and various figurines that have been found. And the capacity to build monumental structures—the engineering and the work force—was there too, and yet no such structures were built. Similarly, there are no palaces present either, much in contrast to the Egyptians and Mesopotamians: 'Another contrast between Egypt and Mesopotamia and the Indus civilization is the absence of palaces, the large abode of the heads of government and their powerful associates charged with managing the fortunes of the political apparatus.'[47] The fact is that nothing conclusive is known about the social organization of the Harappans. Creating a social system completely in contrast to the Mesopotamians and Egyptians, based on the lack of similarity in the structures found in the remains of the Mesopotamian and Egyptian civilizations, is nothing but a sleight of hand—a pure work of fantasy and projection.

Then, what really happened to most of the prominent cities of the Indus civilization? The answer lies in the drying up of the Saraswati. There is a correspondence between the time that the Saraswati dried up and the abandonment or the decline (as the case may be) of the Harappan cities. Shaffer and Lichtenstein write:

> In the early second millennium BC, there was the capture of the Ghaggar-Hakra (or Saraswati) river system (then a focal point of

---

[46] Ibid., 148.
[47] Ibid.

human occupation) by adjacent rivers, with subsequent diversion of these waters eastwards (Shaffer 1981, 1982, 1986, 1993; Mughal 1990, 1997; Shaffer and Lichtenstein 1995, 1999). At the same time, there was an increasing tectonic activity in Sindh and elsewhere. Combined, these geological changes meant *major* changes in the hydrology patterns of the region (Flam 1981, 1993). These natural geological processes had significant consequences for the food producing cultural groups throughout the greater Indus Valley area.[48]

Further, they not only categorically refute the AIT but are also incisive about all attempts to twist data to show Western influences on the rise of prehistoric civilization in India. In their assessment, the most current archaeological records show a remarkable continuity within the Indian subcontinent:

> The modern archaeological record for South Asia indicates a history of significant cultural continuity; an interpretation at variance with earlier eighteenth through twentieth-century scholarly views of South Asian cultural discontinuity and South Asian cultural dependence on western cultural influences.[49]

B. B. Lal validates the above-mentioned contention of Shaffer and Lichtenstein. Lal[50] contends that many aspects and cultural practices, including the city-building plan of the Harappans, continued until historic times, as is evidenced in the excavation of the 600 BCE city of Sisupalgarh and its incorporation into the *Arthashastra* of Kautilya,[51] a text composed in the 4th century BCE. Lal[52] has also shown how farming methods, plans of building houses, ornaments used by the female populace, including artefacts for wedding ceremonies, bedtime tales, lapidary methods, cooking methods,

---

[48] Shaffer and Lichtenstein, 'South Asian Archeology and the Myth of Indo-Aryan Invasions,' 84, italics in original.

[49] Ibid., 93.

[50] B. B. Lal, *Piecing Together: Memoirs of an Archaeologist* (New Delhi: Aryan International Books, 2011).

[51] Kautilya, *The Arthashastra*, Trans. and ed. L. N. Rangarajan (New Delhi: Penguin Books, 1992).

[52] B. B. Lal, *How Deep are the Roots of Indian Civilization? Archaeology Answers* (New Delhi: Aryan Books International, 2009).

including the use of pots and pans, games like chess, toys used by children, writing pads, etc., have continued to find their use in current times in areas surrounding the Harappan civilization. In addition, figurines showing the traditional Hindu greeting namaste, yogic poses later compiled in the *Yoga Sutras of Patanjali*, fire alters used in Vedic ceremonies, seals depicting the Hindu deity Shiva and an iconic representation of Shiva in the form of *shivalinga*, have all been found at various sites of the Harappan culture. The above shows the Vedic and indigenous roots of the Harappan culture, rather than what the mainstream discourse argues for.

Shaffer and Lichtenstein are cognizant of the initiatives of various European nations to bolster their national identity and ego through the appropriation of the Aryan identity and Sanskrit—undertaken in the colonial era but not yet been abandoned:

> The scholarly paradigm of the eighteenth and nineteenth centuries in conflating language, culture, race, and population movements has continued, with historical linguistic scholars still assiduously attempting to reconstruct a proto-Indo-European language, and attempting to link that language to a specific 'homeland,' in order to define population migration away from the seminal geographic base. Suggestions for such a proto-Indo-European homeland range from Siberia to more recent efforts to tracing the homeland to Anatolia (Renfrew 1987) and the Ukraine (Gamkrelidze and Ivanov 1985 a,b; Gimbutas 1985; Mallory 1989; Allchin 1995), and these efforts now incorporate human genetic studies (Cavalli-Sforza et al. 1994) to verify the linguistic chronologies.[53]

Their reasoned view, backed by the analysis of massive amounts of data gathered from various archaeological sites and spread all over the Indian subcontinent, is that neither there is Western influence in the creation and shaping of the Harappan civilization nor are there discontinuities in the cultural record of prehistoric Indian subcontinent.

> The current archaeological and paleoanthropological data simply do not support these centuries old interpretative paradigms

[53] Shaffer and Lichtenstein, 'South Asian Archeology and the Myth of Indo-Aryan Invasions,' 93.

suggesting western, intrusive, cultural influence as responsible for the supposed major discontinuities in the South Asian cultural prehistoric record (Shaffer and Lichtenstein 1999; Kennedy 2000; Lamberg-Karlovsky 2002).... It is currently possible to discern cultural continuities linking specific prehistoric social entities in South Asia into one cultural tradition (Shaffer and Lichtenstein 1989, 1995, 1999; Shaffer 1992, 1993). This is *not* to propose social isolation *nor* deny any outside cultural influence. Outside cultural influence did affect South Asian cultural development in later, especially historic, periods, but an identifiable cultural tradition has continued, an Indo-Gangetic Cultural Tradition (Shaffer 1993; Shaffer and Lichtenstein 1995, 1999) linking social entities over a period of time from the development of food production in the seventh millennium BC to present.[54]

The above by Shaffer and Lichtenstein is conclusive and is in line with the overwhelming amount of archaeological data which have been gathered over time. It also is in contradiction to the contentions of Possehl and Kenoyer, who despite the presence of such data perpetuate the AMT, following linguistics and philology, which continue to remain non-science, despite their bellowing claims to be science—had they been science, the 'Aryan homeland' would not have spanned and continued to span different parts of Europe and most parts of Asia (minus India). It is time that modern academia backs off from perpetuating a colonial myth—either the AIT or the AMT—that continues to be used in textbooks all the way from primary and secondary levels to college and university levels of education. This theory is deeply and profoundly embedded in the racial superiority of Europeans or people with European lineage over the inferiority of Indians. It is quite explicit in the way in which it was crafted. Evidence after evidence keeps emerging, but Western academia, which controls the academic discourse in practically all parts of the world, keeps appropriating it and keeps shifting the goalposts. If it is not the AIT, then it is the AMT; if it is not the AMT, then it will be something else. Once the Aryans come to India, they will keep coming, until we stand up and call out academia for

[54] Ibid., italics in original.

the racist nature of the AIT/AMT discourse. Seeing it any other way is tantamount to ignoring the huge white elephant in the room. *Yes, the elephant in the room has no other colour. It is white—and it is fair, blond and blue-eyed.*

Conclusion: Colonialism and the AIT/AMT Project

The distortion of history has been a mega project of the coloniz-ers. The anticolonial writers were sophisticated enough to under-stand it. Although postcolonial writers have built their legacy on the backs of anticolonial writers, the analysis of distortion of history has not been such a serious undertaking among them, particularly when it comes to India. Eradicating the civilizational contributions of non-European people to humanity was the master note on which the colonizers' representation of colonized cultures and nations played. By distorting history, the colonial project destroyed the identity of the colonized. The destruction of their identity led to the destruction of their faith in themselves and, hence, to the resistance to colonial rule. Whether it was in Africa or in India, the project was the same. Writing an introduc-tion to Aimé Césaire's *Discourses on Colonialism*, Robin D. G. Kelly writes:

> An entire generation of 'enlightened' European scholars worked hard to wipe out the cultural and intellectual contributions of Egypt and Nubia from European history, to whiten the West in order to maintain the purity of the 'European' race. They also stripped all of Africa of any semblance of 'civilization,' using the printed page to eradicate their history and thus reduce a whole continent and its progeny to little more than beasts of burden or brutish heathens.[55]

By removing 'civilization' from the colonized, the European colonizers could turn the colonized 'other' into primitives, which

---

[55] Robin D. G. Kelly, 'Poetics of Anticolonialism,' in *Discourse on Colonialism*, authored by Aimé Césaire and trans. Joan Pinkham (New York, NY: Monthly Review Press, 2000), 7–28, 22.

would then further and justify their civilizing mission. Kelly, commenting on Césaire, elucidates:

> Césaire reveals, over and over again, that the colonizers' sense of superiority, their sense of mission as the world's civilizers, depends on turning the Other into a barbarian. The Africans, the Indians, the Asians cannot posses civilization or culture equal to that of the imperialists, or the latter have no purpose, no justification for the exploitation and domination of the rest of the world. The colonial encounter, in other words, requires a reinvention of the colonized, the deliberate destruction of the past-what Césaire calls 'thingification'.[56]

In the context of India, a systematic *primitivization* of Indian culture and civilization, in particular of the Hindus, began with the publication of *The History of British India* by James Mill[57] in 1817. James Mill was hired by the East India Company (the corporation ruling India till the British crown took over after India's first war of independence in 1857), which funded his research for about 10 years, leading to the publication of his three-volume series on *The History of British India*. Surprising as it may sound today, Mill did not visit India even once to write this work; in fact, he defends it quite vehemently in the opening pages, claiming that it is not necessary for an author to be familiar with the land to write its history. However, his work became an authoritative text on India—thanks to the colonial influence and power of the East India Company—and it was used by the East India Company to train its civil servants serving in India. In *Book II* of *The History of British India: Volume One*, Mill has written seven chapters on the Hindus. His agenda is quite explicit: to prove that Hindus are savages, barbarians, uncivilized, uncouth, rude, brutes, unrefined, coarse, vulgar, etc. One would be hard-pressed to find one positive representation on the Hindus in the entire section. Let us present to you a slice

---

[56] Kelly, 'Poetics of Anticolonialism,' 9.
[57] James Mill, *The History of British India: Volume 1* (London: Forgotten Books, 2015).

of Mill's vitriol in which he defines or should we say denigrates the religion of the Hindus:

> No people, how rude and ignorant soever, who have been so far advanced as to leave us memorials of their thoughts in writing, have ever drawn a more gross and disgusting picture of the universe than what is presented in the writings of the Hindus. In the conception of it no coherence, wisdom, or beauty, ever appears; all is disorder, caprice, passion, contest, portents, prodigies, violence, and deformity. It is perfectly evident that the Hindus never contemplated the universe as a connected and perfect system, governed by general laws, and directed to benevolent ends; and it follows, as a necessary consequence, that their religion is no other than primary worship, which is addressed to the designing and invisible beings who preside over the powers of nature, according to their own arbitrary will, and act only for some private and selfish gratification. The elevated language, which this species of worship finally assumes, is only the refinement, which flattery, founded upon a base apprehension of the divine character, ingrafts upon a mean superstition.[58]

From the very first sentence in chapter one of *Book II*, Mill launches into showing how the Hindus and their civilization are barbaric. He begins with the premise that uncivilized and brutish nations claim a deep antiquity to their existence: 'Rude nations seem to derive a particular gratification from pretensions to a remote antiquity.'[59] For this, he takes the help of the division of time by the Hindus in terms of four *yugas*: *Satya Yuga*, *Treta Yuga*, *Dwapara Yuga*, and *Kali Yuga*, which are arranged in the ratios of 4:3:2:1. If one takes into account the various texts where the *yugas* are described, the only commonality that one finds is that the *yugas* are arranged at the respective ratio of 4:3:2:1, and that the texts differ in terms of the number of years for one unit. For instance, whereas the Vishnu Purana takes one unit as 432,000 years (the number of years in *Kali Yuga*), Manu Smriti and other astronomy/astrology texts such as Surya Siddhanta take

[58] Ibid., 385–387.
[59] Ibid., 154.

the unit as comprising 1,200 years—consequently, *Kali Yuga* from the perspective of these texts consists of 1,200 years. Despite the fact that Mill is deeply familiar with the Manu Smriti—for he has liberally and selectively used the text to show the barbaric nature of the Hindus—he chooses to use the Vishnu Purana in order to substantiate his thesis about claims of antiquity by a collectivity of people and the lack of civilization. Had he used the time data in the Manu Smriti, Hindu civilization would have been only in the range of 12,000 plus years (4,800 years of *Satya Yuga* + 3,600 years of *Treta Yuga* + 2,400 years of *Dwapara Yuga* + 1,200 years of *Kali Yuga*). Ignoring the data, however, he makes the claim that Hindus lack a sense of history and all that they are capable of is writing imaginary fiction:

> The offspring of a wild and ungoverned imagination, they mark the state of a rude and credulous people, whom the marvellous delights; who cannot estimate the use of a record of past events; and whose imagination the real occurrences of life are too familiar to engage. To the monstrous period of years which the legends of the Hindus involve, they ascribe events the most extravagant and unnatural: events not even connected in chronological series; a number of independent and incredible fictions. This people, indeed, are perfectly destitute of historical records.[60]

Given the influence that Mill's work came to have in academia due to the intersection of colonial power and 'knowledge' production, it became engraved in stone consciously and unconsciously that Indians have no sense of history. Although we have only quoted the work of B. B. Lal above, there have been a host of archaeologists from India who have solidly refuted the AIT and AMT; it, however, seems that academia, which is controlled by the Western discourse, does not move the needle. Even a host of their articles in international journals as well as presentations at international conferences do not alter the discourse.

Furthermore, once Mill firmly establishes the connection between Hindus lacking any sense of civilization and

[60] Ibid., 166–167.

barbarianism, he goes on to contend that the early Hindus were nomads and wanderers:

> If we suppose that India began to be inhabited at a very early stage in the peopling of the world, its first inhabitants must have been few, ignorant, and rude. Uncivilized and ignorant men, transported, in small numbers, into an uninhabited country of boundless extent, must wander for many ages before any great improvement can take place.... They wandered probably for ages in the immense plains and valleys of that productive region, living on fruits, and the produce of their flocks and herds, and not associated beyond the limits of a particular family.[61]

The above discourse solidified the description of ancient Hindus as wanderers, nomads and cattle herders and paved the way for these 'Aryans' to get on the horseback as cattle-herding wandering nomads and invade India, perpetuating the AIT without the backing of any hard and conclusive evidence. This is also why, when the cities of the Harappan civilization were discovered, they were not linked to the ancient Hindus because, in the European imagination (logic from their standpoint), it was not possible for a wandering nomadic people to build a massive civilization of such a material scale as the Harappan civilization. It was, therefore, that civilization (again without any hard and conclusive evidence) was linked to the 'indigenous Dravidian' people whom the 'invading Aryans' defeated. This is also despite that the same 'cattle herding nomadic people' in abundance speak about cities in the Vedas.

Now, when the AIT has been shot down, the description of the AMT which is the officially stated or unstated stance of Western academia, surprisingly as it may sound, is only a politically correct and sanitized version of how Mill described the ancient Hindus in the early 19th century. The *2016 California History and Social Science (HSS) Framework for Grade Six—World History and Geography: Ancient Civilization*, which is an official

[61] Ibid., 173–175.

guideline for publishers to put together books for 6th grade students in the state of California, states the following:

> People speaking Indic languages, which are part of the larger Indo-European family of languages, entered South Asia, probably by way of Iran.... The early Indic speakers were most likely animal herders. They may have arrived in India in scattered bands, later intermarrying with populations perhaps ancestral to those who speak Dravidian languages, such as Tamil and Telugu, in southern India and Sri Lanka today.[62]

Why do we say that the above description by the *California HSS Framework* is a sanitized and politically correct version of the James Mill narrative? First, given that the Aryan is a much derided term because of the holocaust that the Nazis caused appropriating the term, the *California HSS Framework* does not use it, but it basically means Aryans, substituting it with 'people speaking Indic languages, which are part of larger Indo-European family of languages.' And when it means Aryans, it does not suggest Aryans indigenous to India. It specifically means Aryans coming to India via Iran from Europe: white, fair-skinned, blond and blue-eyed Aryans. Second, the groups of 'people speaking Indic languages' are essentially nomadic herders and wanderers just like how they were in the James Mill description. It is just that in the current 2016 *California HSS Framework* version, they are not being called barbaric, uncivilized, ignorant and rude, and it does not describe the larger imperial context in which this narrative was framed to begin with. Needless to say, it is this very version that gets recycled in all History textbooks. In higher studies also, the narrative similar to the one mentioned in the *Framework* appears.

To sum up, the AIT or its politically correct sibling, the AMT, is intimately tied with the colonial project. The invasion theory

---

[62] California Department of Education. *Chapter Ten: History Social Science Framework for California Public Schools: Kindergarten through Grade Twelve*, 2016, 162–163, available at https://www.cde.ca.gov/ci/hs/cf/documents/hssfwchapter10.pdf (accessed on 28 June 2021).

was tied directly to colonialism, and the migration theory is entwined with the racial superiority of the European people. The invasion or the migration theory strips the Indians of their agency to conceive, foster, nurture and perpetuate a civilization. It is about denying the indigenous Indian population the creative, intellectual and rational capacity to engender a civilization. The direct colonial rule may have ended but the paradigm running the colonial enterprise that it is only the European people or people with European lineage who are capable of establishing civilizations is solidly intact when we take the AIT or AMT into consideration.

It is in the backdrop of this 'othering,' this turning of the Indian civilization, its culture, history and contribution to humanity into the primitive 'other' that the picture of the early Aryans as wandering and nomadic cattle herders was formulated, and James Mill is the architect-in-chief of this description. Max Müller arbitrarily ascribed the date of 1500 BCE to the coming of the Aryans, and since the day this issue became conflated with the stated and unstated aspirations of White and European supremacy, all reasoned evidence has been thrown to the wind. Scholars worldwide can keep providing evidence after evidence to show that neither the Aryan invasion nor the Aryan migration happened, the theory will remain intact. And it will remain intact until the time the scholars in the field with European ancestry consciously and unconsciously keep believing that it is they and they alone, who can build any civilization of any substance anywhere in the world.

11

Deconstructing the Colonial

Neena Bansal

History is rewritten from time to time not because some new facts are discovered but because new perspectives emerge in the progression of a history, a nation or an interest. India's past was majorly a reconstruction of Western Indology scholars, a fact well corroborated by many. To quote K. M. Panikkar in this context:

> All this reconstruction of India's past and the translation and popularisation of great Indian philosophical and religious classics was the work almost exclusively of European scholars: English, German, French, Swedish, Russian, in fact scholars from every part of Europe. It was only in the last decades of nineteenth century that Indian scholarship began to participate effectively in this work.[1]

Having recognized the claim made by Panikkar and attributing the due praise for the same to the European scholars, the crucial questions that arise are: Do these writings by the Western scholars conform to the indigenous civilizational history, understanding and the identity? Do they grasp their intent and the insight? Can the native history of a civilization be genuinely reconstructed by external sources? The answers to these questions require some

---

[1] K. M. Panikkar, *The Foundations of New India* (London: George Allen Unwin, 1968), 168.

empirical understanding which the present chapter seeks to search using the methodology of *deconstruction*.

Deconstruction

Deconstruction, a term that started being used in late 1960s, is most commonly associated with Jacques Derrida, the Algerian-born French philosopher. It can chiefly be associated with the school of literary criticism, though at a high risk of oversimplification. Whereas, critical reading endeavours to put forth the meaning of a text, deconstructive reading engages in asking questions in order to establish that what the text claims to be saying and what it is actually presenting are two different things. It calls for dismantling our loyalties to any one idea and being open to learn the different aspects of the same truth that may be lying buried in a text. Christopher Norris defines deconstruction as a series of moves, which include the dismantling of conceptual oppositions, hierarchical systems of thought and moments of self-contradiction in philosophy.[2] Loosely held under the umbrella of post-structuralism and postmodernism, it is primarily associated with certain techniques and strategies for interpreting literary texts developed by Jacques Derrida, Paul de Man and others. Another eminent name associated is that of Michel Foucault, although many would not consider him a deconstructionist in the real sense of the term, as he is much more than that.

In Derrida's first book, *Of Grammatology*, published in 1967,[3] the Derridian approach to philosophy threatened the established cannons of the discipline. It viewed texts as a dynamic entity, open to an ongoing plurality of meanings—with the techniques of repeated readings and textual interactions. Meaning that 'deconstruction is concerned with offering an account of what is going on in a text—not by seeking out its meaning, or its component parts,

---

[2] Christopher Norris, *Derrida* (London: Fontana Press, 1987), 19.

[3] Jacques Derrida, *Of Grammatology*, trans. Gayatri Chakravorty Spivak (Baltimore, MD: Johns Hopkins University Press, 1976).

or its systematic implication—but rather by marking off its relation to other texts, its contexts, its sub-texts'.[4] And by examining that how the 'explicit formulations' of the text 'undermine its implicit or non-implicit aspects'.[5] 'It brings out what the text excludes by showing what it includes.'[6] According to Derrida, a text is essentially multi-layered, so the language used is metaphorical. No text has absolute meaning for there is always a possibility of some new interpretations. In one of the well-known texts, 'Letter to a Japanese Friend', Derrida addresses the problem and says,

> ...deconstruction is neither an *analysis* nor a *critique*...It is not an analysis in particular because the dismantling of a structure is not a regression towards a *simple element*, towards an *indissoluble* origin...No more is it a critique, in a general sense or in a Kantian sense.[7]

In one of his famous lectures at Johns Hopkins University in 1968, Derrida critiqued the very idea of structure, questioning the fixity of centres and argued for a free play of centres and margins. According to him, humankind, at least in the Western world, is logo centric that believes in a central principle in which all beliefs and actions are supposed to be grounded, favouring, thus, certain metaphysical ideas over others. Such a centre has been given many names: God, Truth, Platonic Forms and so on. Michael Drolet and others observe:

> While Derrida agreed with Foucault that the traditional approach to human sciences was dead and not worth reviving, he believed Foucault's archaeology and genealogy still adhered to the assumption underpinning Western philosophical tradition that there was an objective body of knowledge or ultimate truth that could be discovered. He concluded that Foucault was unable to accomplish the post-structuralist project and therefore failed to go far enough

[4] Hugh J. Silverman, ed., *Derrida and Deconstruction* (New York, NY: Routledge, 1989), 4.

[5] Ibid.

[6] Ibid.

[7] As quoted in Ian Maclachlan, ed., *Jacques Derrida: Critical Thought* (Farnham: Ashgate Publishing, 2004), 1.

in his efforts to break free from humanism. Derrida aimed for a definitive rupture and the ultimate success of post-structuralism.[8]

Drolet and others seem to have perceptively observed that the way in which Derrida set out to achieve this was alien to conventional philosophy—using strange terminology and numerous long digressions in his narrative thread.[9] This was done deliberately in order to 'push language beyond the boundaries of convention'[10] or, as Derrida himself says, to 'make the limits of language tremble'.[11] The outcome is that, 'The coalescence of these elements makes his work frustratingly difficult to understand.'[12]

Deconstruction is, thus, the enemy of the authorized or an authoritarian text. In general, the revolutionary nature of deconstruction can be seen as challenging the way in which Western civilization has conceived of the world since Plato. In 1970s, deconstructionism was seen as having major influence on literary criticism mainly because of the strong influence of its originator, Derrida, and the precursors, Friedrich Nietzsche and Martin Heidegger. In the USA, deconstruction became closely associated with Yale University for a simple reason that some of its strong advocates were faculty on board. In fact, it was also referred to as the 'Yale school of criticism'.

Not surprisingly, deconstruction has not been welcomed by all readers and concerns were expressed about its obscure and confusing terminology. Also, that it robs literature of its significant import and plays down the texts by wordplay and jargons. On the other hand, its defenders locate it as giving a way to read more critically and objectively than the previous structures have allowed.

B. K. Matilal (1935–1991) once said in one of his essays, 'Today the Indian subcontinent may enjoy political independence,

---

[8] Michael Drolet, ed., *The Postmodernism Reader* (London: Routledge, 2004), 21–22.
[9] Ibid., 22.
[10] Ibid.
[11] As quoted in Ibid.
[12] Ibid.

colonial powers may have faded, the Suez Canal may have been Arabized, but the intellectual superiority of the West has remained unchallenged'.[13] Although this still remains a dominant truth, the fact that *Eurocentrism* today stands severely criticized cannot be denied. Eurocentrism has evinced strong criticism as well as praise ever since it started gathering weight in the 17th century. Many scholars now converge that the Eurocentric inheritance has distorted the capacity of social sciences to deal and analyse the problems of the contemporary world. That today it leaves us languishing for viably sustainable solutions to the indigenous problems and challenges. The question thus arises: Are there any solutions? Or are we just heading towards some kind of an antithesis of the phenomena—extreme nationalism?

Developing somewhat on a similar thesis, Stanziani in his recent work seeks to suggest some kind of a synthesis approach of 'rejecting *none* against the other': *a humankind perspective.* Reflecting on the nation-centric history he writes:

Many historians in Africa as well as Asia, Russia, and Turkey accuse their Western colleagues of using history to reintroduce a strictly western approach, thereby denying the value of the nation, which is the core concern for these countries. This viewpoint... leads to the conclusion that if the history of Africa is written by Africans, the history of Russia by Russians, and so on, alongside the Eurocentric attitude decried....In reality, the critique of Eurocentrism, however defensible, tends to be vague or even, paradoxically Eurocentric itself....The question is not to deny that Western-centric attitudes were imposed in other parts of the world or that, even today, all around the West, students in Chinese or African history are obliged to know the basics of Western history while the reverse is not true. This must be overruled; *however, the solution does not consist in replacing one centrism with another but to overcome the using of history as a clash of civilisation's perspective. Hopefully, several works in global history openly adopt a humankind perspective.*[14] [Emphasis added]

[13] Jonardon Ganeri, *The Collected Essays of Bimal Krishna Matilal: Mind, Language and World* (New Delhi: Oxford University Press, 2002), 370.

[14] Alessandro Stanziani, *Eurocentrism and the Politics of Global History* (London: Palgrave Macmillan, 2018), 13–14.

If we go by the Derridian methodology of deconstruction in this context, Stanziani's proposal is fraught with some pragmatic strains. The *humankind perspective* approach projected as a viable solution by Stanziani is not without problems. One, it is vague and fraught with customary elusiveness. Second, ironically, his analysis of Eurocentrism seems to be Eurocentric itself, for Stanziani essentializes Eurocentrism which he initially starts disapproving with. Third, he gives us an understanding that if the history of Asia is written by Asians, and that of Russia by Russians, the scholars would not be able to keep their Eurocentric pre-dispositions at bay. And finally, that the 'use of history' be better made for developing a 'humankind perspective' rather than for replacing 'one centrism with another' in order to avoid the 'clash of civilizations'.

The point that I submit to make in this context is that the humankind perspective might seem to be a rational approach to adopt, but the questions still remain: Will this be a *viably sustained* solution for the multidimensional problems posed in the world by centuries of Eurocentric dominations? The answer actually needs to be understood more objectively, without playing down the vast field of nation-centric and indigenous researches in every part of the world. When the histories, the psychologies and the politics of imperial dominations still have the stories of painful struggles, devastations and erosions of traditions to tell, the humankind approach suggested by scholars like Stanziani has its own limitations to deal with the compound problems of subjugation. The present chapter seeks to discuss the problem of colonial and pre-colonial histories, especially in the Indian context.

Critically examining the methodologies of 'researches' on the indigenous Maori people of New Zealand, Linda Smith raises some very germane issues in the present context and asks, 'Research as an Extension of Knowledge: Whose Knowledge?'[15] The ideal that particular research projects serve the purpose of helping the humanity with some benefits and emancipatory goal

[15] Linda Tuhiwai Smith, *Decolonizing Methodologies: Research and Indigenous Peoples* (London: Zed Books, 1999), 169.

is as much a 'reflection of ideology' rather than some academic rigour.[16] 'Notions of rationality' and 'conceptualization of knowledge' become 'convenient tools for dismissing' the indigenous cultures and traditions.[17] Highlighting the fallacies of the imperial research projects, she says:

> From the vantage point of the colonized, a position from which I write...the term 'research' is inextricably linked to European imperialism and colonialism. The word itself, 'research', is probably one of the dirtiest words in the indigenous world's vocabulary. When mentioned in many indigenous contexts, it stirs up silence, it conjures up bad memories...it appals us that the West can desire, extract and claim ownership of our ways of knowing, our imagery, the things we create and produce, and then simultaneously reject the people who created and developed those ideas and seek to deny them further opportunities to be creators of their own cultures and own nations.[18]

The Imperial Majesty

'The British idea of themselves as an imperial people charged with governance of others', originated in the process of taking over the 'Tudor state in the sixteenth century'.[19] When in the 1560s and the 1570s, the lieutenants of the Queen set out to overpower Ireland, they faced the dilemma of justifying these expeditions to their conscience and, thus, devised theories that could justify their claims of a superior power.[20] This can well be applied to other colonial subjugations and conquests made by the British to establish their majesty in different parts of the world.

> With the conquest of Ireland, the English thus made of themselves for the first time—but not the last—*new Romans, charged with*

[16] Ibid., 2.
[17] Ibid., 170.
[18] Ibid., 1–2.
[19] Thomas R. Metcalf, *Ideologies of the Raj* (New Delhi: Cambridge University Press, 1998), 2.
[20] Ibid.

civilizing backward peoples. [Emphasis added] Conquest hence-forth found justification not, as in the Crusades, in the punishment of infidels and heretics, though the Irish were of course degraded by their Catholicism, nor as the outcome of dynastic rivalry, but as the product of a conception of civilization whose differing levels secured a place for the English at its apex. The English took this rationale for the subjugation of foreign peoples from Ireland to America, and thence to India and Africa.[21]

The Irish historian, Nicholas Canny, says, 'The English adventur-ers...had little difficulty in satisfying themselves that the Gaelic Irish were pagans,[22] and this became an accepted tenet of all Englishmen'.[23] Explaining the logic of the English adventurers to convince themselves that the Irish were pagans, he says:

English recognised a distinction between Christianity and civiliza-tion, and believed that a people could be civilised without being made Christian but not Christianised without first being made civil....It was admitted that the Romans had been civilised despite being pagans, and sixteenth century Englishmen were not ignorant of the existence of civilizations beyond the boundaries of Christian Europe. Supremacy was claimed for western civilization because it combined the benefits of Christianity with those of civility. To admit that native Irish were Christians would, therefore, have been to acknowledge them as civilised also. By declaring Irish to be pagan, however the English were decreeing that they were culpa-ble....Once it was established that the Irish were pagans, the first logical step had been taken towards declaring them barbarians.[24]

---

[21] Ibid., 3.

[22] According to *Cambridge Dictionary*, 'pagan' means 'belonging or relating to a religion that worships many gods, especially one that existed before the main world religions'. *Collins* mark it as 'beliefs and activities that do not belong to any of the main religions of the world and take nature and a belief in many gods as the basis. They are older, or are believed to be older, than other religions. The synonyms are heathen, infidel, irreligious and polytheistic.

[23] Nicholas Canny, 'The ideology of English Colonization: From Ireland to America', *William and Mary Quarterly* 30, no. 4 (October 1973): 585, available at https://www.jstor.org/stable/1918596 (accessed on 28 June 2021).

[24] Ibid., 585–586.

Coming to the particular reference of India, one of the oft-made claims by the Imperial masters is that Britain has given to the Indian masses better laws and a better judicial system than they ever had before or could create one for themselves and that this service rendered alone, if there were no other, fully justifies her in retaining possession of the land.[25] While such statements well served the purpose of consolidating and legitimizing the British establishment, the actuality of the claim has been researched and studied empirically. Nandini Bhattacharyya Panda in her book, *Appropriation and Invention of Tradition*, brings out a 'seminal discussion' on the 'indigenous knowledge' by the British Indologists as representing an 'instrument' of 'subordinating the subject people'.[26] Her study concludes that the 'whole idea of *Hindu law* was a British administrative invention'.[27] And that, 'the early ideologues and administrators repeatedly referred to this tradition as the legal tradition of the country, ignoring the fact that the primary concern of the Dharmasastras was the community and the individual and not the state'.[28] Bringing in the fact and the claim of the Western Indologists, as also emphasized by Panikkar at the beginning of this work, of exclusively reconstructing, translating and popularizing India's past, it is this understanding, intent and the insight that the present chapter seeks to call in question: Can the native history of a civilization be dependably reconstructed by external scholarship?

An Englishman John Dickinson (1815–1876), who was remembered as 'A Forgotten Friend of India' at the 71st session

---

[25] Elizabeth Kolsky, 'Codification and the Rule of Colonial Difference: Criminal Procedure in British India', *Law and History Review* 23, no. 3 (Fall 2005): 631–683, available at http://www.jstor.org/stable/30042900 (accessed on 28 June 2021).

[26] Nandini Bhattacharyya Panda, *Appropriation and Invention of Tradition: The East India Company and Hindu Law in Early Colonial Bengal* (New Delhi: Oxford University Press, 2008), 3.

[27] Ibid., 243.

[28] Ibid.

of Indian History Congress (2010–2011), had 'vociferously pro-tested in Parliament, press and platform against abuses and the policy of destroying local self-government, and the virtual exclusion of Indians from the jobs in the administration'.[29] He believed that the English people at home were ignorant about the ground situation in India, and that the British policies in India were doing more harm than good to the native people. When the stories of commotion created by the policies of Governor General Lord Dalhousie in India (1848–1856) had reached England, Dickinson had joined the opposition as a protest. He published a book in 1853 with the title *Government of India under a Bureaucracy*, which constitutes one of the most scathing attacks on the imperial British system in India. The chapter titled 'The Judicial System' describes the kind of legal system set up by the British and the result which it produced, thus:

> The English, rashly assumed that the ancient, long-civilised people....[of India] were a race of barbarians who had never known what justice was until we came among them, and that the best thing we could do for them was to upset all their institutions as fast as we could, and among others their judicial system, and give them instead a copy of our legal models at home (in England)....Long before we knew anything of India, the fabric of native society had been characterised by some peculiar and excellent institutions, viz., by a municipal organisation, providing a most efficient police for the administration of criminal laws, while the civil law was worked by a simple process of arbitration, which either prevented litigation, or else insured prompt and substantial justice to the litigants....and now, in lieu of [their own] simple and rational mode of dispensing justice, we have given [them] an obscure, complicated, pedantic system of English law, full of artificial technicalities, which disable the candidates for justice from any longer pleading their own cause, and force them

---

[29] Prabha Ravi Shankar, 'A Forgotten Friend of India, John Dickinson (1815–1876)', *Proceedings of the Indian National Congress*, 71st session (2010–2011): 1302, available at http://www.jstor.org/stable/44147616 (accessed on 28 June 2021).

to have recourse to a swarm of attorneys and special pleaders, by means of which their expenses are greatly increased and the ends of justice are defeated.[30]

There are various other sources to validate the fact that the pre-colonial India had its relevant structures of ruling and dispensing justice well in place. P. N. Bose gives an abundant testimony of several high and esteemed English officers of the early years of British Rule in his book while meaning to say,

> Village self-Government was the vital thing in the country which not only kept society together but made it prosperous despite the division of caste and despite the occasional misrule of tyranni-cally and viciously disposed despots, whether Hindus, Buddhist or Mohemdan. The Central Government might be dead or rotten to the core, but it did not seriously affect the life of the people whose soul lay in the villages.[31]

When the British first entered India as adventurers and traders, did they find a civilization that was low, or one that was high? This question was answered by Sir Thomas Munro, a distin-guished Governor of Madras, in a statement made by him before a committee of the House of Commons in 1813 (*Hansard's Parliamentary Debates*, 12 April) as follows:

> If a good system of agriculture, unrivalled manufacturing skills, a capacity to produce whatever contribute to convenience or luxury; schools established in every village, for teaching, reading, writing and arithmetic; the general practice of hospitality and charity among each other, and above all a treatment of the female sex, full of confidence, respect and delicacy, are among the signs which denote a civilised people, then Hindus are not inferior to the nations of Europe; and if civilization is to become an article of trade between

---

[30] John Dickinson, 'India Reform No. VI: Government of India under a Bureaucracy' (1853): 36–48, available at https://www.jstor.org/stable/60101529 (accessed on 20 July 2019).

[31] Pramatha Nath Bose, *Swaraj: Cultural and Political* (Calcutta: W. Newman & Co. Ltd, 1929), 71.

the two countries, I am convinced that this country (England) will gain by the import cargo.[32]

Imperial Instruments of Legitimization

Legitimization is the need of every ruler and more so for an imperialist one. Soon after the military conquests in Bengal, the British started to look for a variety of ways to legitimize their rule in India, right from the governor generalship of Warren Hastings. Building a narrative principally on the basis of the account given by the European travellers in India, the English officials started preparing their propaganda from the second half of the 18th century. They projected the conditions of the people under the Mughal Empire before Company's rule to exhibit that their conditions actually improved under the colonial empire. And thus, they could easily term the entire medieval period as 'Dark Age', a term that was picked up by the Indian writers later.[33]

The general assumption was that since the people of India were under despotic dispensations, they would reconcile themselves and even support a foreign power that would bring about agricultural improvement, 'rule of property' and law, and a balanced governance.[34] Metcalf says,

> To Legitimate the conquest of India it was necessary, not only to discipline Britain's agent in that country, but to reorder their activities....Imperialism, in other words, could be made moral by a just governance that would reconcile the Indians to their subject status. Such views were to echo down the years to 1947.[35]

[32] Quoted in Jabez T. Sunderland, *India in Bondage: Her Right to Freedom* (Calcutta: Prabasi Press, 1928), 348–349.

[33] Aniruddha Ray, 'Preface', in *The Sultanate of Delhi (1206–1526): Polity, Economy, Society and Culture* (Delhi: Manohar, 2019).

[34] See Ranajit Guha, *A Rule of Property for Bengal: An Essay on the Idea of the Permanent Settlement* (New Delhi: Orient Longman, 1981).

[35] P. J. Marshall, ed., *The Writings and Speeches of Edmund Burke, Vol. 5, India: 1774–1785* (Oxford: Oxford University Press, 1987), 179, 221, 402 as quoted in Metcalf, *Ideologies of the Raj*, 19–20.

The colonial usage of the terms like 'justice' needs to be properly contextualized in order to get the real import of the same. Nandini Panda indicates two clear strands in the policies projected by Hastings and his followers. One, imposition of 'British sovereignty' even in the remotest part of the country by creating a 'supra-local authority' in the form of a strong judiciary, which was expected to weaken the sway of the local zamindars and other influencers. Second, in order to create an impression that the new government wanted to continue with the established system of traditions, the codification and translation of the indigenous 'rules' were taken up with rigour.[36] 'The records of the Mayor's court and the works of five important officials—Luke Scrafton, J. Z. Holwell, Alexander Dow, William Bolts, and Harry Verelst—document the Company's growing awareness of and perceptions regarding indigenous laws and customs.'[37] There were systematic attempts to organize the new found knowledge into an effective instrument of power. For some seven decades (1698–1772), there was a gradual intensification of the urge to undertake a detailed study of the indigenous literature.[38] 'But one notes a new sense of urgency after 1770, when the Company began to exercise effective power over an extensive territory.'[39] The 'administration of justice' with respect to 'property (mainly land)' provided the imperial masters with the much-needed basis of legitimacy required by a ruler.[40] Interestingly, thus, the 'security of property rights was projected as a useful instrument for communicating the message that the Company rule was founded on justice'.[41] Panda amply establishes the intimate relationship between the political and financial wants of the company, and the need to codify the civil and personal rules of the country.[42]

Another interesting instrument of colonial legitimization is highlighted by Ian J. Barrow in his book *Making History,*

---

[36] Panda, *Appropriation and Invention of Tradition,* 82.
[37] Ibid., 37.
[38] Ibid.
[39] Ibid.
[40] Ibid.
[41] Ibid., 37–38.
[42] Ibid., 82.

Drawing Territory: British Mapping in India, c. 1756–1905. His
argument is that the British Map makers often created maps to
justify territorial possessions. 'What is particularly interesting
about this intended use for a map is that, during the British
colonial period in India, maps were among the most effective
resources the British could turn to when they looked for their
legitimacy as a colonial power.'[43] He focuses on different strategies used by the surveyors and the map makers to demonstrate:
one, the history of a territory and second, more importantly, the
justification of the land possessed. The land was converted into
a territory by establishing a history of its possession. This is the
reason why cartography had the leading edge among the tools of
colonial justification.[44] Barrow conveys that between 1756 and
1905, a huge number of 'published and manuscript British maps
of India presented a state-centric perspective'.[45] 'The power of
colonial maps was that they were able to show, in a beguiling
way, that the control was not just over the people and the rights
of trade, but also over the land.'[46]

Recovering the Indic

In a letter written to the chairman of the East India Company
(1730–1794), Nathaniel Smith, on 4 October 1784, Warren
Hastings conveyed a deep concern in the context of lauding the
antiquity and the veneration in which a considerable portion of
human race had held the text of the Bhagavad Geeta for so many
ages.[47] Hastings wrote:

> …Every instance which brings their real character home to observa-
> tion will impress us with a more generous sense of feeling for their

[43] Ian J. Barrow, *Making History, Drawing Territory: British Mapping in India, c. 1756–1905* (New Delhi: Oxford University Press, 2003), 2.
[44] Ibid., 9.
[45] Ibid., 11.
[46] Ibid., 185.
[47] Warren Hastings, 'Letter to Nathaniel Smith, from The Bhagvat Geeta', cited in P. J. Marshall, ed., *The British Discovery of Hinduism in the Eighteenth Century* (London: Cambridge University Press, 1970), 184–191.

natural rights, and teach us to estimate them by the measure of our own. *But such instances can only be obtained in their writings: and these will survive when the British dominion in India shall have long ceased to exist, and when the sources which it once yielded of wealth and power are lost to remembrance.*[48] [Emphasis added]

Well, the significance of these words of Hastings can easily be corroborated today by the fact that students' and researchers' interest on Indic thought and studies is growing. I have been teaching 'Indian Political Thought: Classical and Modern' in my college for several years now. But since the past few years, students' interest in the subject has seen a phenomenal surge. In fact, many of them question as to why they are told so less about their own history and heritage during the years of their education. The upsurge of this interest in the nation-centric histories cannot be sidetracked, rather should be fostered, if we wish to develop a 'humankind perspective' wished by Stanziani. *The idea is not to return to some kind of nationalist orientalism; but at the same time, also not one of suspending all cultural uniqueness in the name of humankind perspective. Rather, a nuanced approach is required to grasp the obscurities of the narrative.*

It was not without reasons that Tagore and Aurobindo laid stress on 'India's distinctiveness' which seemed to them 'threatened by absorption into a universalized Europe'.[49] And they were not the first ones to have underlined the uniqueness of the Indian civilization. Strong and similar voices did exist since the time of the French philosopher, Voltaire, as he was 'attracted to Hinduism in 1760 when he was presented with a manuscript called the *Ezour Vedam*, or commentary on Hindu scriptures'.[50] Referring to his work *Philosophie de l'histoire* that was first published in 1765, Marshall says,

Voltaire asked whether the Jews had taught other nations or whether they had been taught by them and he left his readers in

[48] Ibid., 189.
[49] Peter Heehs, 'Shades of Orientalism: Paradoxes and Problems in Indian Historiography', *History and Theory* 42, no. 2 (May 2003): 195.
[50] As cited in Marshall, *The British Discovery of Hinduism*, 8.

no doubt as to the answer: other peoples had both older and more refined civilizations. Voltaire had hesitated in the past between the claims of India and China, but the 'Ezour Vedam' seems finally to have convinced him that the Indians were the most ancient people on earth.[51]

Nathaniel Brassey Halhed, an excellent linguist and well known for his extensive readings and knowledge of Persian, Bengali and Sanskrit, came to India in 1771 as a writer in the Company's Bengal service.[52] He was astonished to find the similarities of Sanskrit words with those of Persian and Arabic, and even of Latin and Greek and remarked about Sanskrit language:

> ...every part of speech, and every distinction which is to be found in either Greek or Latin, and that in some particulars it is more copious than either...I do not attempt to ascertain as a fact, that either Greek or Latin are derived from this language; but I give a few reasons wherein such a conjecture might be founded: and I am sure that it has a better claim to be the parent than, Phoenician or Hebrew.[53]

However, the linguistic similarities that Halhed pointed out were to be later picked up by scholars like William Jones to develop the *Aryan invasion theory* (AIT), discussed later in the chapter.

The issue of chronology was another vital matter, for if religions of the East were shown to have been established before the birth of Christ, the European claims of being the 'unique instrument of God's providence'[54] would have been contradicted. Marshall further reveals,

> when Halhed set out the theory of four *yugas*, giving them a total of about eight million years...he made it clear that he was not prepared to dismiss these claims out of hand, however irreconcilable they might be with a Christian view of the world's history.

[51] Ibid., 26.
[52] Ibid., 8–10.
[53] Ibid., 10.
[54] Ibid., 25.

He also added that there was no mention of a flood in the Hindu scriptures (an astonishing statement from someone who claimed some acquaintance with the *Puranas*), apparently further proof of their great age.[55]

Bose and Jalal rightly quote Subhas Chandra Bose for stressing two features critical to the understanding of India: first, its history had to be 'reckoned not in decades or in centuries but in thousands of years'; and second, only under British rule, India 'for the first time in her history had begun to feel that she had been conquered'.[56] A 'heritage', dating back to more than five millennia, containing several layers of cultures, history of wars, destruction, assimilation and civilizational influences, was bound to be exceptionally complex and gaping for many interpretations.[57]

To quote Partha Chatterjee in relation to the pre-colonial Bengal:

Ancient India became for the nationalists the classical age, while the period between the ancient and the contemporary was the dark age of medievalism. Needless to say, this was a pattern heartily approved by European historiography. If the nineteenth-century Englishman could claim ancient Greece as his classical heritage, why should not the English-educated Bengali feel proud of the achievements of the so-called Vedic civilization?[58] (Emphasis added)

Orientalism

Interesting to note that, whereas the World History Association was created in the USA in 1982, the *Journal of World History* was founded in 1990, in the wake of a quite unusual historical

---

[55] Ibid., 30.

[56] Quoted in Sugata Bose and Ayesha Jalal, *Modern South Asia: History, Culture, Economy* (New York, NY: Routledge, 2018), 9.

[57] Ibid.

[58] Partha Chatterjee, *Empire and Nation: Essential Writings 1985–2005* (Ranikhet: Permanent Black, 2010, Co-published by Columbia University Press), 79.

context: fall of the Berlin Wall, end of the Cold War, emergence of China and India as potential economic powers, and Bill Clinton and Tony Blair flaunting the gains of free market and globalization.[59] Ironically, 'a vast majority of dissertations and university chairs were still devoted to national history, whereas cultural areas elicited only marginal interest, seemed out of step with the concerns of globalisation.'[60]

What Stanziani draws attention to in this context is not something unfamiliar happening for the first time in world history, for there have been several Oriental philosophies that have similar histories of their genesis. Let us see how. As the Imperial masters set out to create a niche for themselves in colonial India by devising theories for justifying their rule, they had to face a dilemma. Known by their ideals of liberty and democracy, a monocratic rule in India was a sharp contrast with the professed principles of political ethics. 'By what right, the Victorian British had to ask themselves, could a liberal democracy assert a claim to imperial dominion based on conquest.'[61] The dilemma was resolved by adopting different strategies such as creating literary discourses of legitimization and initiating researches on the history, law, religion and the early texts of India. 'Orientalism' in this sense is a discourse about the Orient as the 'Other' of Europe, having its origin in the debate initiated by Edward Said in 1978 in his book *Orientalism*.[62] One of his most debated contentions in this context is that all European Orientalists of the colonial era were directly or indirectly in collusion with the aims of colonial domination supported by institutions, scholarship, colonial bureaucracy and its vocabulary.[63]

Some important historical facts have been highlighted by Ranajit Guha in his remarkable work *Dominance without*

---

[59] Stanziani, *Eurocentrism and the Politics*, 7.
[60] Ibid.
[61] Metcalf, *Ideologies of the Raj*, ix–x.
[62] Edward Said, *Orientalism* (London: Vintage Books, 1978).
[63] Ibid., 2.

Hegemony. The most preliminary exercise in colonialist historiography for laying the foundations of the Raj was to settle the most vital issue of the *relation of property to the empire*, which, in fact, became the matter of controversies.[64] After securing a command over the wealth of the land, started the more mature and sophisticated discourse of a philosophical apparatus of control. Although initiated much before, this ideological pedestal was solidified in the 70 years of vast research from 'Mill's *History of British India* (1812) to Hunter's *Indian Empire* (1882)'.[65]

The Asiatic Society of Bengal, established in 1784, was a research society founded under the patronage of Governor General Warren Hastings. With William Jones as its first president, the well-known intent was one of creating the legitimate base in the country that would enable the English colonial masters a greater control and authority in India. 'To meet these needs ancient scriptures were translated on a massive scale under the editorship of Max Mueller...fifty volumes, some in several parts, were published under the *Sacred Books of the East* series.'[66] With the support of the British finance, Oriental studies were undertaken in Britain's important universities on topics such as political institutions, caste system, status of women and economic life of the people.[67] These Oriental studies set out the tone of a research lineage that became the foundation of a future course of civilizational research of India, as understood and projected by the colonial masters of this land.

> Max Mueller and other western scholars made certain generalisations about the nature of ancient Indian history and society. They stated that the ancient Indian lacked a sense of history, especially of the factor of time and chronology. They stressed that the Indians were accustomed to despotic rule. They added that since

[64] Ranajit Guha, *Dominance without Hegemony: History and Power in Colonial India* (Delhi: Harvard University Press, 1997), 2.

[65] Ibid.

[66] R. S. Sharma, *Rethinking India's Past* (New Delhi: Oxford University Press, 2009), 270.

[67] Ibid., 271.

the Indians were engrossed in the problems of the next world, they felt no concerns about the problems of this world. ...Their emphasis on the Indian tradition of one-man rule could justify the system which vested all powers in the hands of the viceroy. Similarly, if the Indians were obsessed with the problems of the other world, the British colonial masters had no option but to look after their lives in this world. Without any experience of the self-rule in the past, how could the natives manage their affairs in the present?[68]

The sweeping statements about the civilized abilities of the native people in India were necessary to prove that the people of this land were not qualified enough to govern themselves. Matilal's collected essays assertively pronounce the intent of these researches, thus:

It is undeniable that Orientalism began with the spread of Western powers to exploit and dominate the east. From the initial idea of collecting nuggets of information about the 'exotic' Oriental societies, much as the merchants and pirates collected gold, Orientalism became a full-fledged subject for the classical scholars who switched from the study of Greek and Latin to that of Arabic, Persian and Sanskrit....They were not simply satisfied with collecting gold, extracting wealth and leaving the local societies undisturbed. They took to the study of the Orient in a systematic way. The original idea, to be sure, was not to learn anything new or of lasting value but to gather information that would be certainly useful for the administrators, legislators and rulers in their policy formations and decisive actions as far as the Orient was concerned....Thus was the birth of Orientalism in India. [69]

The Revolt of 1857 had given the British a jolt and made them realize that in order to gain a stronghold over India, they needed a better and deep understanding of the norms, manners and the systems of the colonial people. To know the vulnerable points of the Hindu religion was also the need of the Christian missionaries, which were constantly on the lookout to win converts and, thus, strengthen the British Empire.

[68] Ibid.
[69] Ganeri, *The Collected Essays*, 370–371.

Oriental Despotism

The concept of *Oriental despotism* was the natural fallout of Orientalism, arguing that ancient India had experienced *only* despotic rule. Interestingly, in this lineage of despotism, the British researchers mapped the entire heritage of pre-colonial and ancient Indian thought. Referring to the text of *Arthashastra*, V. A. Smith very conveniently remarked, 'The only form of government described in detail by the author was an absolute autocracy'.[70]

Discussing the civilizational history of the early days of Magadha ascendancy in ancient India, Majumdar points out that monarchy was *not* the only form of government either in the East or in the West. No doubt there were powerful kings in places such as Bihar, Oudh, Malwa and Punjab, but these kings were not the undisputed masters for they had to deal with free and war-like tribes, having the monarch-like authority.[71] Also, there were types of kings who led as commanders in the wars but left the business of government to a body of local seniors.[72] He also talks about diarchy or *dvairajya* prevalent, as in Sparta, where the number of ruling kings was two.[73] The raja of the *Madhyadesh* conducted the affairs of his state with the advice and assistance of ministers and nobles. Even in kingdoms where the popular assembly is not much in evidence, the monarch had to defer to the wishes of Brahmanas, elders of corporations and commonality.[74] Some traits seem most modern and relevant even in the present-day context when he says, 'Tyrannical princes were not infrequently expelled from the throne. Even in Magadha, the citadel of imperialism, the king consulted the village headmen. A dynasty was driven out by the citizens because of its delinquencies.'[75] Interesting to note

[70] Vincent A. Smith, *The Early History of India* (London: Oxford University Press), 1924, 145.

[71] R. C. Majumdar, H. C. Raychadhuri, and Kalikinkar Datta, *An Advanced History of India* (New York, NY: Macmillan, 1963), 71.

[72] Ibid.

[73] Ibid.

[74] Ibid.

[75] Ibid.

that, although the monarchies were generally hereditary, cases of election were not unheard of in many cases. 'A Greek writer tells us that in a certain district of the Punjab the handsomest man was chosen as King. Kingship was no longer a monopoly of the Kshatriyas caste, and one of the most powerful dynasties of the age was of Sudra extraction.'[76]

In his another work, *Ancient India*, Majumdar talks about the existence of oligarchic and republican governments in this country in about 6th century BC, finding references not only in ancient literature, coins and inscriptions but also in the travelogues of the Greek travellers. Although not much is known about them, some of them were Lichchhavis, Sakyas and Mallas, out of which the Lichchhavis were very powerful and won great name and fame in ancient India. Buddha talked quite highly of them, and their system of administering justice was remarkably favouring the individual. 'He [individual] could be punished only if seven successive tribunals had unanimously found him guilty, and he was quite safe if but one of them regarded him as innocent.'[77] Majumdar quotes Megasthenes while giving an account of the large number of democratic states that flourished in the 4th century BC, thus:

> Megasthenes says that most of the cities in his time adopted the democratic form of government, and other writers corroborate him. One of the most important democratic States in the 4th century B.C. was that of the Sabarcae, who, like many others, fought with the army of Alexander the Great. Their territory extended along the bank of the Sindhu, and they had a huge army....The city-state of Nysa...had an oligarchical form of government and its governing body consisted of a President and 300 members of the oligarchy. In some other cases the governing body consisted of as many as five thousand councillors. *The Greek writer could not help emphasizing its obvious similarity with the Spartan constitution.*[78] [Emphasis added]

---

[76] Ibid.
[77] R. C. Majumdar, *Ancient India* (Delhi: Motilal Banarsidass, 1952), 158.
[78] Ibid., 158–159.

However, with the establishment of the Mauryan Empire, these non-monarchical states vanished for they were incompatible with the existence of a large, centralized empire. After the downfall of the Mauryan Empire, others arose in their place, but had to succumb to foreign invaders and imperial powers.[79] The point to be emphasized over here is that the state in ancient India does not represent a category of Oriental despotism but has had a long civilizational history of republican trends that needs to be researched and understood without a predisposed understanding of her past.

Partha Chatterjee brings out an interesting fact in the context of 'history' being used as 'play of power' in his *Empire and Nation*. He observes that with the founding of the University of Calcutta in 1857–1858, history textbooks written by British historians were translated into Bengali for use in schools. 'The translations ended with a eulogy to the blessings of Providence which had chosen the East India Company to bring to an end the anarchy and corruption into which the country had fallen.'[80] In order to have a grasp of the informal dispositions of the time in the Bengali society, Chatterjee deliberately uses a set of school textbooks on Indian history from the 19th-century Bengal, written not by any major historians. He says,

> ...the Bengali literati were schooled in the new colonial education. Now Indians were taught the principles of European history, statecraft, and social philosophy. They were also taught the history of India as it came to be written from the standpoint of modern European scholarship...The English-educated class in Bengal, from its birth in the early decades of the nineteenth century, became deeply interested in this new discipline of Indology.[81]

It remains unquestioned though that much of the researches on the Orient were indeed initiated by the European scholars in the latter part of the 18th century, but it goes without saying that these researches produced concepts that have served as the 'bases' for

[79] Ibid., 159.
[80] Chatterjee, *Empire and Nation*, 69.
[81] Ibid., 68–69.

shaping much of the European interpretations of the Asiatic societies. It has very aptly been remarked that the 'rise of Orientalism as
an *ism* is connected in its genesis with the subordination of Oriental
societies to Western powers for the last four hundred years'.[82] The
point that deserves attention and, in fact, serious contemplation in
this context is that even after Independence, not enough researches
were initiated to know the *Indian roots of the Orient*. This can
be the only reason that can be cited for the comments noted by
Narayan Joshi at the annual conference of Indian History Congress
in 2001, where Dr Amartya Sen said that the Ramayana and the
Mahabharata do not have any historical value. These two epics are
simply mythology and nothing but poets' fancy. Also, that neither
Rama nor Krishna was a historical personality.[83]

In a conversation with Professor Himanshu Roy it came
up that these may be mythologies because we do not find any
historical data to substantiate their existence till date, yet they
cannot be outrightly dismissed as the ideas contained in them
are the material force of the Indian civilization, which have
driven its citizens in the everyday existence till date. The ideas on
the statecraft, on the functioning of the different organs of the
state, on public policy, on social relations and a gamut of other
facets of society have been in existence for millennium. In the
Ramayana, we find five elements of state, in the Mahabharata,
there are six, and the subsequent literature on statecraft like
that of Kautilya, Kamandaka or Barani also deal with these
elements, which continued to reflect in the writings till the pre-
colonial days.[84] Another very interesting idea pointed out by
Professor Roy was that in Ramayana, there exists a reflection
of an 'objection' to the application of 'law of primogeniture'[85]

[82] Ganeri, *The Collected Essays*, 370.

[83] Narayan Joshi, 'Mahabharata: History or Myth?' *Annals of the
Bhandarkar Oriental Research Institute* 91 (2010): 49, https://www.jstor.
org/stable/41692159

[84] Himanshu Roy, Professor at Deen Dayal Upadhyaya College, University
of Delhi.

[85] Refers to the law of inheritance, mainly of the real estate, by the oldest
son of the family.

which was again challenged in the Mahabharata. It was finally restored after the violent struggle of the long epic battle. We do not find the application of this principle in India as if the post-Mahabharata development destroyed this law of primogeniture. Whereas the primogeniture system is said to have come under attack in the Western world in the latter part of the 18th century and the British Parliament abolished it in 1925 as the governing rule of inheritance.

The concept of Oriental despotism has shaped the European interpretation and representation of Asiatic governments and societies for centuries. The origins can be traced back to the Aristotelian political philosophy. Nonetheless, its meaning since then has matured due to the theoretical approach of different thinkers, and Europeans had to face confrontation in the Asiatic world.[86] Like many other concepts, Oriental despotism also has its roots in the Greek thought, where it became an effective tool of automatic recognition of the Greek superiority over the other 'barbarous' nations, mainly the great Persian enemy.[87] In many respects, this was a crucial distinction which enabled the Greeks to theoretically justify their future attitudes towards Asiatic societies and political systems.[88]

However, the idea got popularized only when the mercantilist and first-generation industrial powers had acquired colonies in India and other parts of Asia. Among others, the idea of Oriental despotism found itself in the writings of Adam Smith, Montesquieu, Richard Jones and Hegel, and was propagated by James Mill. They highlighted not only the Oriental despotism but also the unchanging and stationary traits of laws, customs, manners and religion of China and India.[89]

[86] Rolando Minuti, 'Preface', in *Oriental Despotism*, European History Online, available at http://ieg-ego.eu/en/threads/backgrounds/european-encounters/rolando-minuti-oriental-despotism (accessed on 28 June 2021).
[87] Ibid., 3.
[88] Ibid.
[89] R. S. Sharma, *Aspects of Political Ideas and Institutions in Ancient India* (Delhi: Motilal Banarsidass, 1996), 77.

Although despotism faded from European concerns after 1789, with the ending of French absolutism, the notion of 'Oriental despotism' had enduring implications for the emerging Raj in India, for it carried with it the connotation that Asian countries had no laws or property, hence its peoples no rights.[90]

Needless to say, the entire approach sprang from the British need to justify their rule in India. They had to devise novel and exceptional theories of governance without which they could not have derived the legitimacy to rule the colonies. In order to have a better hold, the East India Company required that its officers be well versed in the Indian language and should have knowledge about the Indian practices and norms. This led the officers to study Sanskrit, Persian, Bengali, Tamil and various other Indian languages, which also became an essential tool for later translations of important works like Dharmashastras—the norms about social obligations and ritual requirements.[91]

[T]he major British scholars initially associated with them were William Jones, Henry Colebrooke, Nathaniel Halhead, Charles Wilkins and Horace Hyman Wilson. Some of the initial research and seminal papers were published as monographs, with many more in Asiatic Researches, a periodical of Asiatic Society of Bengal established in 1784. There was much discussion at the meetings of the Asiatic Society in Calcutta, focusing largely on the origins and the reconstruction of language and on the religion and customs. *But, curiously, membership of the Society was not open to Indians for many years, even those presenting their findings were being trained by Indian scholars.*[92] [Emphasis added]

In fact, there were some bids to relate the chronology of the Puranas with that of the Biblical, which was somehow not successful. 'A son of Noah was said to have migrated to India to establish the Indian population but evidence for this was found

[90] Metcalf, *Ideologies of the Raj*, 7.
[91] Romila Thapar, *The Penguin History of Early India: From the Origins to AD 1300* (New Delhi: Penguin Books, 2002), 2–3.
[92] Ibid., 3.

wanting.'[93] Later, in the 19th century, one sees the emphasis grad-ually getting crystalized on the innate superiority of the European civilization. This was made possible by declaring that 'Oriental civilizations' have once been great but are now in decline. Thus, different phases of Orientalism shaped the European insight about the India's past into some specific and peculiar patterns of understanding.[94]

These ideas started getting vehemently attacked by the Indian scholars in the early 20th century. Dr Radhakrishnan once said, Macaulay's policy is loaded on one side, 'While it is so careful as not to make us forget the force and vitality of Western culture, it has not helped us to love our own culture and refine it where necessary'.[95] It is interesting to note that in response to such kind of denunciations by the Indian scholars, the Western Indologists developed what Sharma calls 'a kind of *neo-Orientalism* based on sociology', and as a concession to the independent republican status of India, they modified the idea of perpetual despotism and skilfully placed undue emphasis on the *role of religion*, particularly rituals, and on the divinity of kingship.[96] This phe-nomenon of an unwarranted and complimentary prominence that was accorded to 'role of religion' needs careful attention and proper understanding for it forms one of the rudimentary edifice on which some of the subsequent philosophies of nation-building were erected. One such structure is that of 'secularism'[97] in India. The whole idea of secularism that comfortably sits on this premise today, ironically, seems to be a 'colonial construct of convenience', when studied from an Orient perspective of its genesis. In order to comprehend this, we need to fathom out the relationship between 'religion' and 'dharma'.

[93] Ibid., 3–4.

[94] Ibid., 4.

[95] S. Radhakrishnan, *Indian Philosophy*, vol. 2 (New Delhi: Oxford University Press [1923] 2008), 726.

[96] Sharma, *Aspects of Political Ideas*, xxvi.

[97] For details see, Himanshu Roy, *Secularism and Its Colonial Legacy in India* (New Delhi: Manak Publications, 2009).

Religion and Dharma

In her address to the annual convention of the Theosophical Society in 1898, Annie Besant described *dharma* as the most valuable contribution of India to the world, as *religion* is by Egypt, *purity* is by Persia, *beauty* is by Greece and *law* is by Rome.[98] This amply signifies that the two terms 'religion' and 'dharma' are understood to be separate. But the irony is that despite this awareness, the two are generally used interchangeably not only in the common parlance but also in some important academic narratives. The result is that even after 70 years of independence, India still grapples with the right connotations of some of its basic premises which carry not the indigenous but the European stated underpinnings. The concept of dharma is not only a philosophical concept but the bedrock, rather, the 'core' of Indian thought that requires detailed understanding for its proper comprehension. Malhotra remarks, 'Dharma has no equivalent in the Western lexicon'.[99] Most of the times, it is commonly translated into 'religion' which is especially misleading. An 'atheistic religion' would be a paradoxical preposition, but actually Buddhism, Jainism and Carvaka systems of dharma do not believe in the existence of God.[100] In fact, a debate is said to have been ensued for more than 100 years about the existence and the status of God in some Hindu systems. Then the question is, what is 'dharma' and how to define it.

The dictionary meaning of the term 'dharma' would include duty, conduct, right, justice, virtue, good work, morality, religion and so on. But they actually fail to convey the real meaning of the same. P. V. Kane, the well-known authority on *Dharmasastra Series* and a professor of Indology, asserts that this word 'escapes all ventures at a precise meaning in English or any other

[98] Annie Besant, *Dharma*, 5th ed. (Chennai: Theosophical Publishing House, 2000), 1.
[99] Rajiv Malhotra, *Being Different: An Indian Challenge to Western Universalism* (New Delhi: HarperCollins, 2011), 260.
[100] Ibid.

language'.[101] In his well-researched and authoritative series on the *History of Dharmasastra*, he reveals that in the Rigveda hymns, the word is used as an 'adjective' or as a 'noun' and occurs at least '60 times'. He also states that it is amply difficult to find out what was the 'exact meaning of the word Dharma in the most ancient period of the Vedic language'.[102] While quoting the different ancient texts such as Atharvaveda, *Aitareya Brahamana*, *Brihadaranyaka Upanishad*, *Taittiriya Upanishad*, the Bhagavad Gita and Manusmriti, Kane observes how the word dharma has passed through numerous alterations of meanings and finally the most pronounced import came to be 'the privileges, duties and obligations of a man, his standard of conduct as a member of the Aryan community, as a member of one of the castes, as a person in a particular stage of life'.[103] It is in this sense of the term that dharma is mostly used in the eminent texts such as *Taittiriya Upanishad*, Manusmriti and the Bhagavad Gita.[104] However, he does confirm that the word clearly originates from Sanskrit *dhr* which means 'to uphold or to support or nourish'.[105]

It is rightly stated, thus, by Dr Radhakrishnan that it is difficult to neatly define dharma for it signifies differently in different contexts. It signify beliefs, morals, prejudices, practices and institutions that outlines the identity of the individual as a member of a society. 'While the spiritual perfection of man is the aim of all endeavour, the Hindu society does not insist on any religious belief or form of worship.'[106]

---

[101] A. Pandurang Vaman Kane, *History of Dharamsastra: Ancient and Medieval Religious and Civil Law in India*, vol. 1, 2nd ed., pt 1, Government Oriental Series, Class B, No. 6 (Poona: Bhandarkar Oriental Research Institute, 1968), 1.

[102] Ibid.

[103] Ibid., 3.

[104] Ibid.

[105] Ibid., 1.

[106] S. Radhakrishnan, 'The Hindu Dharma', *International Journal of Ethics* 33, no. 1 (October 1922): 1–2, available at http://www.jstor.org/stable/2377174 (accessed on 28 June 2021).

To cite one example: there are several philosophical, political and normative overtones in the underlying plot of the epic's narrative, the basic premise of the text of the Mahabharata is the struggle between dharma and adharma. This kind of supposed admixture of state and dharma may have led the early 18th and the 19th century European scholars to popularize India as a land of religion, superstitions, sectarianism, spiritualism and Oriental despotism. Badrinath Chaturvedi has simply and profoundly put it, thus:

> [T]here is perhaps no other word that has been misunderstood more than 'dharma'. It has always been translated, wrongly, as 'religion'. The result is that, since our perceptions are governed by that incorrect translation, the statement that dharma is the foundation of law and governance, is quickly interpreted to mean that the foundation is 'religious' in character, which it is not.[107]

It seems a little surprising to learn that while the major civilizations of the world were able to locate their *great* histories, India was so inept to have preserved its past despite marvellous knowledge systems that were located and interpreted by travellers, historians and philologists from other countries. Although there are answers to this enquiry, one of the points that may be made here is that the perspectives about 'what to hold' or 'encompass' as history are different with different people. Some may remember the entire event in its chronology, some may retain the exact dates or some other might grasp the important message from the same event. This is a natural phenomenon of the human mind. If this is true, then same can also be true with different cultures of the world. This brings us to another related discussion that is worth our attention.

Historiography and Itihasa

Itihasa is a Sanskrit word, which when split as *iti-h-aas* means 'so it has been' or 'thus indeed in the tradition'. There is an emphasis on the 'utilitarian' aspect of the history embedded in the term

---

[107] Badrinath Chaturvedi, *The Mahabharata: An Inquiry in the Human Conditions* (Delhi: Orient Longman, 2006), 418–419.

itihasa, linking the narration to the legendary tradition of the land that need not be in the order of chronology.

Ranjan Ghosh brings out the nuanced understanding of India's distinctiveness of *itihasa* and argues,

> ...what Indians would claim as *itihasa* need not be rudely frowned upon because it does not chime perfectly with what the West or the Chinese know as history. Accepting the truth that our ways of understanding the past, the sense of the past, and historical sense-generation, vary with different cultures and civilizations will enable us to consider *itihasa* from a perspective different from the Hegelian modes of doing history and hence preclude its subsumption under the totalitarian rubric of world history.[108]

What marks the difference between the two is that history in ancient India did not care much to chronicle the dates or the names of the authors who wrote the texts but gave importance to the experience or the truth that was evinced. 'What the Hindus felt worth preserving was the meaning of events, not a record of when events took place.'[109] In fact, this raked up the entire debate in the later Vedic age about the authorship and, thus, the authenticity of the Vedas because the names of the authors and the dates were wanting. Peter Heehs's observes in this context, 'Precolonial Indian scholars were for the most part uninterested in the historical origin of the Vedas, regarding them eternal and uncreated'.[110] A. B. Keith observes in this context:

> What interests writers is not questions of the opinions of predecessors as individuals, but the discussion of divergences of doctrine all imagined as having arisen ex-initio. The names of some great authorities may be preserved, as in the case of schools of philosophy, but nothing whatever with any taint of actuality is recorded regarding their personalities, and we are left to grope for dates. This indifference to chronology is seen everywhere in India, and

[108] Ranjan Ghosh, 'India, Itihasa and Inter-historiographical Discourse', *History and Theory* 46, no. 2 (May 2007), 210.

[109] Troy Wilson Organ, *The Hindu Quest for the Perfect Man* (Athens: Ohio University Press, 1970), 30–31.

[110] Heehs, 'Shades of Orientalism'.

must be definitely connected, in the ultimate issue, with the quite secondary character ascribed to time by the philosophies.[111]

Metcalf quotes Alfred Lyall, a careful research student in the British government who had come close to throwing up his hands in despair while researching on Indian religion, thus, '...an ancient religion, still alive and powerful, which is a mere troubled sea, without shore or visible horizon, driven to and fro by the winds of boundless credulity and grotesque'. Finding the answer to the *why* of the same, Lyall says, this is because of the 'absence of a central ecclesiastical structure capable of disciplining popular practice'.[112] Lyall is, in fact, not mistaken, for the ancient Indian texts are so voluminous that this may be normal even for some Vedic student of Hindu religion.

Ranjan Ghosh rightly argues, 'History is a medium for articulating one's own cultural identity in respect to its difference from the identity of others',[113] and not corroborating to some patterns of universal or dominant cultural evolution. India has had a resonant past and 'writing the *itihasa* of India would demand acknowledging her wide diversity (histories of history) and thus the little narratives and attitudes that have come through in her making'.[114]

Even though there were intermittent wars and invasions, famine, floods and diseases that killed millions, comments by Basham are worth noting when he says,

> ...in no part of the ancient world were the relations of man and man, and of man and the state, so fair and humane. In no other civilization were slaves so few in numbers, and in no other ancient law book are the rights so well protected as in *Arthasastra*. No other ancient lawgiver proclaimed such noble ideals of fair play

[111] A. B. Keith, *A History of Sanskrit Literature* (London: Oxford University Press, 1920), 146–147.

[112] Metcalf, *Ideologies of the Raj*, 136.

[113] Ghosh, 'India, Itihasa', 216.

[114] Ibid., 217.

in battle as did Manu. In all her history of warfare Hindu India has few tales to tell of cities put to the sword or of the massacre of the non-combatants.[115]

Unfortunately, the Western Orientalist studies that focused largely on chronology, documents and records could not appreciate India's *itihasa* tradition which did not offer much in terms of organized chronologically arranged data of the events.

Good Governance and Rajdharma

The fact that the Hindu political thinkers distinguished the king from the state falsifies the Orientalist theory of perpetual despotism in ancient India. The society was conceived as an organic whole, and the ruler was an integral part of the same. Parekh notes,

> The ruler was...an integral part of a highly differentiated and un-centralised social order. He did not stand above the social order. He was one of its several parts, albeit an important one, but still only a part. His authority was hedged in by the relatively inviolable authority of the various autonomous centres of power, and regulated by his own specific dharma. Since he was never seen as outside of, leave alone above society, the very conceptual framework required by the idea of Oriental Despotism was absent.[116]

It is important to note that not only was the king a part of a differentiated social order, surrounded by diverse limitations, but *he was also regulated by his own dharma of discharging the duties of his incumbency known as rajdharma.*

Initially expressed in a 1989 World Bank publication, the concept of 'good governance' got popularized after the World

---

[115] A. L. Basham, *The Wonder That Was India* (New York, NY: Grove Press, 1959), 8–9.

[116] Bhikhu Parekh, 'Some Reflections on the Hindu Tradition of Political Thought' in *Political Thought in Modern India*, eds Thomas Pantham and Kenneth L. Deutsch (New Delhi: SAGE Publications, 1986), 22.

Bank Report of 1992, titled 'Good Governance'. However, good governance has been the concern of all humans of all civilizations and their theoretical projections, whether Occident or Orient. The theories may differ regarding the sustenance of the state, but a point where all history meets is invariably the idea that the state made its origin to provide good governance. The similar concerns of good governance are found in *Nitisara* of Shukracharya, *Ashtadhyayi* of Panini, the Ramayana of Valmiki, *Arthashastra* of Kautilya and the *Shantiparva* of the Mahabharata.

Apart from the other texts mentioned above, *Shantiparva* of the Mahabharata especially contains a detailed philosophical discourse on politics emphasizing the varied aspects of the characteristics, nature and the extent of the duties of a good king. There are 18 *parva* or sections in the Mahabharata, and *Shantiparva* is the 12th *parva* of the epic. *Shantiparva* is further divided into three sub-sections, namely *Rajdharamanusasana parva*, *Aapaddharma parva* and *Mokhshadharma parva*. In total, *Shantiparva* has 365 chapters consisting of 13,716 *shlokas*. The discourse on *rajdharma* alone runs into 130 chapters consisting of 4,716 *shlokas*.

The concerns of the Mahabharata are usual concerns of everyone even today, where the moot question broadly comes to be, 'how to be happy', 'satisfied' and 'contented'. Against such an unpretentious framework, the text gives a valuable political discourse on the dharma of the king that takes place between Bhishma and Yudhisthira in the periphery of the war field, when the war is over but the tragic memories are still alive. When Bhishma, one of the celebrated teachers and a political guardian of an iron will, is about to leave his body after being badly injured in the war, Yudhisthira asks his great grandfather to guide him in the perusal of his dharma as a king. Most appropriately placed in the text, the chapter that deals with politics after the war is *Shantiparva*—the book of peace. The placement and the contents of the chapter in the epic signify the following: one, that a war should always be followed by peace, and two, it is politics that leads to peace with the efforts of a good king. *Shantiparva* is, thus, a compilation of erudite writings on statecraft, political obligation and human conduct, representing the two broad mainstream traditions of ancient Indian political thought, 'dharma' and 'danda'.

Shantiparva clearly states 'protection of the people from all fears' as king's highest dharma. Varma quotes Krishna Dwaipayana to emphasize that if there is a theft and the king is not able to restore the property to the owner, he should compensate it from his own treasury.[117] This kind of order is to be restored by the king with the implementation of *danda* (punishment, penalizing, order...) to protect dharma. But *danda* should be so used by the king as would bring about the welfare of all his subjects. 'Although the king is invested with the authority and power of governance, the true sovereignty belongs to *dharma*, not to him. *Mahabharata* states this again and again in many ways.'[118] Even though monarchy prevailed, the theory of divine rights of the king is not proposed as the basis of king's rule. *Rajdharma* or the prescribed code of conduct was superior to the will of the ruler and, thus, governed all his actions.[119] *Arthashastra* while highlighting the principle of good governance declares, 'In the happiness of his people lies king's happiness, in their welfare his welfare, whatever pleases himself he shall not consider as good, but whatever pleases his people he shall consider as good.'[120] Thus, it follows that the king who acts against *rajdharma* loses his legitimacy to govern, since that would make the subjects unhappy and would provide the scope for a rebellion by them.

It is worth mentioning that 'there is in *Mahabharata* the simultaneous presence of two languages: *the language of experience and the language of transcendence*. Each when separated

---

[117] V. P. Varma, *Studies in the Hindu Political Thought and Its Metaphysical Foundations* (Delhi: Motilal Banarsidass, 1974), 229.

[118] Chaturvedi, *The Mahabharata*, 424.

[119] Subhash C. Kashyap, 'Concept of Good Governance and Kautilya's Arthasastra' in *Good Governance and Strategies*, eds Rajiv Sharma and Ramesh K. Arora (Jaipur: Aalekh Publishers, 2010), 31.

[120] *Arthashastra*, Book 1, Chapter xix, p.39.

from the other leads to *anrta*, untruth, and to its violence, as it always has.'[121] Although deficient in date, location and site, the Mahabharata represents one of the most compelling knowledge sources for a wide spectrum of people of not only India but also of the world, signifying, thus, the actual tradition of *itihasa*.

The Aryan Invasion Theory

The reason why the theory of Aryan invasion figures last in the array of the Indic recovery is the intense controversy that long surrounds the debate, hardly shorn of any personal predispositions, leading scholars like Trautmann (2005) to remark:

> Now, India is a free country, and everyone is entitled to publish any interpretation of history they wish. If one wants to say that the Taj Mahal was built by the Vedic rishis, or that the moon is made of green cheese, or that the earth is flat, one is entirely free to do so. But not all views of history are equal, or deserve to be taken seriously by scholars....We need not despair and conclude that the Aryan debate will continue unresolved forever...A convincing decipherment of the Indus script might end the Aryan debate, but it might not, because facts and interpretations are always open to challenge and the results of historical investigations are always provisional.[122]

The Aryan debate is majorly about the question whether the 'Sanskrit-speaking Aryans enter India from the north-west in about 1500 BC, or were they indigenous to India and identical with the people of the Indus Civilisation of 2600–1900 BC?'[123] AIT used the linguistic similarities that were located between Sanskrit and European languages. *It holds that the Indus civilization*

---

[121] Chaturvedi, *The Mahabharata*, 21.

[122] Thomas R. Trautmann, 'Introduction', in *The Aryan Debate*, ed. Thomas R. Trautmann (New Delhi: Oxford University Press, 2005), xvii, xliii.

[123] Thomas R. Trautmann, 'Constructing the Racial Theory of Indian Civilisation', in *The Aryan Debate*, ed. Thomas R. Trautmann (New Delhi: Oxford University Press, 2005), xiii.

ceased to exist with the arrival of the invading Aryans, either due to the destruction caused by them or by the environmental factors. Sir Mortimer Wheeler had made further archaeological investigations of the Indus civilization and interpreted groups of skeletons which were carelessly buried in Mohenjo-daro as the victims of a massacre by the invading Aryans.[124] On this basis, he concluded that this invasion caused the collapse of the civilization. However, in the absence of any substantial archaeological evidence of the invasion, the theory has been toned down to a modified version, as Aryan migration theory without proposing any change in the projected dates.

One of the earliest projections of AIT were made by Max Muller[125] which Trautmann calls the formation of the *racial theory of Indian civilization*, where the Indian civilization is supposed to have been caused with a 'big bang', as a result of the conquest of 'light-skinned Aryan civilized invaders, over the dark-skinned savage aboriginal Indians'.[126] He further says:

> Max Muller, engaged as he was in editing the Rigveda for publication, was the first to interrogate the text by means of this theory. Subsequently, the proof texts were published *in extenso* by John Muir,[127] in an important collection that was intended not only to solidify the new view of Indian history in the West but to propagate it among Indians as well. By the time of the Vedic Index (1912), in which A.A. Macdonell and A.B. Keith summarised the results of a century of Orientalist research on the Veda, it was firmly established.[128]

[124] Sir Mortimer Wheeler, *Civilizations of the Indus Valley and Beyond* (London: Thames and Hudson, 1966), 83.

[125] F. Max Muller, *The Sacred Books of the East: Vol. 32, Vedic Hymns, Part 1* (reprint, Delhi: Motilal Banarsidass [1891] 1964).

[126] Thomas R. Trautmann, ed., *The Aryan Debate* (New Delhi: Oxford University Press, 2005), 100.

[127] J. Muir, *Original Sanskrit Texts on the Origin and History of the People of India, Their Religion and Institutions*, 5 vols (London: Trubner & Co., 1874–1884), quoted in Trautmann, *The Aryan Debate*.

[128] Trautmann, *The Aryan Debate*.

British anthropologist, Colin Renfrew, raises a quite valid question in this regard. While agreeing that the historical linguistics can be used to establish a relationship between languages, he questions its accuracy in determining the homeland of the original speakers of the Indo-European language family.[129] AIT has been controversial till date, although many scholars opposed it since the 19th century itself. A well-researched study by T. S. R. Prasanna, a scientist from the field of metallurgy and material sciences, provides evidence against the theory, from the field of Vedic literature, astronomy, mathematics and metallurgy.[130] He also cites many archaeologists who do not support AIT.[131]

In a lecture delivered on the occasion of the 34th anniversary of Shri Ramkrishna Gopal Bhandarkar in 1959, R. C. Majumdar publicly expressed his deep concerns regarding the same. He was referring to the 'International Commission for Writing a History of the Scientific and Cultural Development of Mankind' under the aegis of UNESCO, where the portion concerning India was written by Sir Leonard Woolley, an eminent international scholar. He says,

> The whole volume consists of more than 1500 typed pages and covers the period from the very beginning down to 1200 B. C. It is admitted in the draft of this volume that the Aryans came to India about 1500 B. C. Nevertheless, everything concerning the Aryans and their culture is contained in about ten lines.[132]

[129] Colin Renfrew, *Archaeology and Language: The Puzzle of Indo-European Origins* (London: Penguin Books, 1987), 77.

[130] T. S. R. Prasanna, 'Vedic Rituals and Aryan Invasion theory', *Current Science* 109, no. 10 (25 November 2015): 1882–1888; T. S. R. Prasanna, 'There Is No Scientific Basis for the Aryan Invasion Theory', *Current Science* 103, no. 2 (25 July 2012), 216–221.

[131] K. K. Klostermaier, *A Survey of Hinduism* (Albany, NY: Sunny Press, 2007); E. F. Bryant, *The Quest for Origins of Vedic Cultures* (Oxford: Oxford University Press, 2001); E. F. Bryant and L. L. Patton, *The Indo-Aryan Controversy* (London: Routledge, 2005); D. K. Chakrabarty, *The Oxford Companion to Indian Archaeology* (Oxford: Oxford University Press, 2005).

[132] R. C. Majumdar, 'Rigvedic Civilization in the Light of Archaeology', *Annals of the Bhandarkar Oriental Research Institute* Vol. 40, no. 1/4 (1959): 2–3.

In one of the articles, another scholar, Padma Manian gives an interesting argument pointing out the fallacies of AIT, thereby questioning it:

One conclusion to which these scholars arrived was that the Aryans were pastoral nomads since the hypothetical vocabulary that they had created many words for domesticated animals and fewer words for cereal grains. They then tried to identify the homeland where the Aryans first practiced nomadic pastoralism. Various widely separated places for the Aryan homeland were suggested such as northern Europe, the Balkans, Anatolia, Southern Russia and the Caucasus; *but India was not one of them* [emphasis added]. Therefore, it was believed that the first speakers of Indo-European languages in India must have come outside...Thus was born the theory that India had been invaded by the Aryans. [133]

Various scholars also write about the research developments related to river Saraswati, which challenge AIT. Manian says:

...the river Saraswati, and not the Indus river, was the most prominent and sacred river in the Rig Veda (playing the same role there as the River Ganges in later Hinduism). The Vedas described the Saraswati as a mighty river flowing from the mountains to the sea. But today the Saraswati, known now as the Ghaggar, is a much smaller stream which gets lost in the Thar desert. A large number of Harappan sites have been found along the banks of the now-dry Saraswati or Ghaggar (see for example the map from McNeill). Recent geological investigations have shown that the Saraswati was indeed once a very substantial river flowing to the sea but that it dried up around 1900 BCE when the Yamuna ceased flowing into it, and instead flowed east to join the Ganges. The decline of the urban phase of the Harappan civilization seems to be correlated to that event.[134]

Ram Vilas Sharma has made very pertinent points in this context. While discussing the methodology of empirical historical research

---

[133] Padma Manian, 'Harappans and Aryans: Old and New Perspectives of Ancient Indian History', *The History Teacher* 32, no. 1 (November 1998), 23.

[134] Ibid., 28.

in determining the time period of the ancient civilizations, he emphasized the reliability on the 'remains of the monuments', rather than on the 'texts', for the obvious reasons of objectivity. Among these monuments, he categorically brings out the historical remains of the river bed of the now-dry Saraswati. He mentions various archaeological and other scientific studies that give ample testimony to show the historical existence of the river, along with the reasons of its disappearance. The inhabitants living around river Saraswati had to move away due to its drying up. Sharma quotes B. K. Thapar to designate the time period to such developments as 1750 BC.[135]

Sharma establishes that in Rigveda, Saraswati is shown as a very powerful and an abundant river flowing between Ganges on one side and the Indus on the other, catering to a huge spread of landmass—Harappa. This makes one thing very clear that since the text of Rigveda is making such a mention, it could possibly not have been written after the decline of the Harappan civilization. The text must have been written much before 1750 BC. Second, flourishing in the same region and being fed by the same rivers, the two civilizations—Harappa and Vedic—were disconnected seems impossible.[136]

In this context, the crucial turn that he gives to the entire debate is by posing a question about the direction of the civilizational spread. His enquiry is whether the expansion of the Harrapan civilization happened 'from the West to the East or from the eastern centres to the West?' In this context he quotes Bhagwan Singh, who is of the view that the Vedic civilization began and blossomed in the Saraswat region, and from there started spreading majorly towards the West and, to some extent, in the East.[137] Ram Vilas

[135] Ram Vilas Sharma, *Bhartiya Sanskriti Aur Hindi Pradesh*, trans. Neena Bansal (New Delhi: Kitab Ghar, 1999), 133–35.

[136] Ibid., 135.

[137] Bhagwan Singh, *Harappa Sabhyata Aur Vedic Sahitya*, vol. 2 (Agra: Radhakrishna Prakashan), 20–21, as quoted in Sharma, *Bhartiya Sanskriti*, 135–136.

Sharma emphasizes the point that the Harappan culture is very much the extension of a matured civilization already mentioned in the Rigveda, where the extra agricultural produce provided inspiration for trading. With the kind of developments in the field of agriculture and skills, that find mentions in the text, it is quite natural that the people thought of trading. That the means of communication for the same were absent from such a developed civilization is doubtful, Sharma opines.[138]

Rakhigarhi, a village in Haryana, hit the headlines when DNA extracted from a woman who lived in the village around 4,500 years ago yielded clues to ancient Indian ancestry, establishing the fact that, 'The population has no detectable ancestry from Steppe pastoralists or from Anatolian and Iranian farmers, suggesting farming in South Asia arose from local foragers rather than from large scale migration from the West.'[139] This refers to the most recent study published in the science journal, *Cell*, after a five-year-long excavation at Rakhigarhi by a team of researchers led by Vasant Shinde, vice-chancellor of Pune's Deccan College Post Graduate and Research Institute. The studies showing that the woman was not of Aryan descent highlights at least one fact that, if at all there was any Aryan migration to the region, it happened after the Indus Valley Civilization declined. The studies also showed a genetic continuity from the ancient hunter-gatherers to the present-day South Asians. Skeletal remains found in the upper part of the citadel area of Mohenjo-daro belonged to those who died in floods, and not in any massacre by the Aryans as 'hypothesised by Sir Mortimer Wheeler', the study says.[140]

---

[138] Sharma, *Bhartiya Sanskriti*, 136.

[139] Vasant Shinde et al., 'An Ancient Harappan Genome Lacks Ancestry from Steppe Pastoralists or Iranian Farmers', *Cell* 179, no. 3 (October 2019), available at https//doi.org/10.1016/j.cell.2019.08.048 (accessed on 28 June 2021).

[140] https://www.hindustantimes.com/india-news/rakhigarhi-excavation-study-says-not-enough-proof-of-aryan-invasion-theory/story-ityRI9x66FZgO4J2KC2QYL.html

Conclusion

Imperialism is an accepted evil, but the garbs that it advances in, are even more dreadful. It assumes different shades of exploitation and colonialism is a crude form of that. This monster assumes elusive forms that can silently subsume cultures and still write histories of its own development. Once this history passes down through ages, *time* tends to become its solidifier. It is here that techniques like deconstruction are most helpful in bringing out the facts through critical enquiry and research. To simply assume that history is an established fact, or becomes one with the passage of the time, is absolving from the responsibility of carrying out empirical researches to bring out the alternative views. India's traditional heritage is so vast that even after major efforts in the direction, a lot remains to be researched—in India. The axiom, *broadening the vision and deepening the roots* can search better solutions for the mankind.

Conclusion

Himanshu Roy

Indic thought has been in constant flux reflecting the ideas of the times. Two broad themes, however, have remained constant: one, how the state should better its function in order to strengthen itself, particularly in the structurally divisive society in the post-Rigvedic eras. Rarely, there is a reflection or an argument for its abolition. What we do find is a reflection of an imaginary ideal state or a society, a *Ram Rajya* or a social desire to return to *Satya Yuga*, *Dwapara Yuga* and *Treta Yuga* which are equated with an ideal society with social bliss. This desire reflected in the writings of academics, organic intellectuals of the time, focuses on the suggestions to monarchs and the elite to improve governance; the second theme has been justice, both social and administrative, for which there has always been individual and social emancipatory praxis best reflected in the *baanis* of the saints. The emancipatory praxis has been collective and democratic as well as plural focusing on the social change to adapt, adopt, co-opt and accommodate the social marginals—meritorious and skilled. In the process, it democratized the society, created space for social mobility and positional shift. It also, simultaneously, widened the social and political legitimacy of the state. Hegel, therefore, remarked about the 'fame of Indian wisdom' and a 'land of desire'.[1]

Being a trading hub of the world, the political-economic elite in India lived in opulence with the bullion coming from all over the world. Those who came to India for trade carried this image of Indian opulence to their home countries which fuelled a desire among their elite to possess India's wealth. This prompted the invaders and immigrants to come to India. This opulence also percolated downwards, kept the skilled labour engaged in manu-facturing and a section of the population mobile with trade across the country that checked the social upsurge from becoming pan Indic. What emerged in protests was co-optation of the marginals, which was confined to regions and localities. This co-optation of pluralism was the premise of famed Indian wisdom, and the prosperity from the trade made India the land of desire.

India has been a trading hub long before Alexander invaded India; his invasion was, in fact, the result of the image of India as the land of desire. Indian state, as per the hitherto written his-tory, was not old in existence. In *Digha Nikaya* (Aggann Sutta), during Buddha's time, we find the emergence of the state,[2] private property and social division. We do not know about the state and society of Indus valley which preceded it, much earlier than the state referred to here. In the Rigveda, in the last *mandalam*, we find the emergence of the state; however, it was in nebulous form, or at best, elementary in functioning. It was an elected body, not yet specialized or hierarchical, but was in the process of becoming. We do not know who wrote the Rigveda, when it was written or where it was written. The two epics, the Ramayana and the Mahabharata, which are considered as post-Rigvedic, reflect more developed forms of state—the Mahabharata reflecting more

---

[1] Hegel, 'Introduction', in *Lecture on the History of Philosophy*, vol.1 (New York, NY: Humanities Press, 1974); Hegel, 'Indian Philosophy', in *Lecture on the History of Philosophy*, vol.1 (New York, NY: Humanities Press, 1974).

[2] For details, see Himanshu Roy and M. P. Singh, eds. *Indian Political Thought*, 3rd ed. (Delhi: Pearson, 2020), 5.

developed form than the Ramayana. These reflections are premised on the contents of the texts. It is not known when they were
written, where they were written and who were the authors. Most
of the claims about these three texts are assumptions, without
any historical support, documentary or evidential. Therefore,
Hegel had remarked that 'the Hindus have no history....In their
poems kings are often talked of: these may have been historical
personages, but they completely vanish in fable'.[3]

Texts, however, present interesting reflections of society of the
time, the subsequent interpretations by different generations in
different eras notwithstanding. While the Rigveda, from second to
seventh *mandalams*, reflect social bliss, absence of social division
and property relations, the two epics reflect hereditary monarchy,
property relations, structured social division and state. Within the
two epics, the Mahabharata reflects a violent usurpation of law of
primogeniture which was muted in the Ramayana. The elements
of the state, therefore, are more developed in the Mahabharata.
We find more nuanced organs of state and a desire for a more
professional knowledge among its functionaries because it had
become the requirement of the time. The moral dimension, so
prominently commented upon, was the reflection of the subterranean changes taking shape in the property relations, best reflected
in the *Digha Nikaya*.

By the time Kautilya wrote his *Arthashastra*, the state in India
had reached its full-blown form, reflecting the existence of politics of the age in its developed stage. It was a long journey from
democracy, universal citizenship and participatory collective
administration of the Rigveda to a developed state with hereditary
monarchy and absence of citizenship. It was also the development
of caste as hereditary, specialized work that impacted the development of monarchy as hereditary, specialized work or the development of state as a specialized organ. More appropriately, these
impacted and strengthened each other and reduced the citizens
to subjects. In territories where the private property, monarchy

[3] Hegel, *Lecture on the History of Philosophy*.

and state were yet to develop or had not developed in their full form, the democratic space, citizens' freedom and the civil society continued to function till they were marginalized or eliminated in the course of history. Therefore, philosophy proper, as Hegel had argued, ceased to develop as an independent branch of knowledge after Buddha unlike political thought, which as an allied branch of philosophy had a long continual history in India. Philosophy became 'identical with its religion' in the course of the formation and development of hereditary monarchies. The withering away of the free institutions, which existed due to the 'connection between political freedom and freedom of thought', created conditions for the philosophy proper—the absolute universal of self-consciousness—to lose its vitality. The idea weakened and could not fructify into objective. The external and the objective could not be comprehended as a full-blown form in accordance with the idea. However, the epistemology about the concepts of an ideal polity, civil laws, justice, property, sovereignty and secularism as the six allied branches of philosophy proper blossomed over the centuries. This was because these concepts were necessitated by and required for the existence of state and for its expansion in different forms in different regions according to the then prevalent social structure. The content and the contours of these themes, however, lacked substantive or sharp formulation when compared to the consistent evolution seen in Greco-Roman political philosophy; however, an intensive reading of the available historical material in India leads us to interesting conclusions that are conceptually similar in content to the European formulations while simultaneously being distinct with a discernible Indian imprint. The similarities and differences in the political philosophy are, broadly, the results of the similarities and differences in the pre-capitalist social formations of India and Europe, of their state structures, of Episcopal orders and of variegated pattern of landholdings. In fact, one of the basic factors of distinction in India was the wide prevalence of landholdings and of property rights among the peasantry in customary forms whose vast numerical existence for centuries created conditions for the emergence of distinctive inputs into the conceptual paradigms of political thought. It provided an ontological base over which many philosophical discourses emerged as different branches of knowledge and fructified into independent/autonomous/related disciplines.

The colonial rule under the planned design interpreted this epistemological history, the famed Indian wisdom, as fables, deceit and untruth once it acquired the sovereign state power; before it, India was the land of desire and its wisdom was to be learnt. From the 1780s, the Brahmins became 'immoral', they lost 'conscience in respect to truth'. Hindus became 'cunning'; their fundamental characteristics became 'cheating, stealing, robbing, murdering'. Manu's code of morals became 'the basis of Hindu legislations'. No doubt, geometry, astronomy, algebra and grammar were advanced but history was 'altogether neglected', in fact, it was 'rather non-existent'. For, 'history required understanding—the power of looking at an object in an independent objective light and comprehending it in its rational connection with other objects'.[4] Hindus lacked this power of comprehension as they had not yet arrived at the stage of development where they possessed this 'self-consciousness', this made them 'incapable of writing history'.[5]

This colonial, and subsequently, European interpretation phrased in Hegelian metaphors continues to haunt the Indians, particularly the Left and their academics. Ignoring the colonial motives, the framework of contempt under the rubric of critical analysis is still deployed by them to interpret the pre-colonial history of Indic thought. The famed Indian wisdom, so famous among the foreigners, is either deliberately ignored or is still beyond their comprehension. Even the prosperity, as the land of wealth, has rarely been discussed and appreciated in their academic works. What is rather posited about pre-colonial India is the fragmentary discourse on the destitute, Dalits and women, which is framed in the Hegelian language as if they had miserable existence, as if it happened under the yoke of social and

[4] Ibid.
[5] Paraphrased, Ibid.

economic oppression of Brahmins and not under the regime of the Company. The Company Raj is projected as the epitome of modernity, which arrived with the British East India Company rule, that liberated them socially. The Company Raj, thus, was projected as a providence for the Indians which provided them governance and development. The loot, one of the first words to enter into English lexicography, is rarely discussed which was responsible for the poverty of the Indians impacting their education, social lives and psyche. A. D. Campbell, collector of Bellary, confessed this impact of the loot when he wrote in 1823 that under the rule of the Company, the grants coming from the society had dried up for education leading to the closure of the schools. In pre-colonial India, education was the responsibility of the society which was funded charitably by the individuals and religious organizations.

The foundation of the Asiatic Society in 1784 at Calcutta was the beginning of the systematic destruction of the Indic history famed for its wealth and wisdom. The British military officers and judges determined the publications of the manuscripts, their selections and translations. The pundits and the maulvis chosen by them determined the importance of the manuscripts, which manuscripts represent Hinduism and which represent Islam. The colonial publications of these texts transformed them to acquire pan-Indian status, made them universal Indic history transcending the localities and regions in which they were written, of which there was impact on the texts, which were so plural, regional and local representing the diversities of Hinduism. Hinduism was converted into a uniform, unilinear systemic religion, like Christianity and Islam having one book. This manufacturing of Hinduism around which emerged an academic discourse in colonial and post-colonial India and in the world was the real problem which needs deconstruction. William Jones, the president of the Asiatic Society and a friend of Hegel, had already prepared a framework of his work to be actuated which had 15 themes. The printing press and the publication of these manuscripts made them widely available to the reading public. The translations into English were more a result of interpretations of the interpreters who were versed as per their social and religious backgrounds of England. The Sanskrit texts written in different epochs with multiple meanings of different words were interpreted, out of their historical and regional contexts, in the framework of Bible and Quran. Consequent to these publications, Hinduism and its history were portrayed in comparative terms with Christianity and Islam.

Had the Company been like any other invaders, the facets of Indic history would have been different. But being representative of mercantile capitalism and operating in colonial mode, it changed the Indic society irrevocably. Islamic invaders had changed the Indic history too, but the changes even after their centuries of rule were not so ruptured and profound as they became during the Company Raj within a century. The brutality of the *bania*, both economic and coercive, actuated the pulverization of the diversities of different facets of Indic society including the production of knowledge. The constant arrival of new technologies supplemented this destruction and actuated uniformity and the integrative process which were lacking at the time of earlier invaders.

India as the manufacturing and trading hub of the world was always linked to the world. The diverse knowledge traditions of the world were integral parts of the Indic society which was receptive to the diverse new ideas required to cater to the diverse needs of different parts of the world.[6] The social divisions of the works performed by the *jatis* were the skilled labour who manufactured the products for the world. The economy generated wealth which kept the population mobile and engaged, providing opportunities to livelihood and checking ruptured social disorder. Immigrants willing to cater to the requirements of the economy were accommodated through different social mechanisms. Parsis, Greeks,

---

[6] New archaeological discoveries in India prove this point conclusively. For details, see 'Pattanam sites's importance is not confind to Kerala or India… it tells us the world was here 3000 years ago', *Times of India*, New Delhi edition, 16 November 2020, 14. The archaeological excavation at Pattanam near Kochi in Kerala, now a small village, adds to this knowledge of India being the trading hub.

Jews, Arabs and others have been coming to India for centuries ringing in localized changes and specialized skills in business, production and knowledge. Foreign travellers who recorded Indic history, as they observed it in their times and passed it on to their mother countries, created legends about India fuelling desires across the world to possess its wealth. The arrival of the Company in the 17th century and the seizure of power in the 18th century were part of this desire. The intent to rule over this wealth—the labour and the resources—led to the distortion of Indic history under the planned design. The education policy and the subsequent foundations of different institutions to map this labour and resources were intended under this design.

There were three major social characteristics in the pre-colonial Indic society which were required for the economy to be vibrant or in other words, the economy created these distinct character-istics for its operation: these were civic freedom of the subjects, rights to own property and constant production of skilled labour. The existence of mass property rights provided, even within the matrix of inscriptive precapitalist social formations, a restricted public sphere, a limited civil society and some basic functional civil laws.[7] These involved a large urban and rural populace of different caste/religion/gender (including the lowest desideratum) who had considerable operational and ideological autonomy as far as their customary rights were concerned. However, it must be noted here that these groups were not a political community yet.

These civic features remained, by and large, intact despite change of monarchies. Islam brought in discord, both at the elite and popular level, but demographically, it was insignifi-cant; the impact, therefore, was not denting to the economy. The social mobility, positional shift, internal and external migrations for livelihood, education and skill development and ownership rights for everyone in cultivable land, business, houses, livestock

[7] See Farhat Hasan, 'Forms of Civility and Publicness in Pre-British India', in *Civil Society, Public Sphere and Citizenship*, eds Rajeev Bhargava and Helmut Reifeld (New Delhi: SAGE, 2005).

were integral parts of this economy. The fragmentary discourse on gender and depressed classes that emerged in the colonial India and continued in post-colonial times was crafted by the colonial masters, was the result of the destruction of this economy by them which continued as legacy in post-colonial India. In a trading economy, it is structurally in built to have the three features, referred above, for vibrancy. Once the trade dries up, the society is likely to break up or become stagnant, conservative and ossified, generating all kinds of fragmentary discourses, competing for limited, fixed resources. That was precisely what the colonial rule did, looting the resources constantly, in different forms, for 150 years, not ever done by any invader. After the battle of Plassey, the property of Nawab of Bengal was carted away in 100 boats from Murshidabad palace to the Company's headquarters at Calcutta. That was the magnitude of their loot after one act.[8] As late as the 1780s, Paolino Da San Bartolomeo, an Austrian missionary, was eulogetic about the Indian society in the Malabar region that reflected the social condition of the women and depressed classes manifested in the educational system. Seven hundred years earlier, Al-Biruni had commented similarly about the Indic society,[9] about her civic freedom and skilled labour. The trade had definitely benefitted the elite far more than the peasants: there was a wide gap between the two classes.

Once India became the colony and drain of its resources began, the lower classes were affected more severely; their social mobility, positional shift and economic engagement shrunk. Social hierarchy became rigid, education and skill upgradation slowed down. From the 'land of wisdom' and 'land of desire' as Hegel had posited about India, the Company sucked its wealth to the maximum and created its image as the land of snake charmers. Within a short span of 190 years, its wealth had gone and image was in tatters; also, a new fragmentary discourse was set in motion in public domain which led to divisive social and political

[8] William Dalrymple, *The Anarchy* (London: Bloomsbury, 2019), xxviii.
[9] Both Bartolomeo and Al-Biruni have been cited extensively in different chapters.

contestation that checked political unity against the colonial rule: Manusmriti was posited as the dominant text representing the Brahmanical values; the professional skilled labour representing different *jatis* and *shrenis* were presented as the unchanging untouchable castes and women became the unfree part of Indic history who lacked civic freedom. In short, it was posited by the colonial regime as if there was no India. It was just a land of unfree, oppressed subjects working for the changing rulers who were the invaders, from the Aryans to the British.

Many of these fragmentary discourses continue to haunt independent India bereft of their historical contextualization.

About the Editor and Contributors

Editor

Himanshu Roy is Atal Bihari Vajpayee Senior Fellow, Nehru Memorial Museum and Library, Teen Murti House, New Delhi. His publications include *Peasant in Marxism; Secularism and Its Colonial Legacy in India, State Politics in India* (ed.); *Indian Political System* (ed.); *Indian Political Thought* (eds.) and *Patel: Political Ideas and Policies* (ed., SAGE).

Contributors

Neena Bansal is Associate Professor of Political Science, Kamala Nehru College, University of Delhi. Her recent publication includes 'Dara Shukoh's Pluralism' in Himanshu Roy and M. P. Singh (eds.) *Indian Political Thought: Themes and Thinkers* (3rd edition).

Vijaylakshmi Brara is Associate Professor, Centre for Manipur Studies, Manipur University, Imphal. Her publications include *Politics, Society and Cosmology in India's North-East*.

Prakash S. Desai is Assistant Professor of Political Science, Goa University, Goa. His recent publication includes 'Karnataka: BJP's Spectacular Victory over the Congress and JD(S)' (ed.) in Paul Wallace (ed.) *India's 2019 Elections: The Hindutva Wave and Indian Nationalism* (SAGE, 2020).

Bhuwan Kumar Jha is Assistant Professor of History (Selection Grade) at Satyawati College and Fellow, Developing Countries Research Centre, University of Delhi. He has been a Fellow at the

Nehru Memorial Museum and Library. He has recently authored a book on the history of CRPF titled *Nation First* (Rupa, 2021) and co-authored *Hindu Nationalism in India: Ideology and Politics* (Routledge, 2020).

Bijayalaxmi Nanda is Officiating Principal, Miranda House, University of Delhi. Her recent publication includes *Discourse on Rights in India: Debates and Dilemmas* (co-editor).

Nandini Bhattacharyya Panda was Senior Fellow, Nehru Memorial Museum and Library, Teen Murti House, New Delhi. Her publications include *Appropriation and Invention of Tradition: The English East India Company and Hindu Law in Early Colonial Bengal* and *Culture, Heritage and Identity: The Lepcha and Magar Communities of Sikkim and Darjeeling*.

Balaji Ranganathan is Professor of Comparative Literature, Central University of Gujrat. His recent publication includes 'Gujarat Sabha, Kheda Satyagraha and the Contesting Masculinities: Evaluating the Early Sardar Patel' in Shakti Sinha in Himanshu Roy (eds.) *Patel: Political Ideas and Policies*.

Kundan Singh is Professor, Sofia University, Palo Alto, California, USA. His publications include *Making Children Hinduphobic: A Critical Review of McGraw Hill's World History Textbooks* (co-author) and *The Evolution of Integral Yoga: Sri Aurobindo, Sri Ramakrishna and Swami Vivekananda*.

K. Srinivasulu is Senior Fellow, Indian Council of Social Science Research, New Delhi. His recent publications include 'Social and Political in Vemana's Thought' in Himanshu Roy and M. P. Singh (eds.) *Indian Political Thought: Themes and Thinkers* (3rd edition) and 'State Building in India: Sardar Patel's Reflections on Civil Service' in Shakti Sinha and Himanshu Roy (eds.) *Patel: Political ideas and Policies*.

Index